STAR WARS®

THE OLD REPUBLIC™

VOLUME THREE
THE LOST SUNS

THE OLD REPUBLIC

(25,000–1,000 YEARS BEFORE THE BATTLE OF YAVIN)

The Old Republic was the legendary government that united a galaxy under the rule of the Senate. In this era, the Jedi are numerous, and serve as guardians of peace and justice. *The Old Republic* comics series takes place in this era, chronicling the immense wars fought by the Jedi of old, and the ancient Sith.

The events in these stories take place approximately
3,600 years before the Battle of Yavin.

STAR WARS®
THE OLD REPUBLIC™

VOLUME THREE
THE LOST SUNS

SCRIPT
ALEXANDER FREED

INKS
MARK MCKENNA

PENCIL ROUGHS (PAGES 7–50, 73–116)
DAVE ROSS

COLORS
MICHAEL ATIYEH

PENCIL FINISHES (PAGES 7–50, 73–116)
GEORGE FREEMAN

LETTERING
MICHAEL HEISLER

PENCILS (PAGES 51–72)
DAVID DAZA

FRONT COVER ART
BENJAMIN CARRÉ

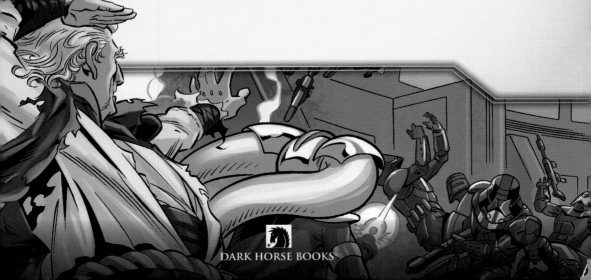

DARK HORSE BOOKS

PRESIDENT AND PUBLISHER
MIKE RICHARDSON

COLLECTION DESIGNER
STEPHEN REICHERT

ASSISTANT EDITOR
FREDDYE LINS

EDITOR
DAVE MARSHALL

Special thanks to Daniel Erickson, Rob Chestney, Hall Hood, Deborah Shin, and Leo Olebe at BioWare; Hez Chorba, Rob Cowles, Anne Marie Hawkins, and Douglas Reilly at LucasArts; and Jennifer Heddle, J. W. Rinzler, Leland Chee, Troy Alders, Carol Roeder, Jann Moorhead, and David Anderman at Lucas Licensing.

EXECUTIVE VICE PRESIDENT NEIL HANKERSON · CHIEF FINANCIAL OFFICER TOM WEDDLE · VICE PRESIDENT OF PUBLISHING RANDY STRADLEY · VICE PRESIDENT OF BUSINESS DEVELOPMENT MICHAEL MARTENS · VICE PRESIDENT OF BUSINESS AFFAIRS ANITA NELSON · VICE PRESIDENT OF MARKETING MICHA HERSHMAN · VICE PRESIDENT OF PRODUCT DEVELOPMENT DAVID SCROGGY · VICE PRESIDENT OF INFORMATION TECHNOLOGY DALE LAFOUNTAIN · DIRECTOR OF PURCHASING DARLENE VOGEL · GENERAL COUNSEL KEN LIZZI · EDITORIAL DIRECTOR DAVEY ESTRADA · SENIOR MANAGING EDITOR SCOTT ALLIE · SENIOR BOOKS EDITOR CHRIS WARNER · EXECUTIVE EDITOR DIANA SCHUTZ · DIRECTOR OF DESIGN AND PRODUCTION CARY GRAZZINI · ART DIRECTOR LIA RIBACCHI · DIRECTOR OF SCHEDULING CARA NIECE

STAR WARS: THE OLD REPUBLIC • Volume 3—THE LOST SUNS

This volume collects issues #1 through #5 of the series
Star Wars: The Old Republic—The Lost Suns, published by Dark Horse Comics.

Published by
Dark Horse Books
A division of Dark Horse Comics, Inc.
10956 SE Main Street
Milwaukie, OR 97222

DarkHorse.com | StarWars.com

To find a comics shop in your area, call the Comic Shop Locator Service toll-free at 1-888-266-4226

Library of Congress Cataloging-in-Publication Data

Freed, Alexander.
The lost suns / script, Alexander Freed ; pencil roughs, Dave Ross ; pencil finishes, George Freeman ; pencils, David Daza ; inks, Mark McKenna ; colors, Michael Atiyeh ; lettering, Michael Heisler ; front cover art, Benjamin Carr. -- 1st ed.
    p. cm. -- (Star Wars--the Old Republic ; v. 3)
"This volume collects issues #1 through #5 of the series Star Wars: The Old Republic-The Lost Suns, published by Dark Horse Comics."
    ISBN 978-1-59582-637-4
1. Graphic novels. [1. Graphic novels. 2. Science fiction.] I. Ross, Dave, 1949- II. Freeman, George, 1951- III. Daza, David. IV. McKenna, Mark, 1957- V. Atiyeh, Michael. VI. Heisler, Michael. VII. Carr, Benjamin (Benjamin C.) VIII. Title.
    PZ7.7.F74Los 2012
    741.5'973--dc23
                        2011041520

First edition: April 2012
ISBN 978-1-59582-637-4

1 3 5 7 9 10 8 6 4 2
Printed at Midas Printing International, Ltd., Huizhou, China

THE LOST SUNS

The Galactic Republic had led civilization into a golden age—its trillions of citizens governed by a democratic Senate and protected by the mystical Jedi Order.

Then the Sith Empire returned. Born of Jedi Knights who had fallen into darkness, this ancient enemy of the Republic had become a powerful and terrifying nation beyond the edges of known space. The Empire struck blow after blow against the free peoples of the galaxy, conquering territory and exacting revenge against the Jedi.

It was nearly three decades before the war ended, and even then, neither side could claim total victory . . .

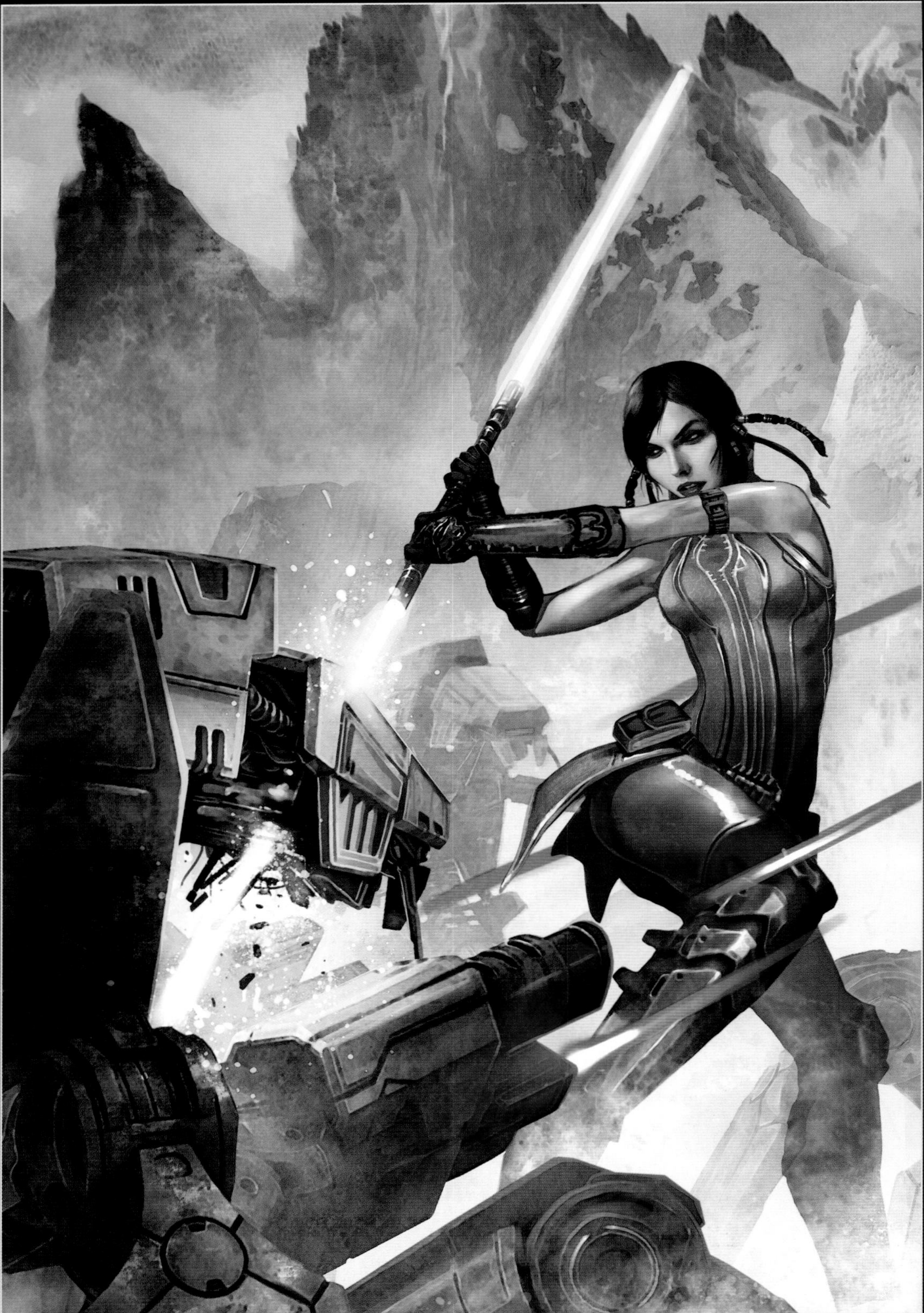

ILLUSTRATION BY
BENJAMIN CARRÉ

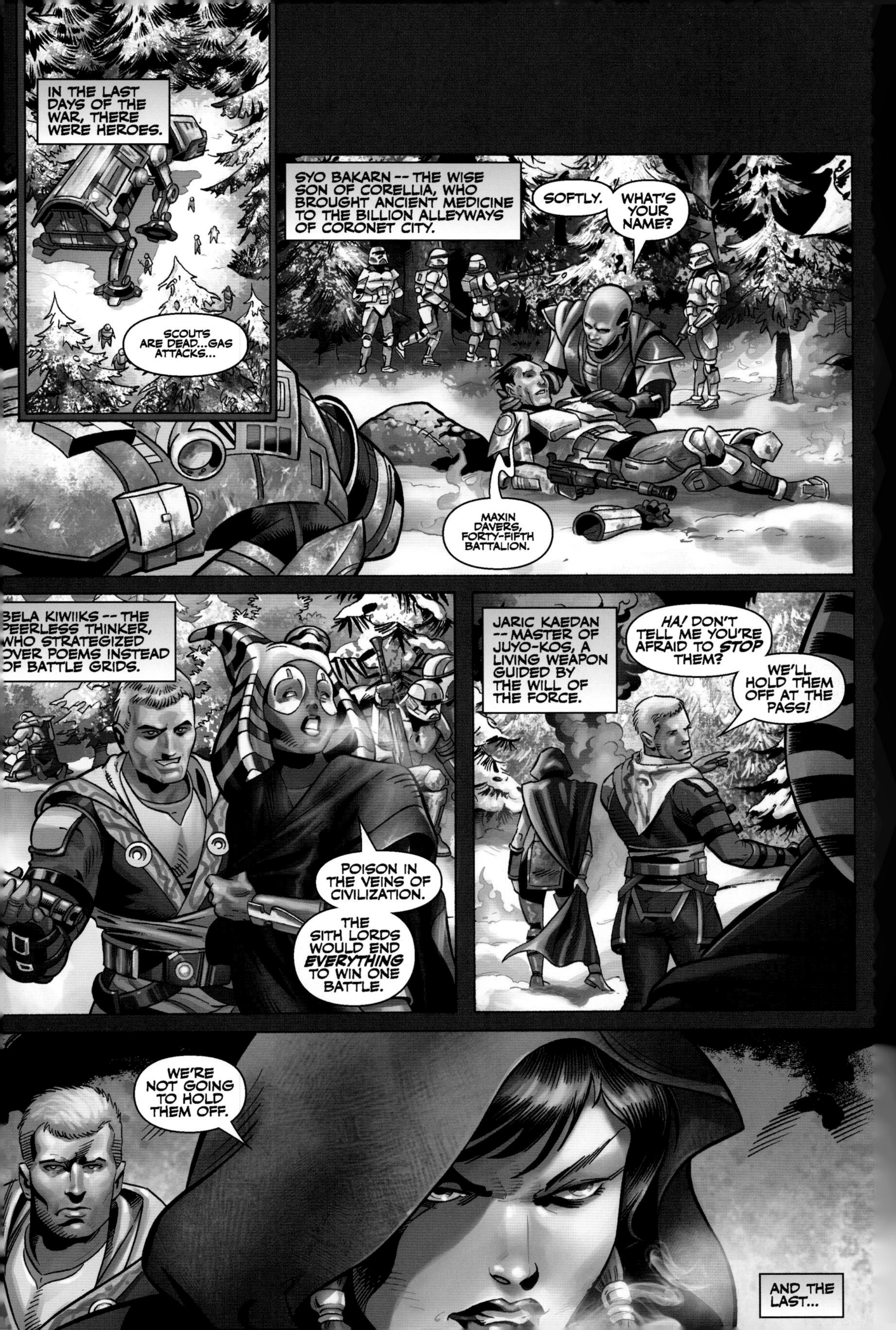
IN THE LAST DAYS OF THE WAR, THERE WERE HEROES.
SCOUTS ARE DEAD...GAS ATTACKS...
SYO BAKARN -- THE WISE SON OF CORELLIA, WHO BROUGHT ANCIENT MEDICINE TO THE BILLION ALLEYWAYS OF CORONET CITY.
SOFTLY.
WHAT'S YOUR NAME?
MAXIN DAVERS, FORTY-FIFTH BATTALION.
BELA KIWIIKS -- THE PEERLESS THINKER, WHO STRATEGIZED OVER POEMS INSTEAD OF BATTLE GRIDS.
POISON IN THE VEINS OF CIVILIZATION.
THE SITH LORDS WOULD END EVERYTHING TO WIN ONE BATTLE.
JARIC KAEDAN -- MASTER OF JUYO-KOS, A LIVING WEAPON GUIDED BY THE WILL OF THE FORCE.
HA! DON'T TELL ME YOU'RE AFRAID TO STOP THEM?
WE'LL HOLD THEM OFF AT THE PASS!
WE'RE NOT GOING TO HOLD THEM OFF.
AND THE LAST...

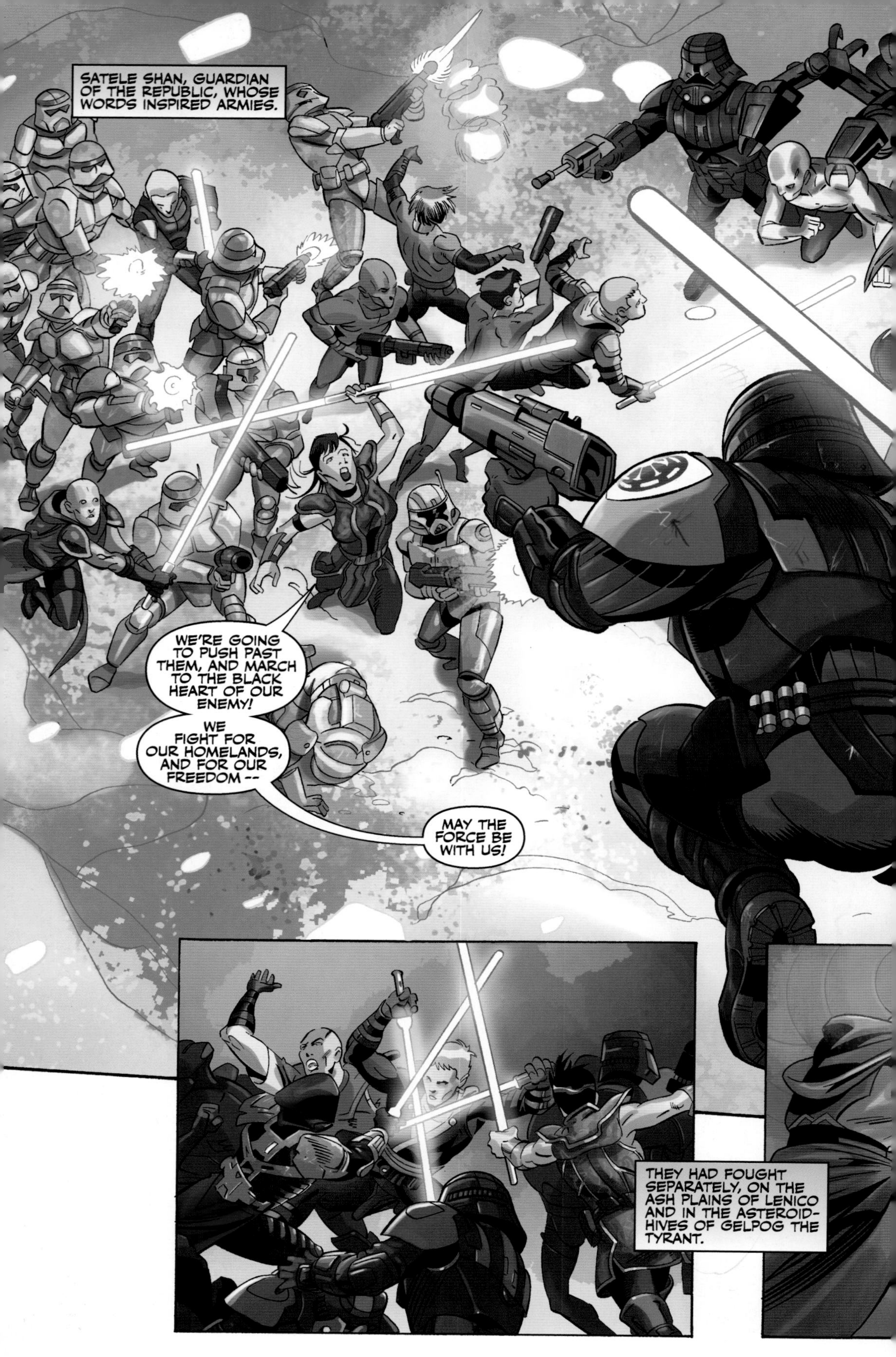
SATELE SHAN, GUARDIAN OF THE REPUBLIC, WHOSE WORDS INSPIRED ARMIES.
WE'RE GOING TO PUSH PAST THEM, AND MARCH TO THE BLACK HEART OF OUR ENEMY!
WE FIGHT FOR OUR HOMELANDS, AND FOR OUR FREEDOM --
MAY THE FORCE BE WITH US!
THEY HAD FOUGHT SEPARATELY, ON THE ASH PLAINS OF LENICO AND IN THE ASTEROID-HIVES OF GELPOG THE TYRANT.

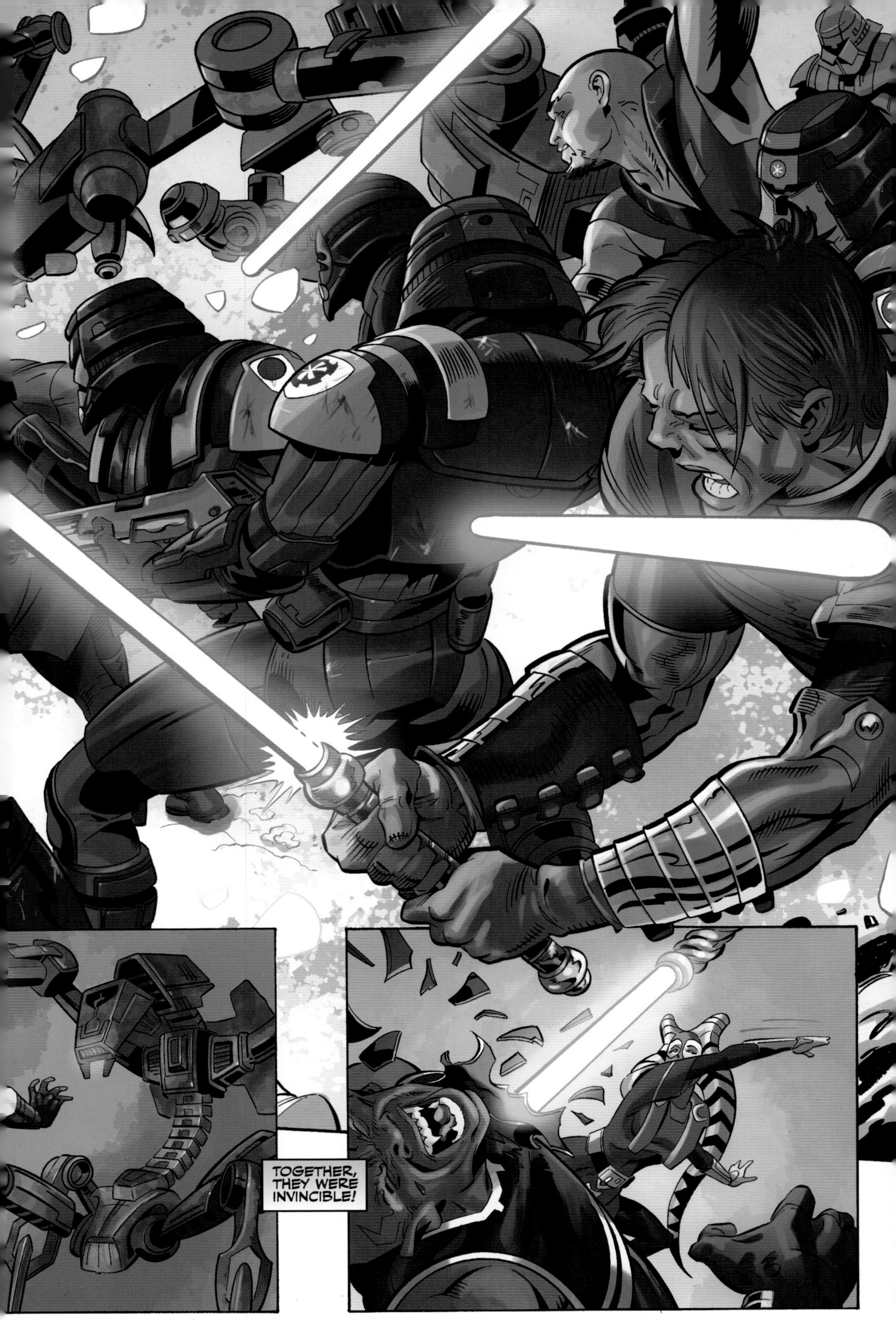
TOGETHER, THEY WERE INVINCIBLE!

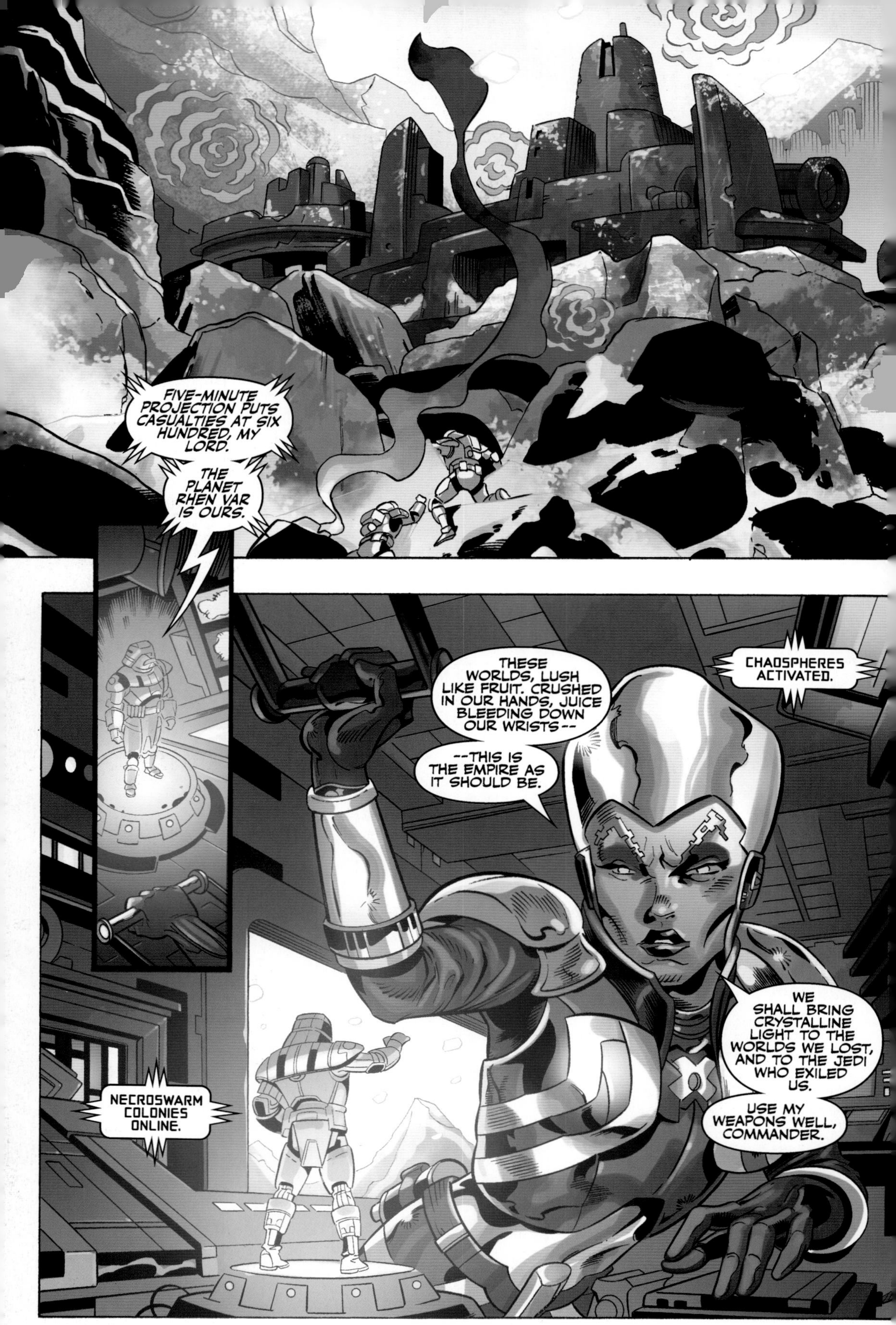
FIVE-MINUTE PROJECTION PUTS CASUALTIES AT SIX HUNDRED, MY LORD.
THE PLANET RHEN VAR IS OURS.
THESE WORLDS, LUSH LIKE FRUIT. CRUSHED IN OUR HANDS, JUICE BLEEDING DOWN OUR WRISTS--
--THIS IS THE EMPIRE AS IT SHOULD BE.
CHAOSPHERES ACTIVATED.
WE SHALL BRING CRYSTALLINE LIGHT TO THE WORLDS WE LOST, AND TO THE JEDI WHO EXILED US.
USE MY WEAPONS WELL, COMMANDER.
NECROSWARM COLONIES ONLINE.

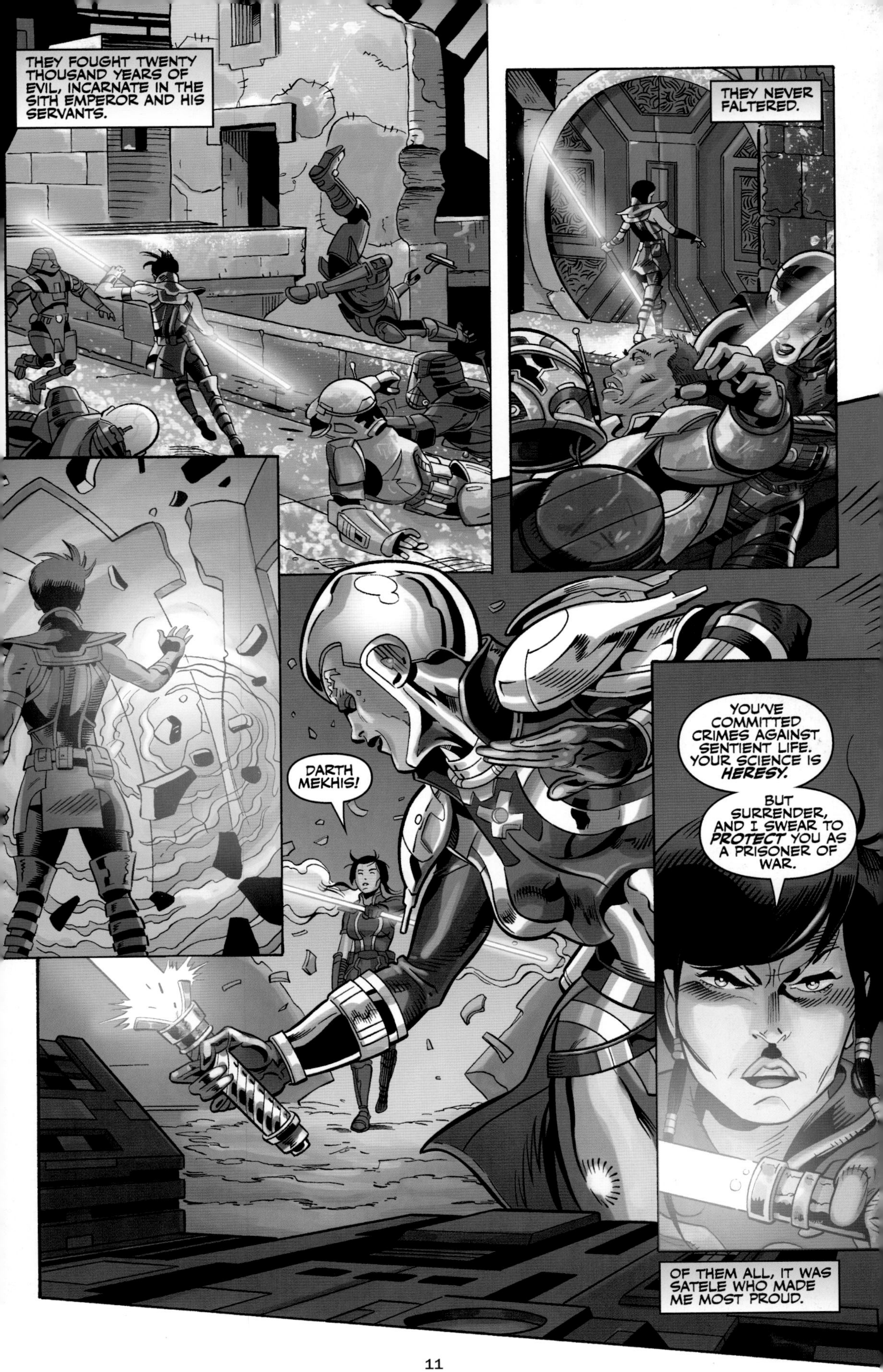
THEY FOUGHT TWENTY THOUSAND YEARS OF EVIL, INCARNATE IN THE SITH EMPEROR AND HIS SERVANTS.
THEY NEVER FALTERED.
DARTH MEKHIS!
YOU'VE COMMITTED CRIMES AGAINST SENTIENT LIFE. YOUR SCIENCE IS *HERESY.*
BUT SURRENDER, AND I SWEAR TO *PROTECT* YOU AS A PRISONER OF WAR.
OF THEM ALL, IT WAS SATELE WHO MADE ME MOST PROUD.

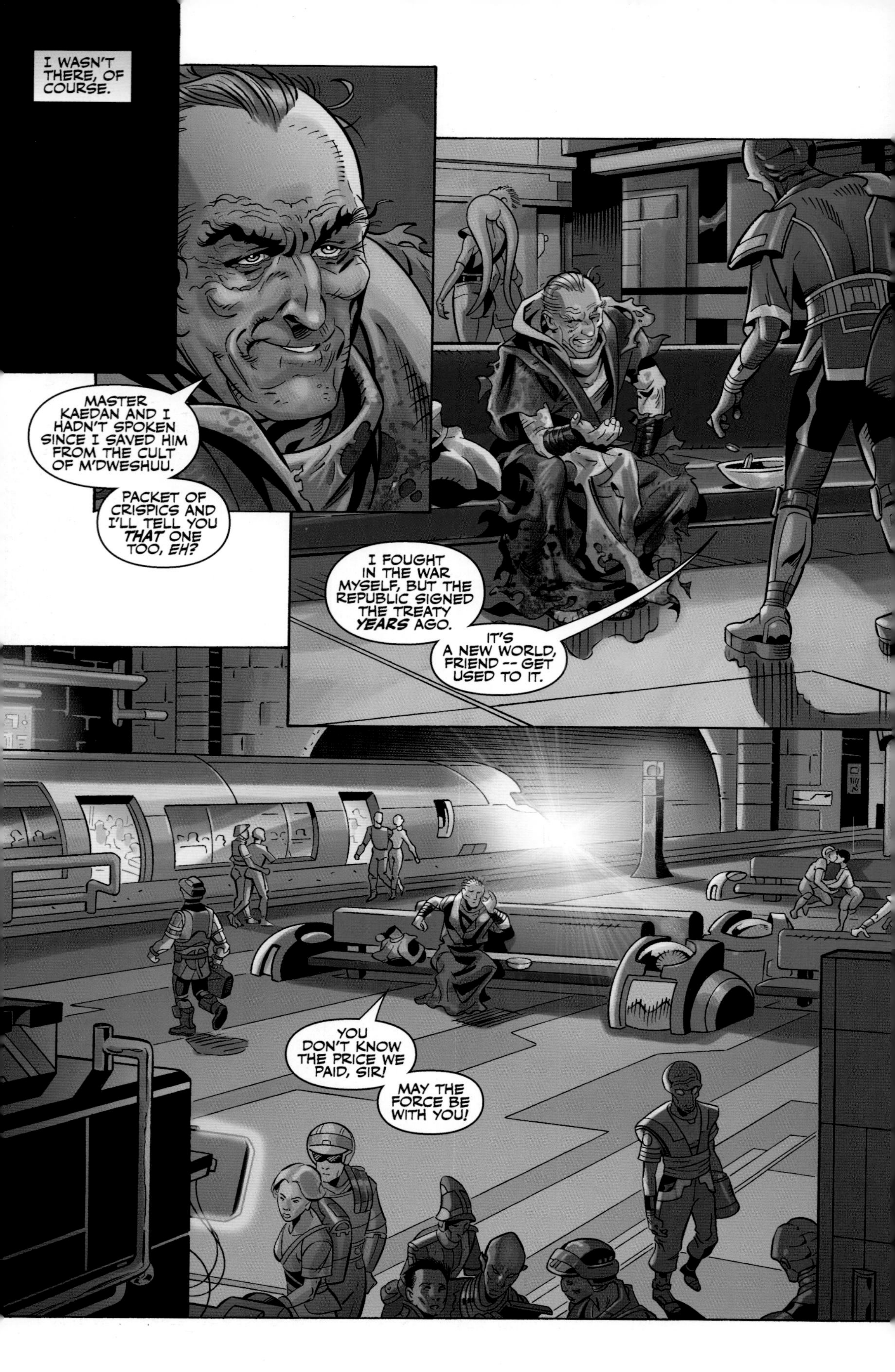
I WASN'T THERE, OF COURSE.
MASTER KAEDAN AND I HADN'T SPOKEN SINCE I SAVED HIM FROM THE CULT OF M'DWESHUU.
PACKET OF CRISPICS AND I'LL TELL YOU *THAT* ONE TOO, *EH?*
I FOUGHT IN THE WAR MYSELF, BUT THE REPUBLIC SIGNED THE TREATY *YEARS* AGO.
IT'S A NEW WORLD, FRIEND -- GET USED TO IT.
YOU DON'T KNOW THE PRICE WE PAID, SIR!
MAY THE FORCE BE WITH YOU!

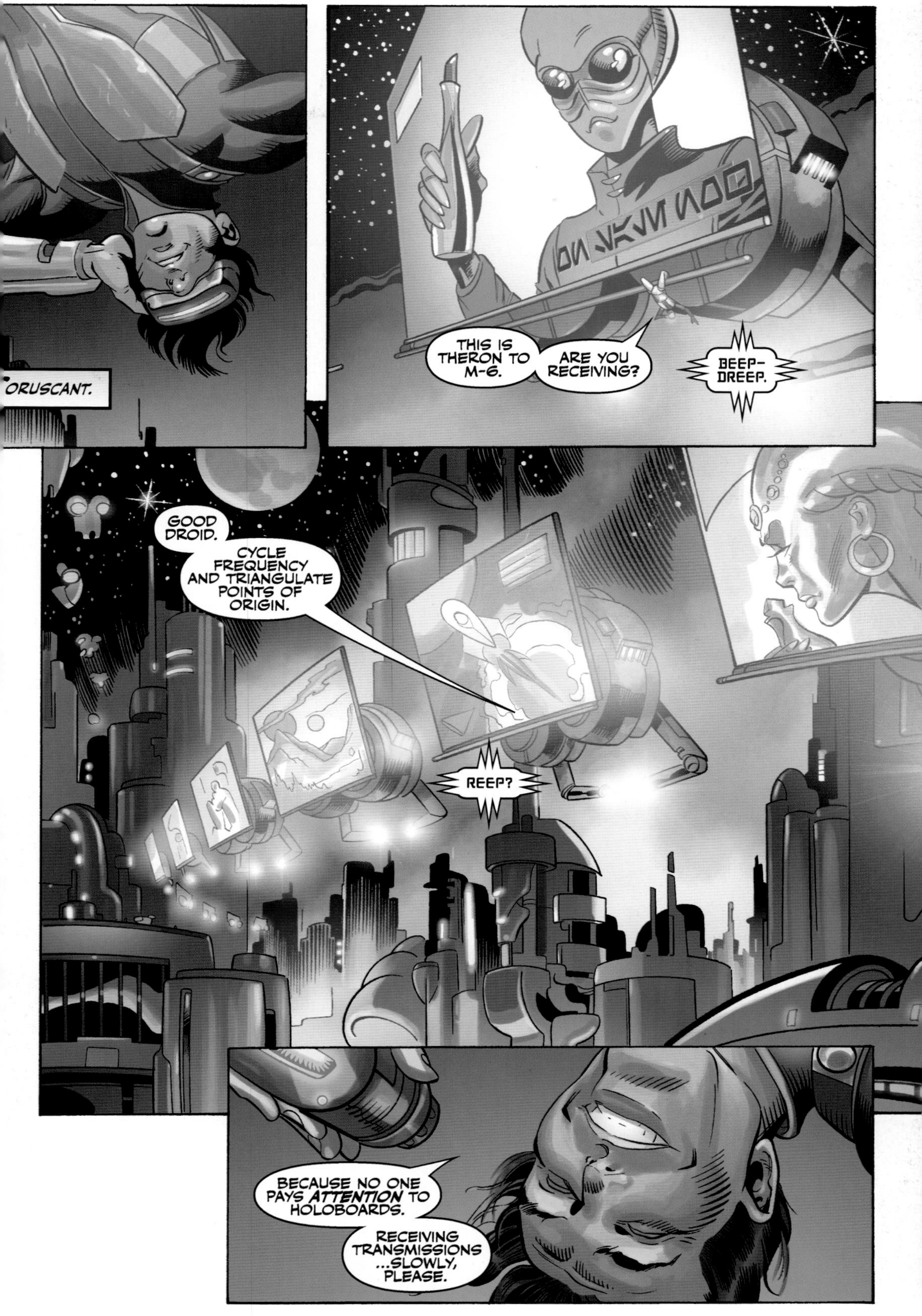
ORUSCANT.
THIS IS THERON TO M-6.
ARE YOU RECEIVING?
BEEP-DREEP.
GOOD DROID.
CYCLE FREQUENCY AND TRIANGULATE POINTS OF ORIGIN.
REEP?
BECAUSE NO ONE PAYS *ATTENTION* TO HOLOBOARDS.
RECEIVING TRANSMISSIONS ...SLOWLY, PLEASE.

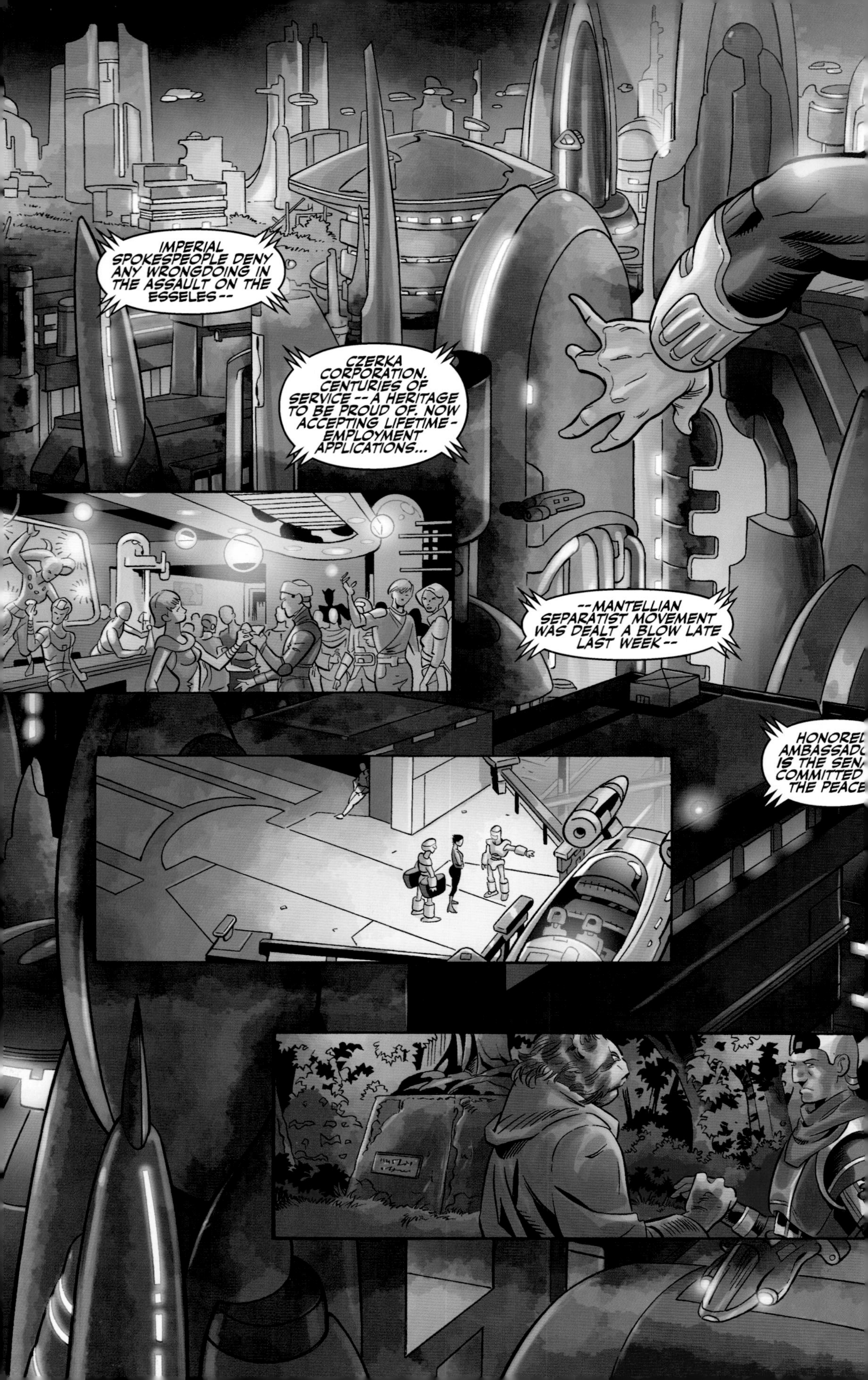
IMPERIAL SPOKESPEOPLE DENY ANY WRONGDOING IN THE ASSAULT ON THE ESSELES--
CZERKA CORPORATION. CENTURIES OF SERVICE -- A HERITAGE TO BE PROUD OF. NOW ACCEPTING LIFETIME-EMPLOYMENT APPLICATIONS...
--MANTELLIAN SEPARATIST MOVEMENT WAS DEALT A BLOW LATE LAST WEEK--

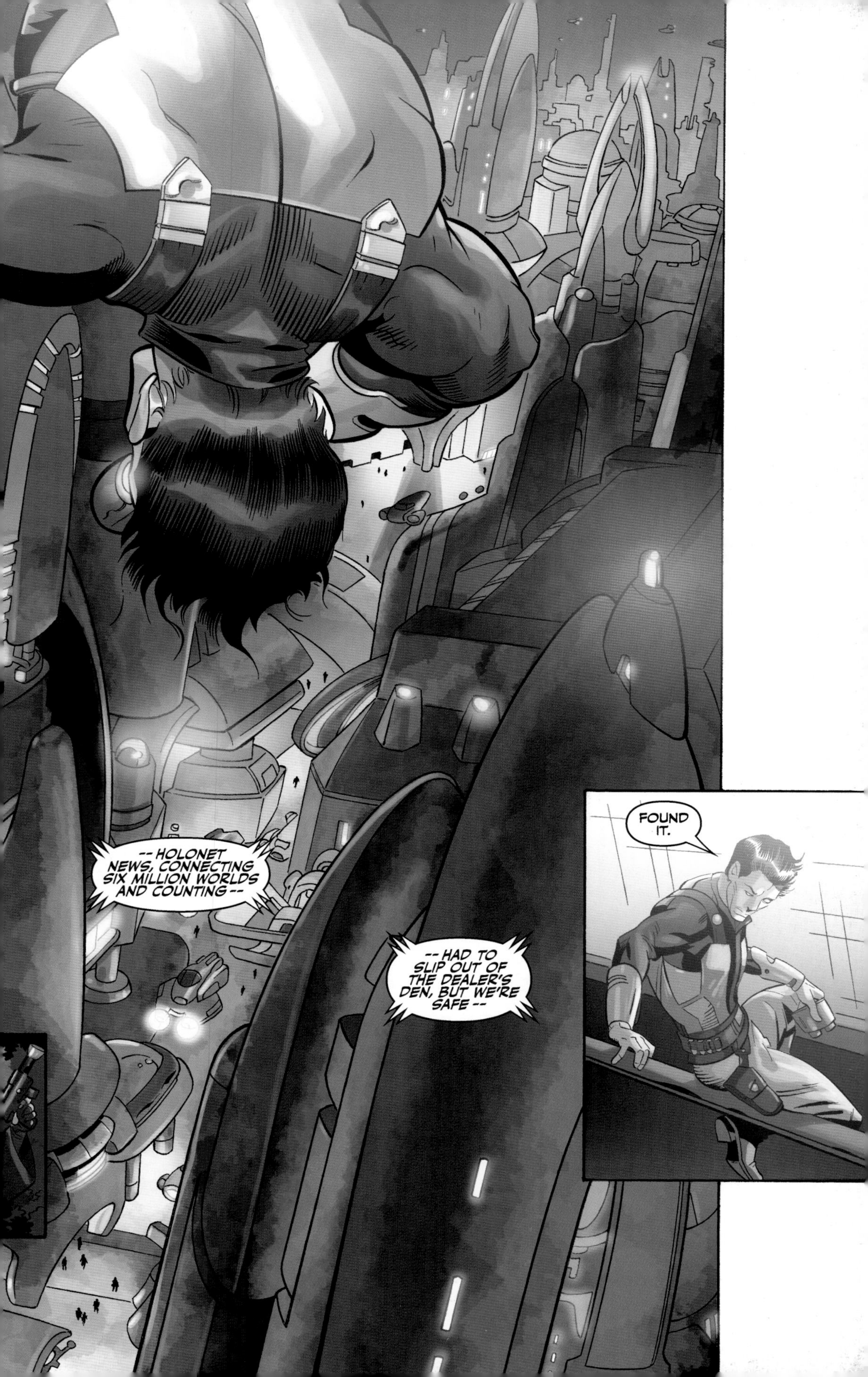

-- HOLONET NEWS, CONNECTING SIX MILLION WORLDS AND COUNTING --
-- HAD TO SLIP OUT OF THE DEALER'S DEN, BUT WE'RE SAFE --
FOUND IT.

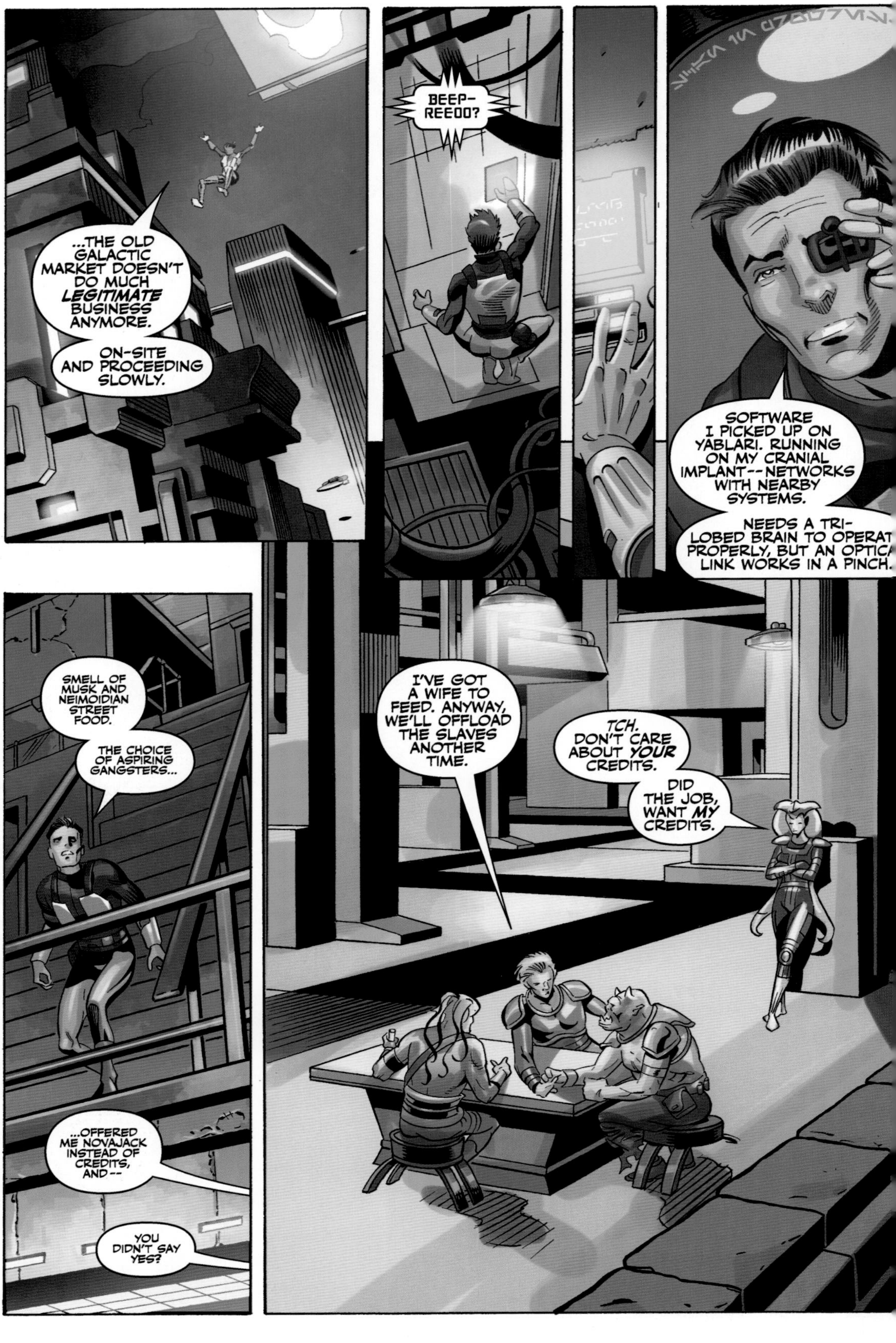
...THE OLD GALACTIC MARKET DOESN'T DO MUCH *LEGITIMATE* BUSINESS ANYMORE.
ON-SITE AND PROCEEDING SLOWLY.
BEEP-REEOO?
SOFTWARE I PICKED UP ON YABLARI. RUNNING ON MY CRANIAL IMPLANT--NETWORKS WITH NEARBY SYSTEMS.
NEEDS A TRI-LOBED BRAIN TO OPERAT PROPERLY, BUT AN OPTICA LINK WORKS IN A PINCH.
SMELL OF MUSK AND NEIMOIDIAN STREET FOOD.
THE CHOICE OF ASPIRING GANGSTERS...
...OFFERED ME NOVAJACK INSTEAD OF CREDITS, AND--
YOU DIDN'T SAY YES?
I'VE GOT A WIFE TO FEED. ANYWAY, WE'LL OFFLOAD THE SLAVES ANOTHER TIME.
TCH. DON'T CARE ABOUT *YOUR* CREDITS.
DID THE JOB, WANT *MY* CREDITS.

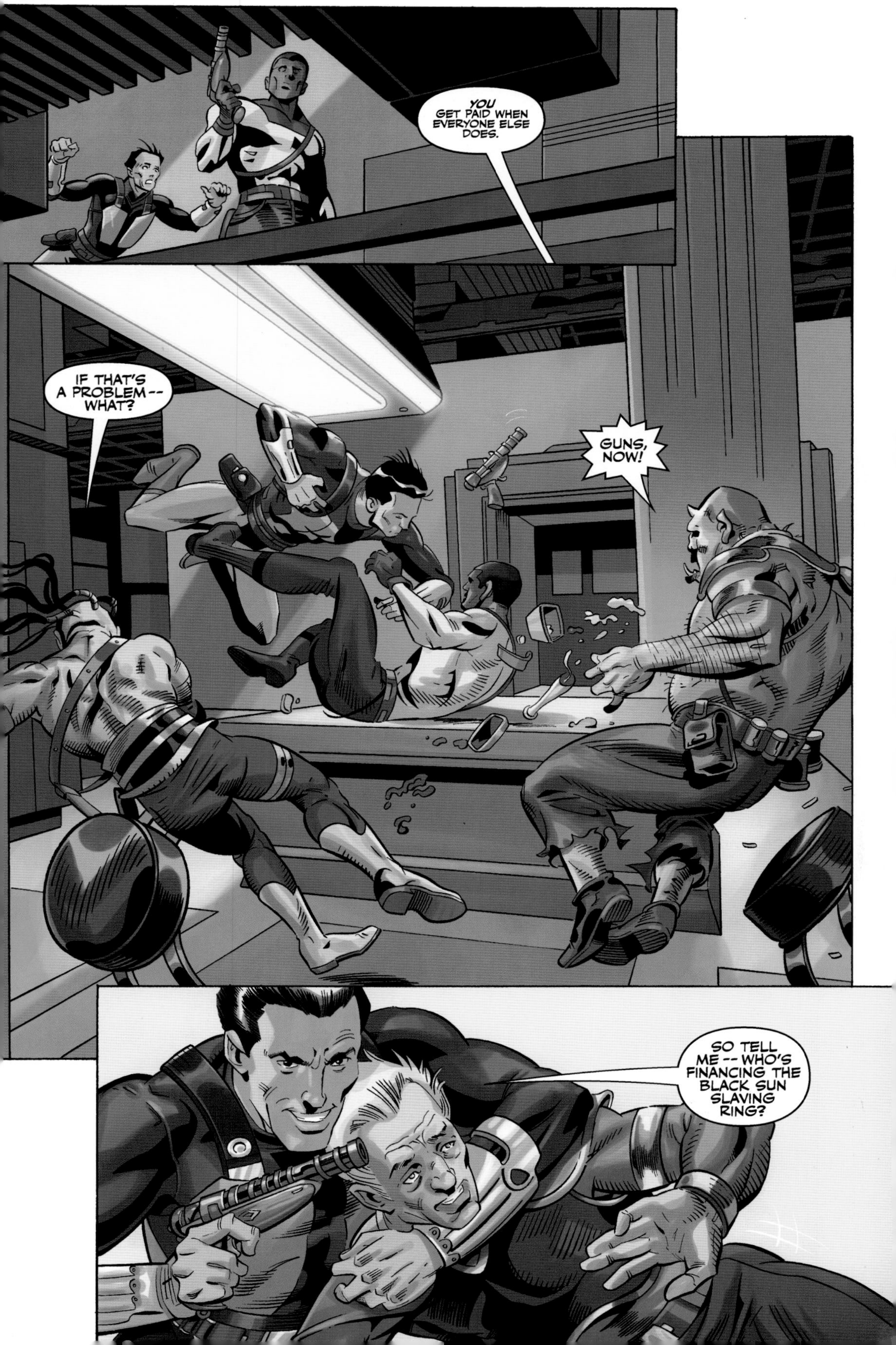
YOU GET PAID WHEN EVERYONE ELSE DOES.
IF THAT'S A PROBLEM -- WHAT?
GUNS, NOW!
SO TELL ME -- WHO'S FINANCING THE BLACK SUN SLAVING RING?

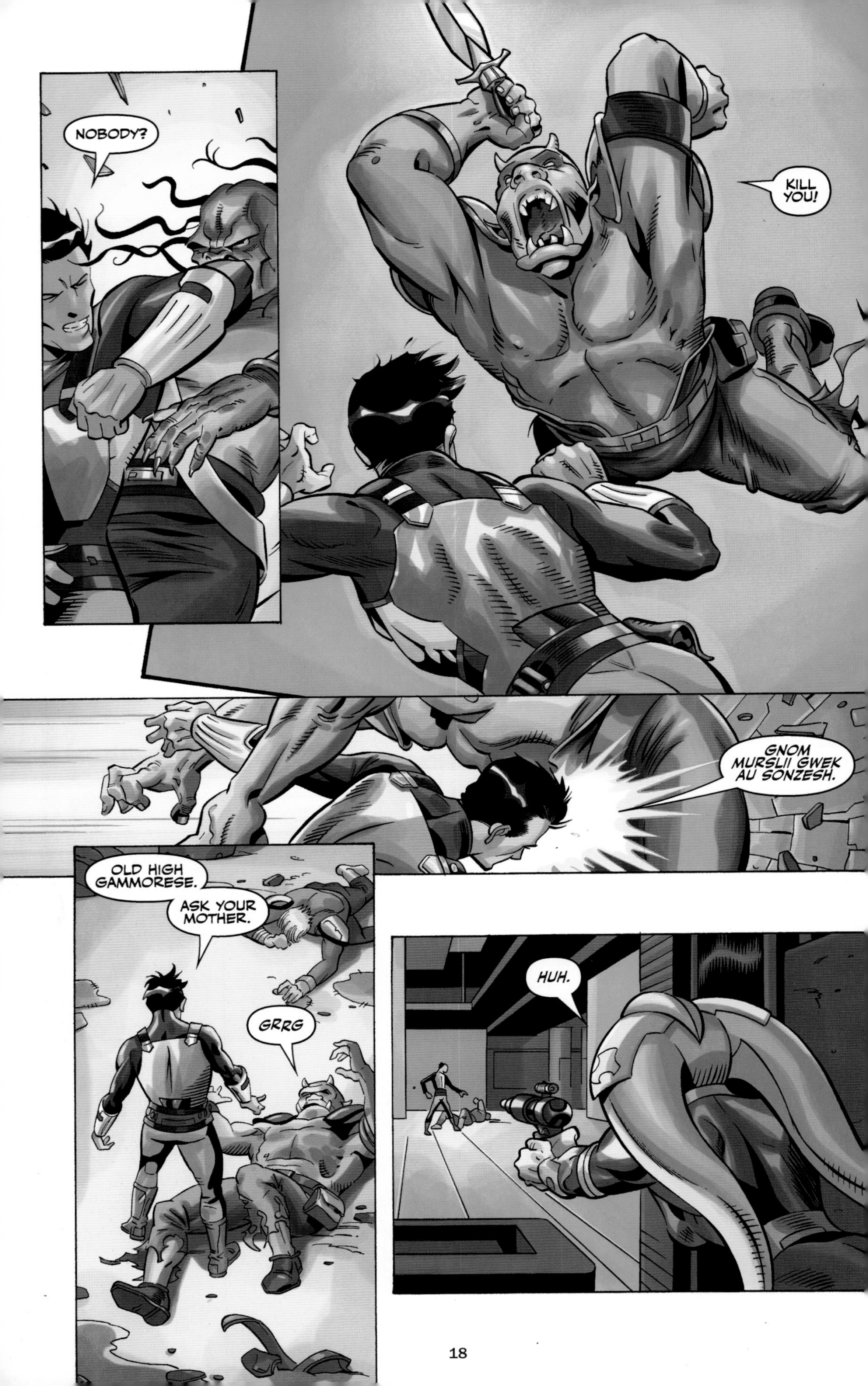
NOBODY?
KILL YOU!
GNOM MURSLII GWEK AU SONZESH.
OLD HIGH GAMMORESE.
ASK YOUR MOTHER.
GRRG
HUH.

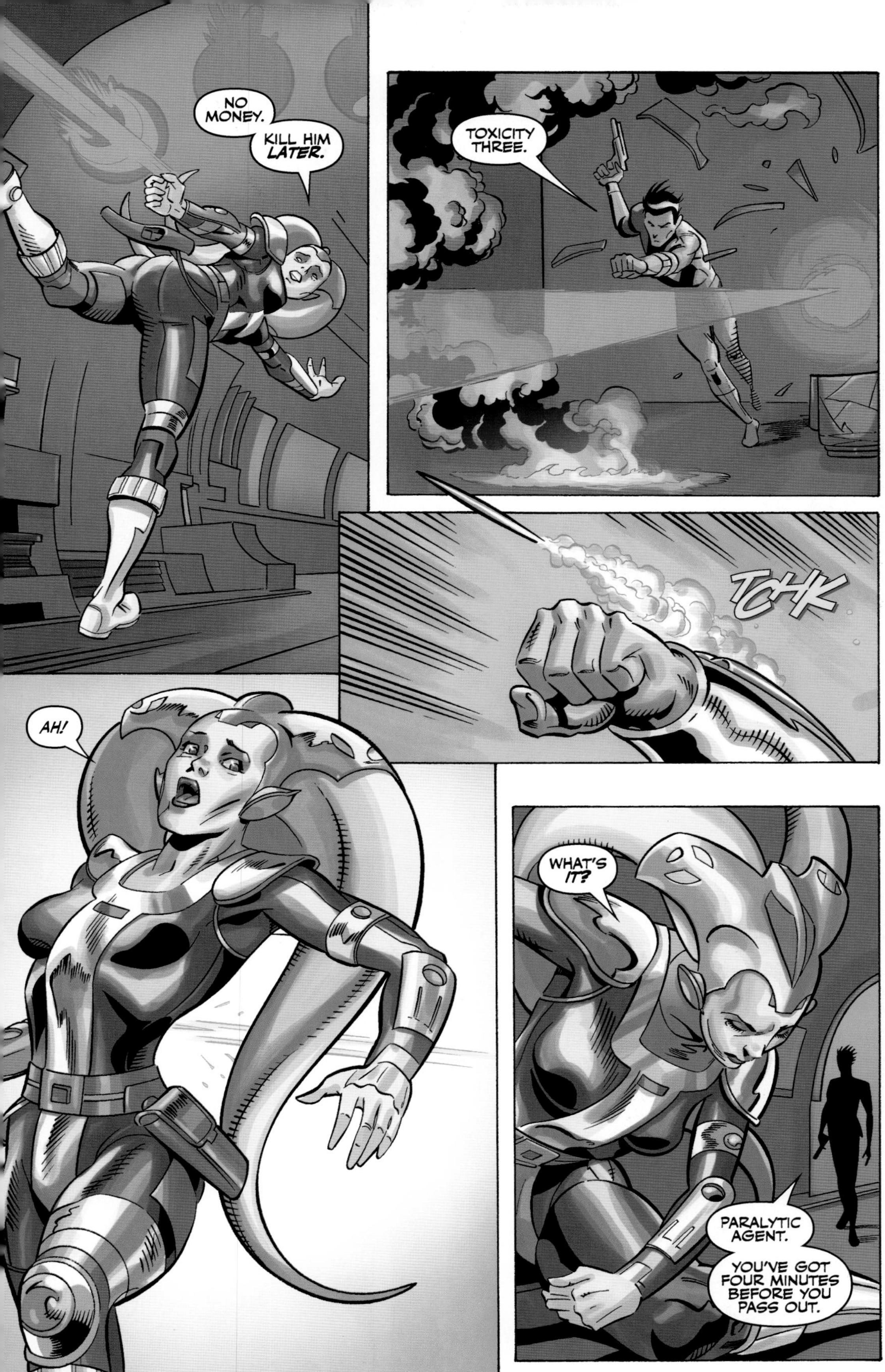

NO MONEY.
KILL HIM LATER.
TOXICITY THREE.
TCHK
AH!
WHAT'S IT?
PARALYTIC AGENT.
YOU'VE GOT FOUR MINUTES BEFORE YOU PASS OUT.

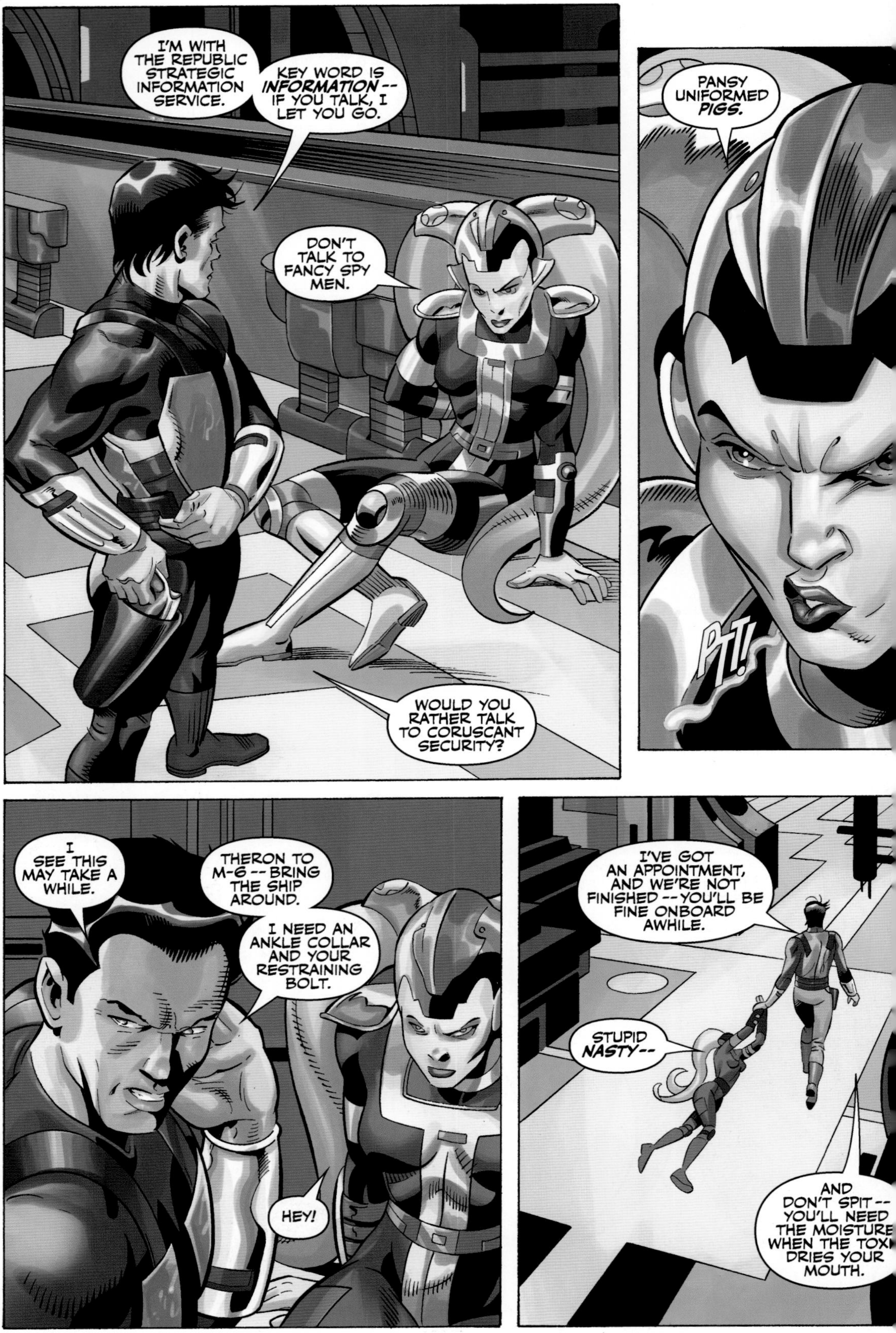
I'M WITH THE REPUBLIC STRATEGIC INFORMATION SERVICE.
KEY WORD IS *INFORMATION* -- IF YOU TALK, I LET YOU GO.
DON'T TALK TO FANCY SPY MEN.
WOULD YOU RATHER TALK TO CORUSCANT SECURITY?
PANSY UNIFORMED *PIGS.*
PTT!
I SEE THIS MAY TAKE A WHILE.
THERON TO M-6 -- BRING THE SHIP AROUND.
I NEED AN ANKLE COLLAR AND YOUR RESTRAINING BOLT.
HEY!
I'VE GOT AN APPOINTMENT, AND WE'RE NOT FINISHED -- YOU'LL BE FINE ONBOARD AWHILE.
STUPID *NASTY* --
AND DON'T SPIT -- YOU'LL NEED THE MOISTURE WHEN THE TOXI DRIES YOUR MOUTH.

THIS IS MY LIFE.

OBSERVE AND FIGHT.

INTERROGATE AND MEDITATE.

ON THE BAD NIGHTS, SKIP THE MEDITATION. HARD TO FOCUS WITH SIXTY LEVELS OF TRAFFIC ECHOING BELOW...

...NOT TO MENTION THE BRUISES AND OTHER DISTRACTIONS.

BEOO-REEP!

HE'S UP EARLY.

TELL THE DIRECTOR I'M ON MY WAY.

STRANGE, THE THINGS THAT STOP FEELING SPECIAL.

...THE GIRL'S NAME IS TEFF'ITH, AND SHE'S EITHER A NASTY *LOCAL THUG* OR AN UNSPECTACULAR *GALACTIC MENACE.*

I PLAN TO KEEP HER OFF-BOOKS FOR A WHILE--

DID YOU ORDER BREAKFAST?

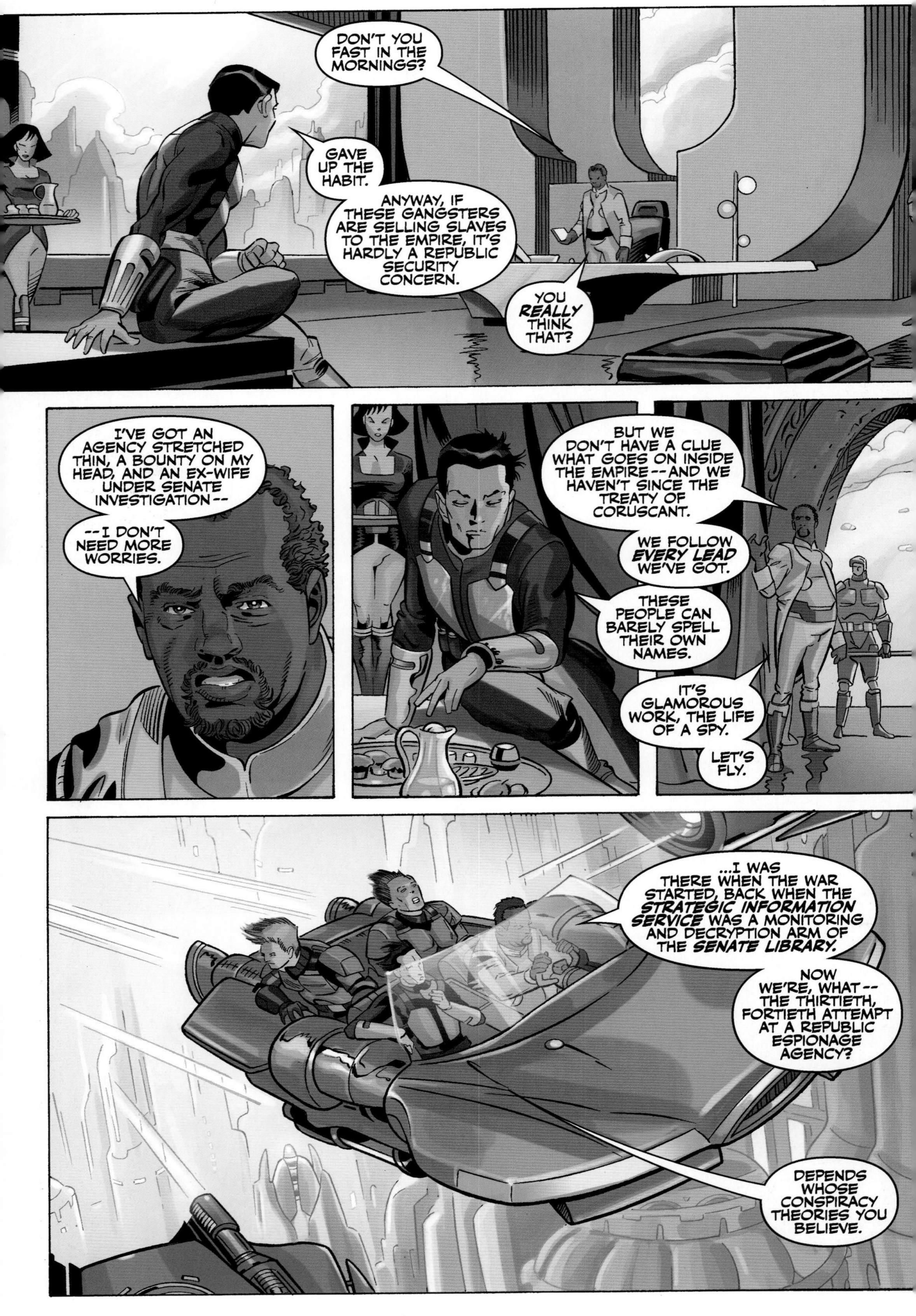
DON'T YOU FAST IN THE MORNINGS?
GAVE UP THE HABIT.
ANYWAY, IF THESE GANGSTERS ARE SELLING SLAVES TO THE EMPIRE, IT'S HARDLY A REPUBLIC SECURITY CONCERN.
YOU *REALLY* THINK THAT?
I'VE GOT AN AGENCY STRETCHED THIN, A BOUNTY ON MY HEAD, AND AN EX-WIFE UNDER SENATE INVESTIGATION--
--I DON'T NEED MORE WORRIES.
BUT WE DON'T HAVE A CLUE WHAT GOES ON INSIDE THE EMPIRE--AND WE HAVEN'T SINCE THE TREATY OF CORUSCANT.
WE FOLLOW *EVERY LEAD* WE'VE GOT.
THESE PEOPLE CAN BARELY SPELL THEIR OWN NAMES.
IT'S GLAMOROUS WORK, THE LIFE OF A SPY.
LET'S FLY.
...I WAS THERE WHEN THE WAR STARTED, BACK WHEN THE *STRATEGIC INFORMATION SERVICE* WAS A MONITORING AND DECRYPTION ARM OF THE *SENATE LIBRARY.*
NOW WE'RE, WHAT--THE THIRTIETH, FORTIETH ATTEMPT AT A REPUBLIC ESPIONAGE AGENCY?
DEPENDS WHOSE CONSPIRACY THEORIES YOU BELIEVE.

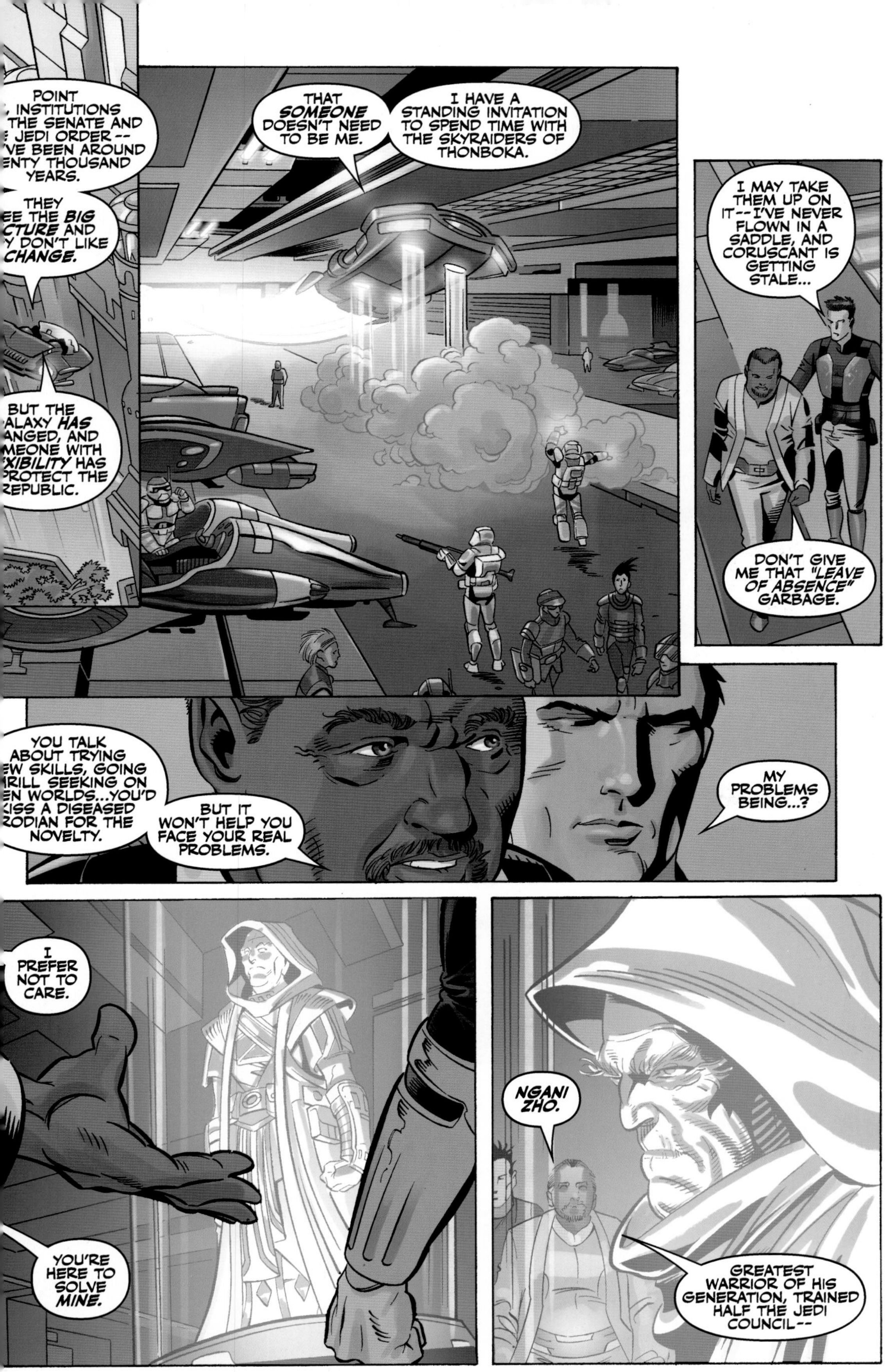
POINT
, INSTITUTIONS
THE SENATE AND
JEDI ORDER--
'VE BEEN AROUND
ENTY THOUSAND
YEARS.
THEY
EE THE BIG
CTURE AND
Y DON'T LIKE
CHANGE.
BUT THE
ALAXY HAS
ANGED, AND
MEONE WITH
XIBILITY HAS
PROTECT THE
REPUBLIC.
THAT SOMEONE DOESN'T NEED TO BE ME.
I HAVE A STANDING INVITATION TO SPEND TIME WITH THE SKYRAIDERS OF THONBOKA.
I MAY TAKE THEM UP ON IT--I'VE NEVER FLOWN IN A SADDLE, AND CORUSCANT IS GETTING STALE...
DON'T GIVE ME THAT "LEAVE OF ABSENCE" GARBAGE.
YOU TALK
ABOUT TRYING
EW SKILLS, GOING
RILL SEEKING ON
EN WORLDS...YOU'D
KISS A DISEASED
RODIAN FOR THE
NOVELTY.
BUT IT WON'T HELP YOU FACE YOUR REAL PROBLEMS.
MY PROBLEMS BEING...?
I PREFER NOT TO CARE.
YOU'RE HERE TO SOLVE MINE.
NGANI ZHO.
GREATEST WARRIOR OF HIS GENERATION, TRAINED HALF THE JEDI COUNCIL--

--INCLUDING GRAND MASTER SATELE SHAN.

I'M FAMILIAR WITH HIS CREDENTIALS.

I BET YOU ARE.

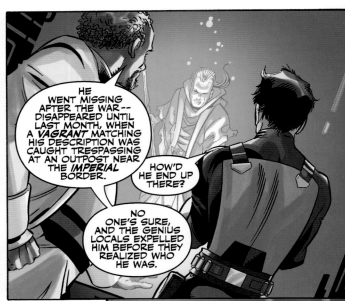

HE WENT MISSING AFTER THE WAR-- DISAPPEARED UNTIL LAST MONTH, WHEN A *VAGRANT* MATCHING HIS DESCRIPTION WAS CAUGHT TRESPASSING AT AN OUTPOST NEAR THE *IMPERIAL* BORDER.

HOW'D HE END UP THERE?

NO ONE'S SURE, AND THE GENIUS LOCALS EXPELLED HIM BEFORE THEY REALIZED WHO HE WAS.

SAID HE DEMANDED FOOD AND CREDITS --CLAIMED HE WAS ON HIS WAY BACK FROM THE VESLA SYSTEM.

VESLA'S A BLACK SECTOR -- CEDED TO THE EMPIRE IN THE TREATY...

...AND TOTAL SILENCE SINCE THEN.

SENT A FEW AGENTS THERE YEARS AGO, BUT NOBODY CAME BACK.

IF NGANI ZHO'S BEEN BEHIND ENEMY LINES, THAT MAN COULD BE THE EDGE WE'RE LOOKING FOR.

I WANT YOU TO RENDEZVOUS WITH HIM, FIND OUT EVERYTHING HE KNOWS.

HUH.

EVEN AT HIS BEST... ZHO WAS NEVER *RELIABLE.*

IF I PLANNED TO *RELY* ON HIM, I'D TRUST THE JEDI COUNCIL TO HANDLE THIS JOB.

I'M SENDING YOU TO FIND TH*TRUTH*--

--UNLES YOU STIL WANT THA VACATION

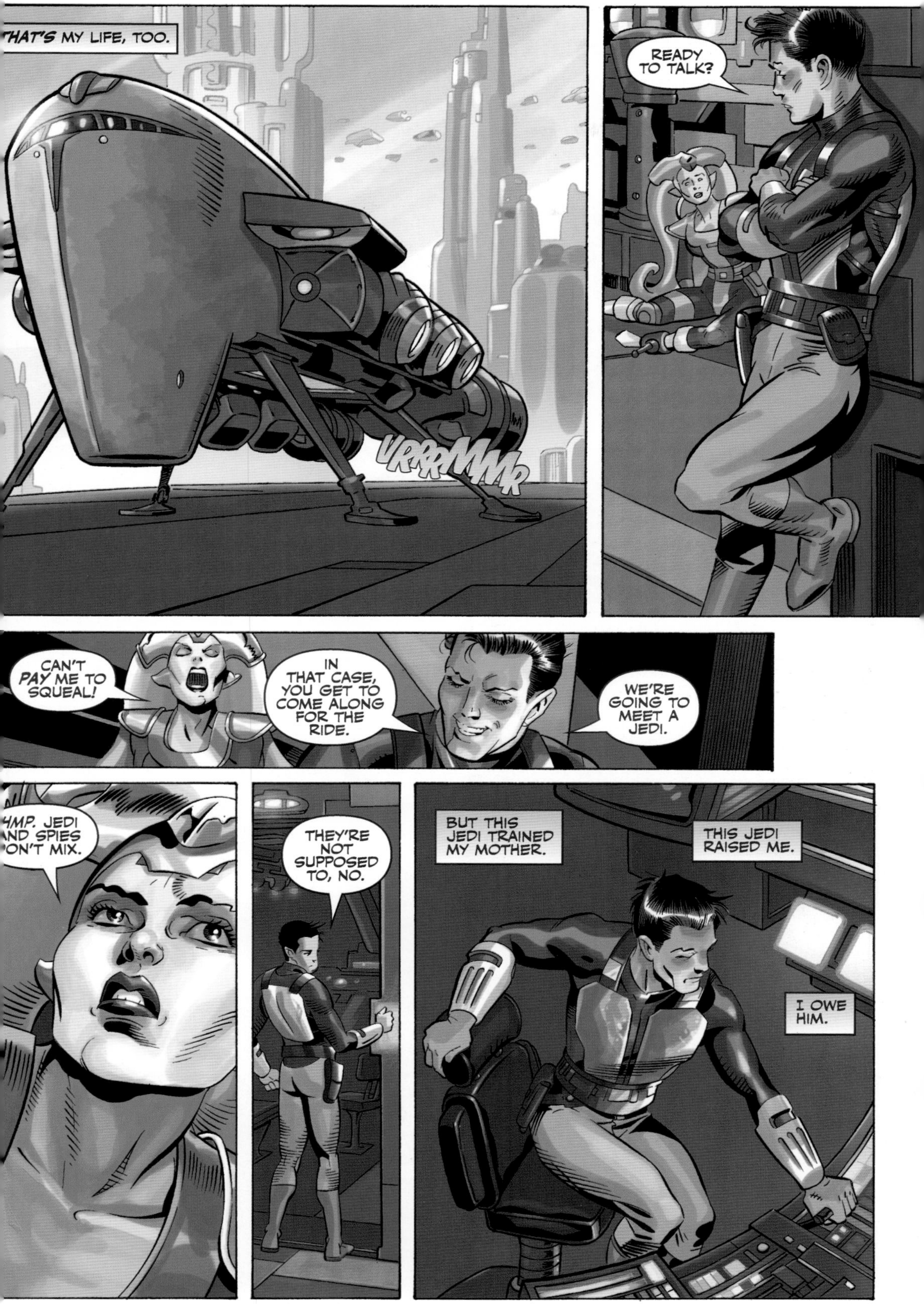
THAT'S MY LIFE, TOO.
URRRMMMR
READY TO TALK?
CAN'T PAY ME TO SQUEAL!
IN THAT CASE, YOU GET TO COME ALONG FOR THE RIDE.
WE'RE GOING TO MEET A JEDI.
HMP. JEDI AND SPIES DON'T MIX.
THEY'RE NOT SUPPOSED TO, NO.
BUT THIS JEDI TRAINED MY MOTHER.
THIS JEDI RAISED ME.
I OWE HIM.

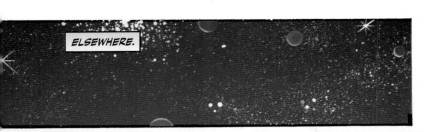

ELSEWHERE.

SSSSSSSS

BATTERY
RECALIBRATIONS
ARE WORKING.

EXCESS
ENERGY RADIATES
THROUGH THE SHIELDS,
SANITIZING EVERYTHING
WITHIN THREE
KILOMETERS.

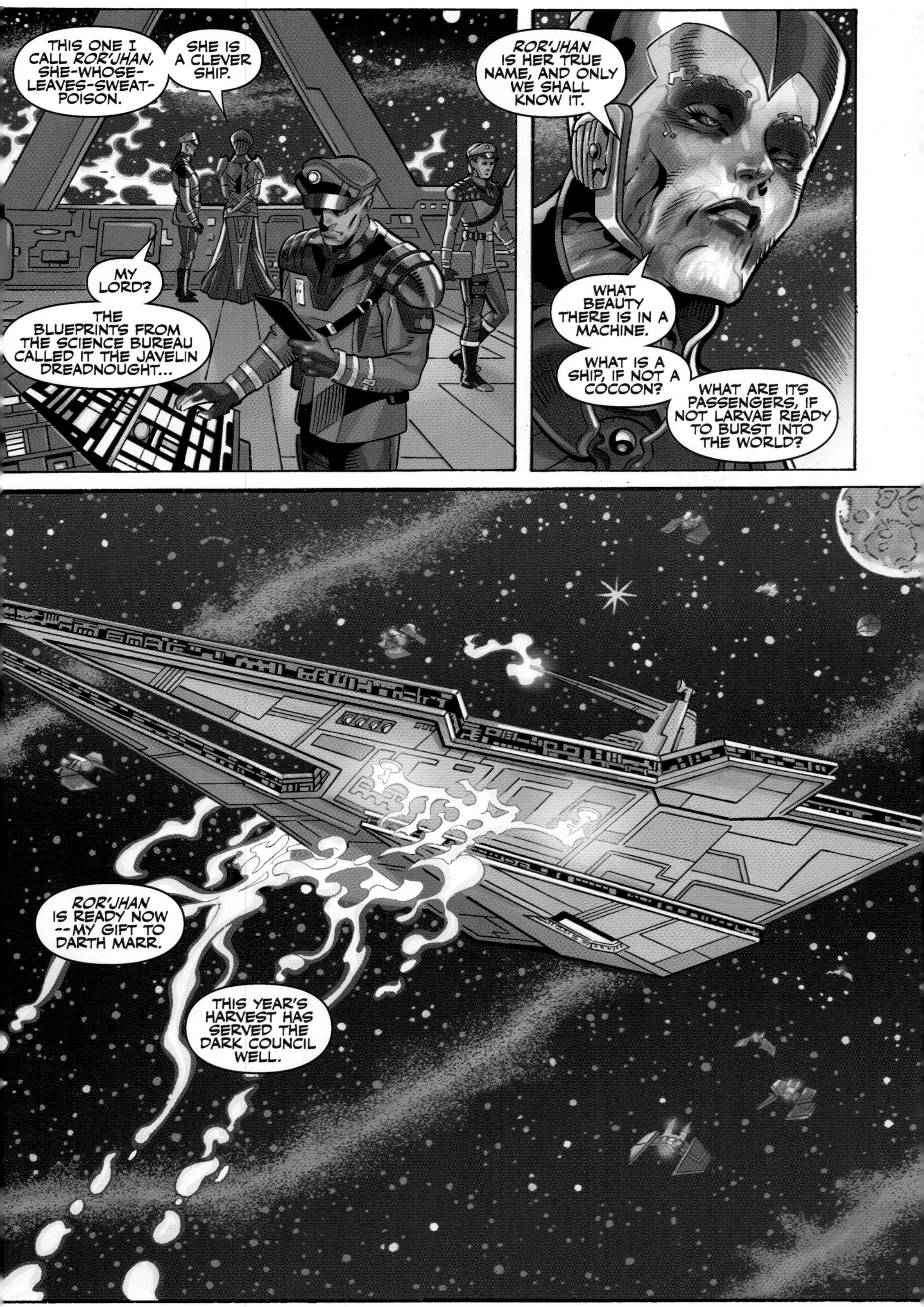
THIS ONE I CALL *ROR'JHAN,* SHE-WHOSE-LEAVES-SWEAT-POISON.
SHE IS A CLEVER SHIP.
MY LORD?
THE BLUEPRINTS FROM THE SCIENCE BUREAU CALLED IT THE JAVELIN DREADNOUGHT...
ROR'JHAN IS HER TRUE NAME, AND ONLY WE SHALL KNOW IT.
WHAT BEAUTY THERE IS IN A MACHINE.
WHAT IS A SHIP, IF NOT A COCOON?
WHAT ARE ITS PASSENGERS, IF NOT LARVAE READY TO BURST INTO THE WORLD?
ROR'JHAN IS READY NOW --MY GIFT TO DARTH MARR.
THIS YEAR'S HARVEST HAS SERVED THE DARK COUNCIL WELL.

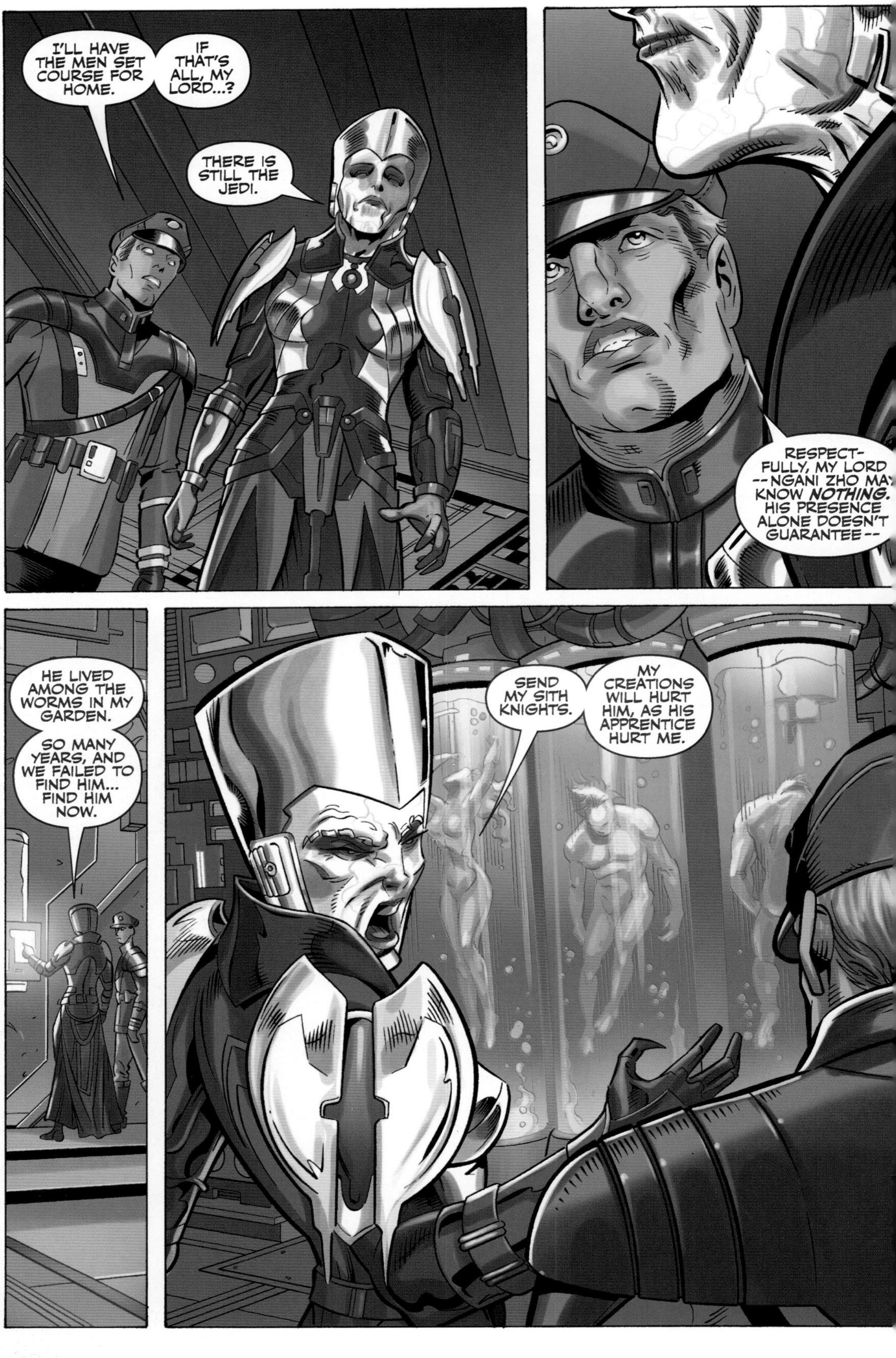
I'LL HAVE THE MEN SET COURSE FOR HOME.
IF THAT'S ALL, MY LORD...?
THERE IS STILL THE JEDI.
RESPECT-FULLY, MY LORD --NGANI ZHO MA KNOW NOTHING. HIS PRESENCE ALONE DOESN'T GUARANTEE--
HE LIVED AMONG THE WORMS IN MY GARDEN.
SO MANY YEARS, AND WE FAILED TO FIND HIM... FIND HIM NOW.
SEND MY SITH KNIGHTS.
MY CREATIONS WILL HURT HIM, AS HIS APPRENTICE HURT ME.

LET ME TELL YOU HOW THE WAR ENDED.

THE EMPIRE HAD EMERGED FROM THE DARK OF THE GALAXY TO CAPTURE A THOUSAND STAR SYSTEMS.

THE REPUBLIC'S GOLDEN AGE TURNED TO FIRE AND ASH...

...AND AS THE WAR WENT ON, THE ENEMY SUBJUGATED *MORE* PLANETS, BUILT *MORE* SHIPS IN THEIR LUST FOR CONQUEST.

BUT TO START A WAR -- TO SEIZE A MAN'S HOME -- IS ONE THING.

TO FIGHT FOR YEARS -- TO HOLD ONE'S PRIZE AND PUT DOWN REBELLION AFTER REBELLION -- IS ANOTHER.

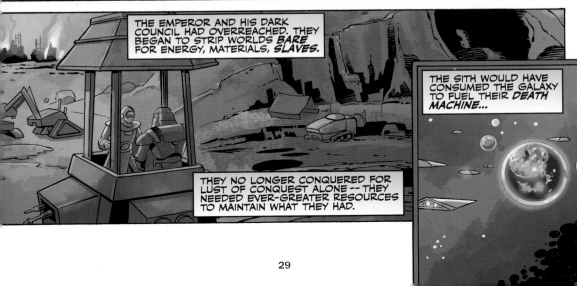

THE EMPEROR AND HIS DARK COUNCIL HAD OVERREACHED. THEY BEGAN TO STRIP WORLDS *BARE* FOR ENERGY, MATERIALS, *SLAVES.*

THE SITH WOULD HAVE CONSUMED THE GALAXY TO FUEL THEIR *DEATH MACHINE*...

THEY NO LONGER CONQUERED FOR LUST OF CONQUEST ALONE -- THEY NEEDED EVER-GREATER RESOURCES TO MAINTAIN WHAT THEY HAD.

...HAD WE NOT *STOPPED* THEM AT ALDERAAN AND RHEN VAR.

THE MEMORIAL DROIDS TOOK THREE DAYS TO RECITE THE NAMES OF THE FALLEN --

-- BUT THE ENEMY'S *EXPANSION* HAD BEEN HALTED.

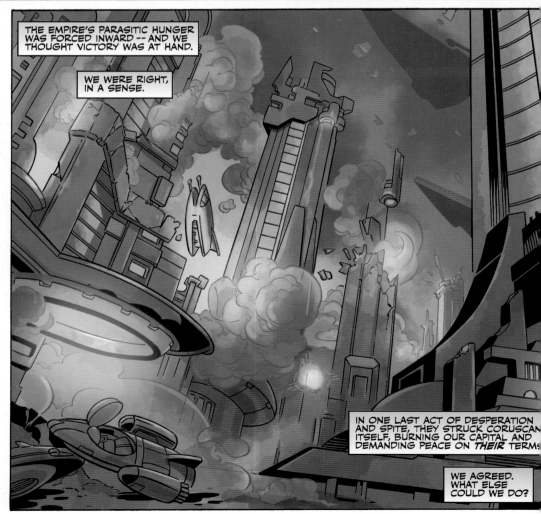

THE EMPIRE'S PARASITIC HUNGER WAS FORCED INWARD -- AND WE THOUGHT VICTORY WAS AT HAND.

WE WERE RIGHT, IN A SENSE.

IN ONE LAST ACT OF DESPERATION AND SPITE, THEY STRUCK CORUSCANT ITSELF, BURNING OUR CAPITAL AND DEMANDING PEACE ON *THEIR* TERMS.

WE AGREED. WHAT ELSE COULD WE DO?

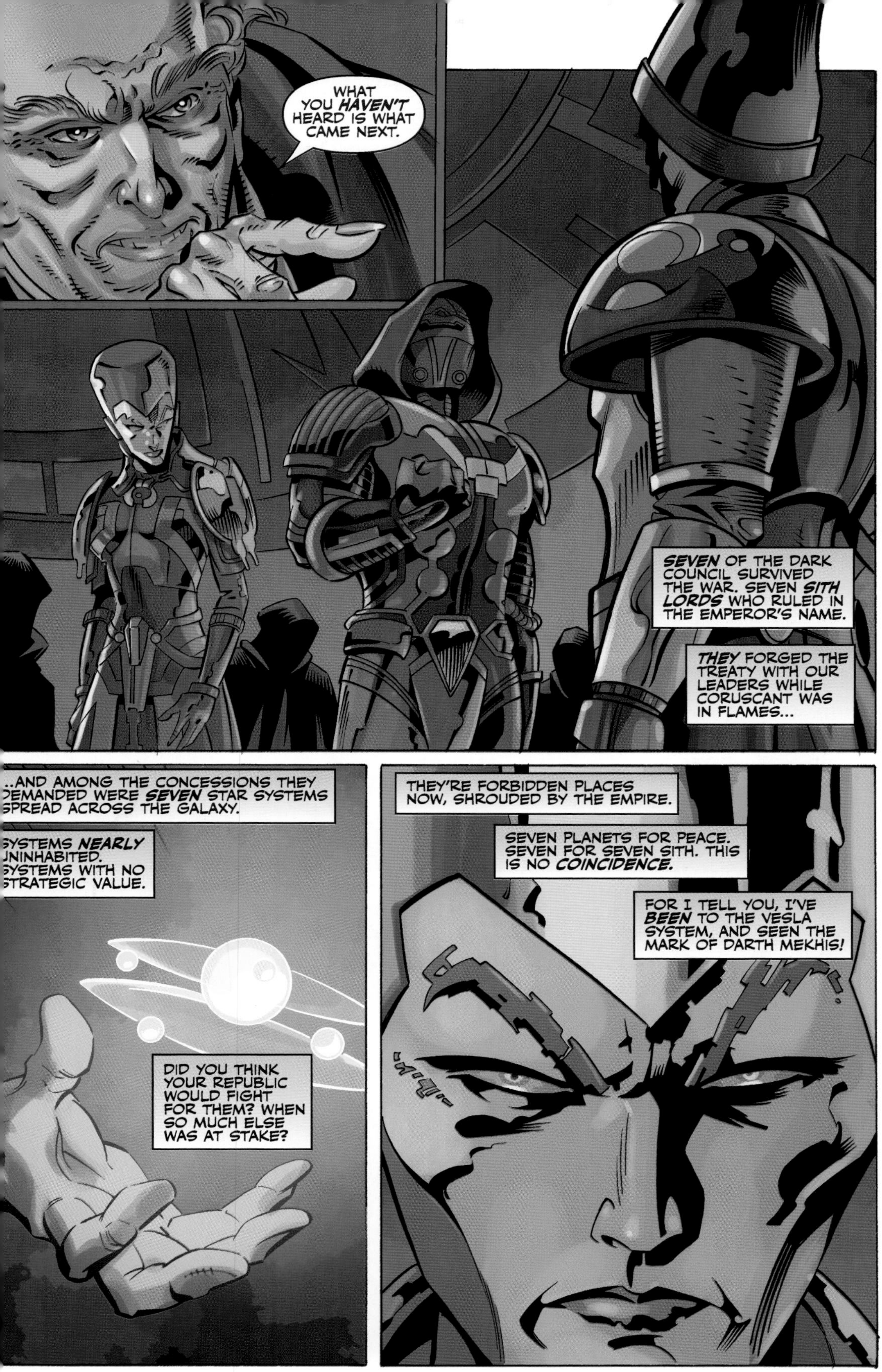
WHAT YOU HAVEN'T HEARD IS WHAT CAME NEXT.
SEVEN OF THE DARK COUNCIL SURVIVED THE WAR. SEVEN SITH LORDS WHO RULED IN THE EMPEROR'S NAME.
THEY FORGED THE TREATY WITH OUR LEADERS WHILE CORUSCANT WAS IN FLAMES...
...AND AMONG THE CONCESSIONS THEY DEMANDED WERE SEVEN STAR SYSTEMS SPREAD ACROSS THE GALAXY.
SYSTEMS NEARLY UNINHABITED. SYSTEMS WITH NO STRATEGIC VALUE.
DID YOU THINK YOUR REPUBLIC WOULD FIGHT FOR THEM? WHEN SO MUCH ELSE WAS AT STAKE?
THEY'RE FORBIDDEN PLACES NOW, SHROUDED BY THE EMPIRE.
SEVEN PLANETS FOR PEACE. SEVEN FOR SEVEN SITH. THIS IS NO COINCIDENCE.
FOR I TELL YOU, I'VE BEEN TO THE VESLA SYSTEM, AND SEEN THE MARK OF DARTH MEKHIS!

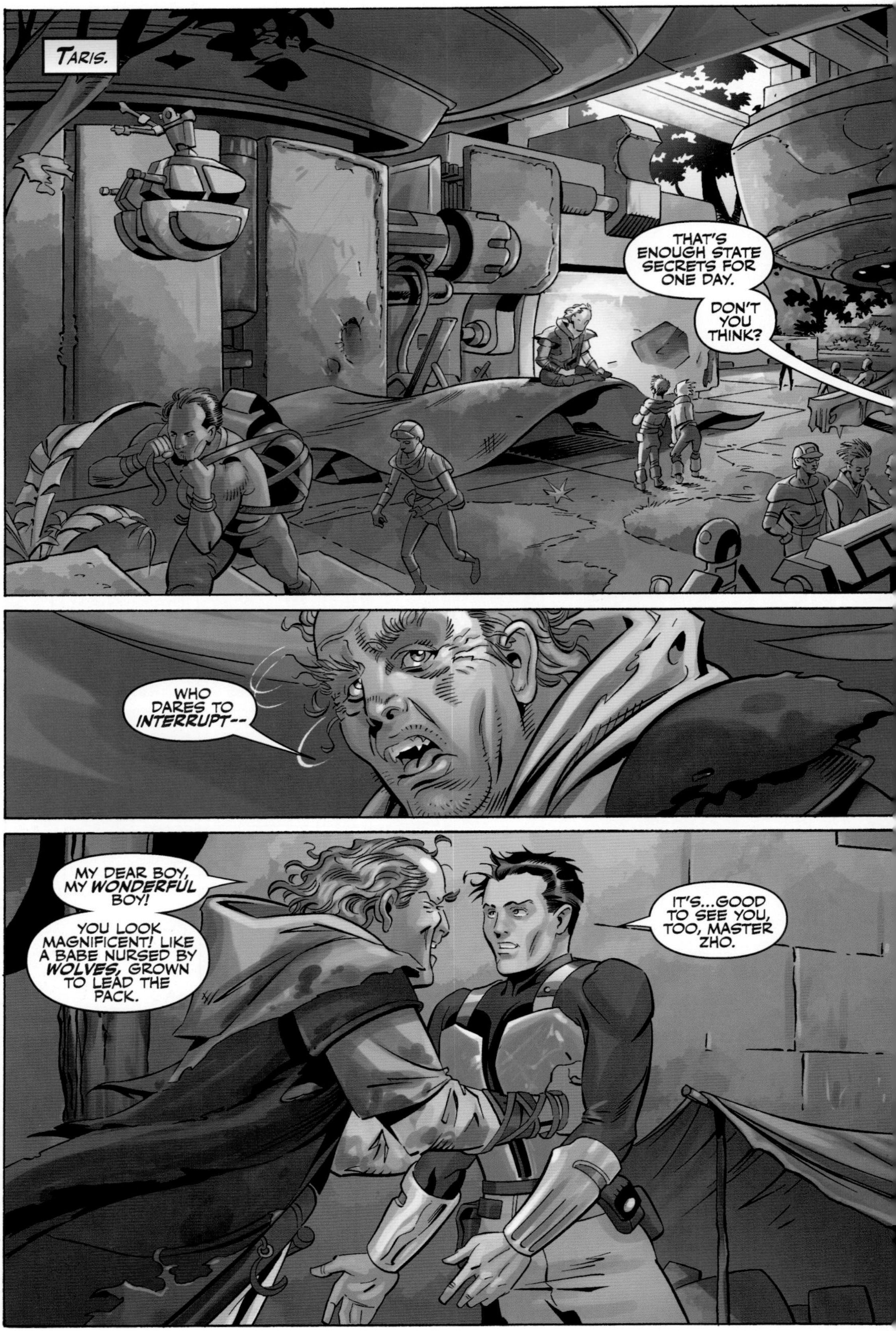
TARIS.
THAT'S ENOUGH STATE SECRETS FOR ONE DAY.
DON'T YOU THINK?
WHO DARES TO *INTERRUPT--*
MY DEAR BOY, MY ***WONDERFUL*** BOY!
YOU LOOK MAGNIFICENT! LIKE A BABE NURSED BY ***WOLVES,*** GROWN TO LEAD THE PACK.
IT'S...GOOD TO SEE YOU, TOO, MASTER ZHO.

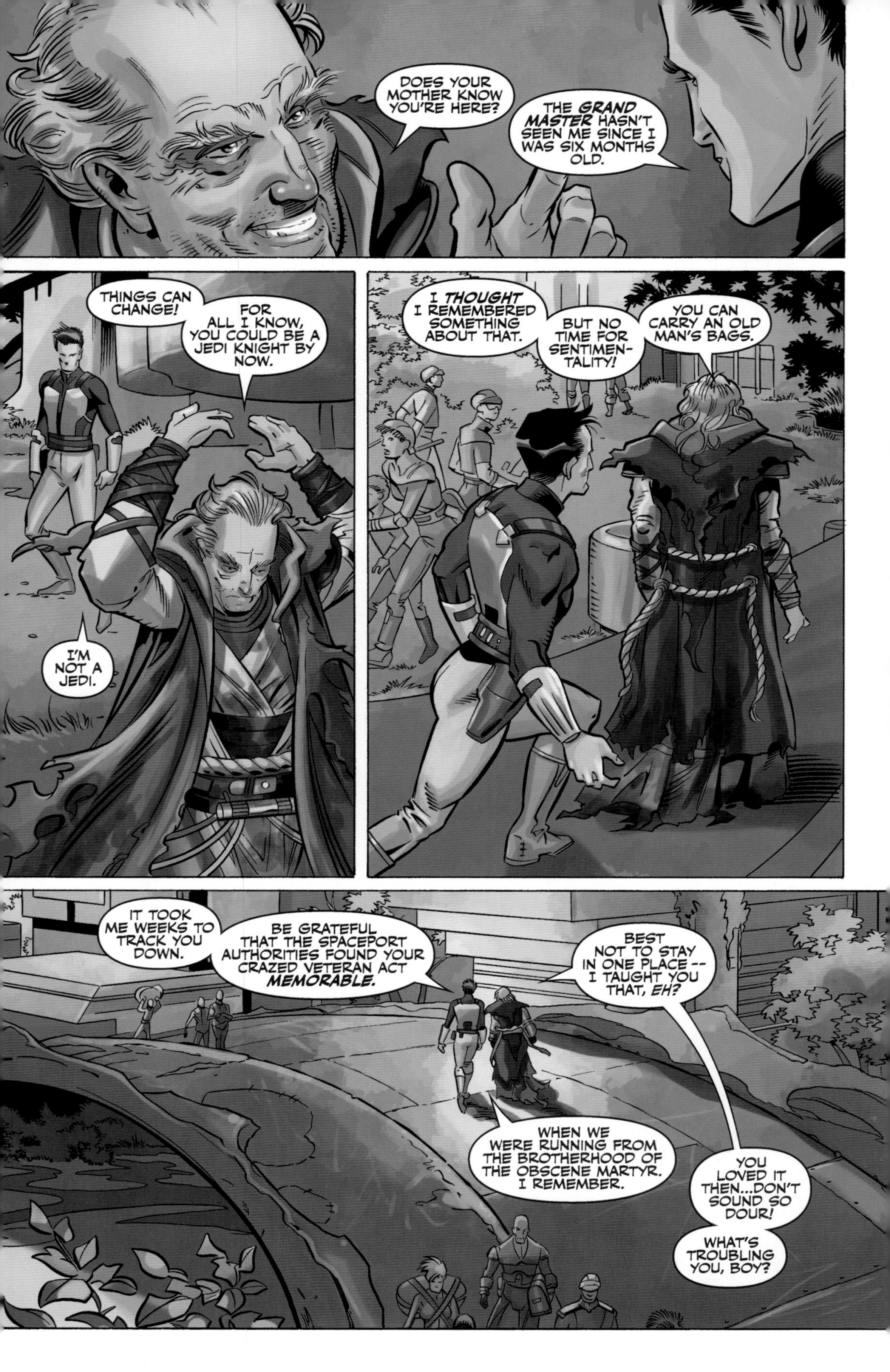
DOES YOUR MOTHER KNOW YOU'RE HERE?
THE GRAND MASTER HASN'T SEEN ME SINCE I WAS SIX MONTHS OLD.
THINGS CAN CHANGE!
FOR ALL I KNOW, YOU COULD BE A JEDI KNIGHT BY NOW.
I'M NOT A JEDI.
I THOUGHT I REMEMBERED SOMETHING ABOUT THAT.
BUT NO TIME FOR SENTIMENTALITY!
YOU CAN CARRY AN OLD MAN'S BAGS.
IT TOOK ME WEEKS TO TRACK YOU DOWN.
BE GRATEFUL THAT THE SPACEPORT AUTHORITIES FOUND YOUR CRAZED VETERAN ACT MEMORABLE.
BEST NOT TO STAY IN ONE PLACE -- I TAUGHT YOU THAT, EH?
WHEN WE WERE RUNNING FROM THE BROTHERHOOD OF THE OBSCENE MARTYR. I REMEMBER.
YOU LOVED IT THEN...DON'T SOUND SO DOUR!
WHAT'S TROUBLING YOU, BOY?

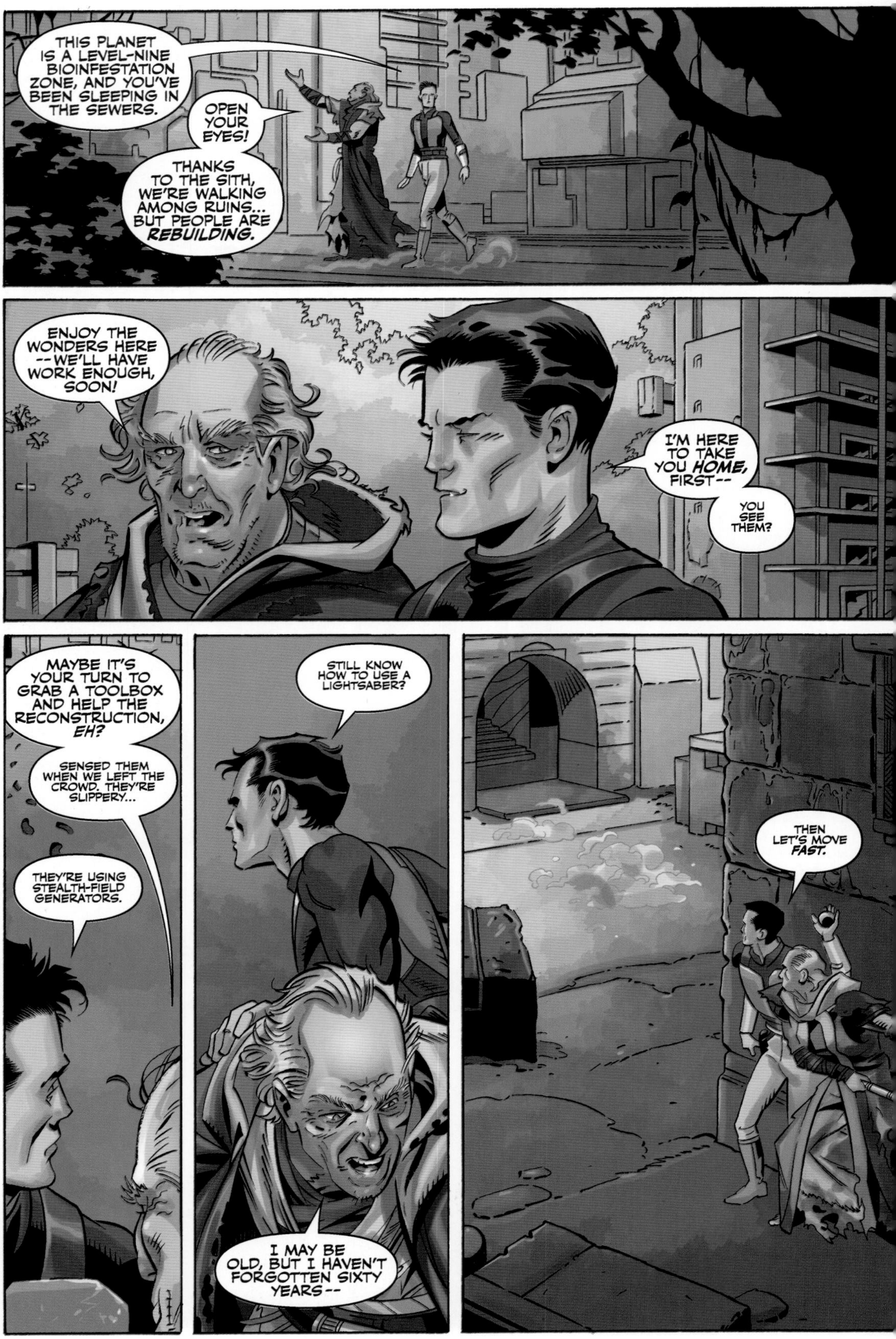
THIS PLANET IS A LEVEL-NINE BIOINFESTATION ZONE, AND YOU'VE BEEN SLEEPING IN THE SEWERS.
OPEN YOUR EYES!
THANKS TO THE SITH, WE'RE WALKING AMONG RUINS... BUT PEOPLE ARE *REBUILDING.*
ENJOY THE WONDERS HERE --WE'LL HAVE WORK ENOUGH, SOON!
I'M HERE TO TAKE YOU *HOME,* FIRST--
YOU SEE THEM?
MAYBE IT'S YOUR TURN TO GRAB A TOOLBOX AND HELP THE RECONSTRUCTION, *EH?*
SENSED THEM WHEN WE LEFT THE CROWD. THEY'RE SLIPPERY...
THEY'RE USING STEALTH-FIELD GENERATORS.
STILL KNOW HOW TO USE A LIGHTSABER?
I MAY BE OLD, BUT I HAVEN'T FORGOTTEN SIXTY YEARS--
THEN LET'S MOVE *FAST.*

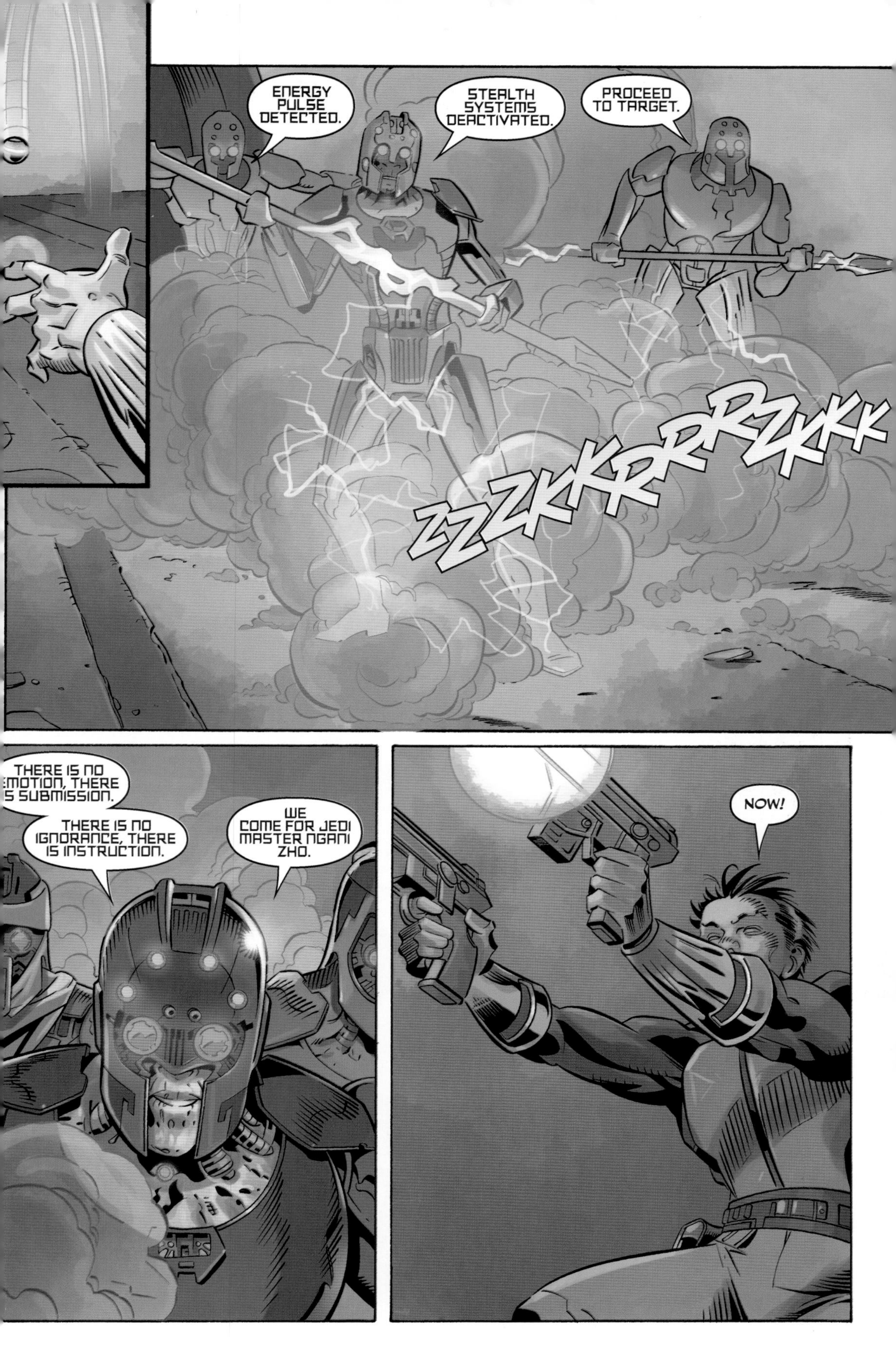
ENERGY PULSE DETECTED.
STEALTH SYSTEMS DEACTIVATED.
PROCEED TO TARGET.
ZZZKKRRRZKKK
THERE IS NO EMOTION, THERE IS SUBMISSION.
THERE IS NO IGNORANCE, THERE IS INSTRUCTION.
WE COME FOR JEDI MASTER NGANI ZHO.
NOW!

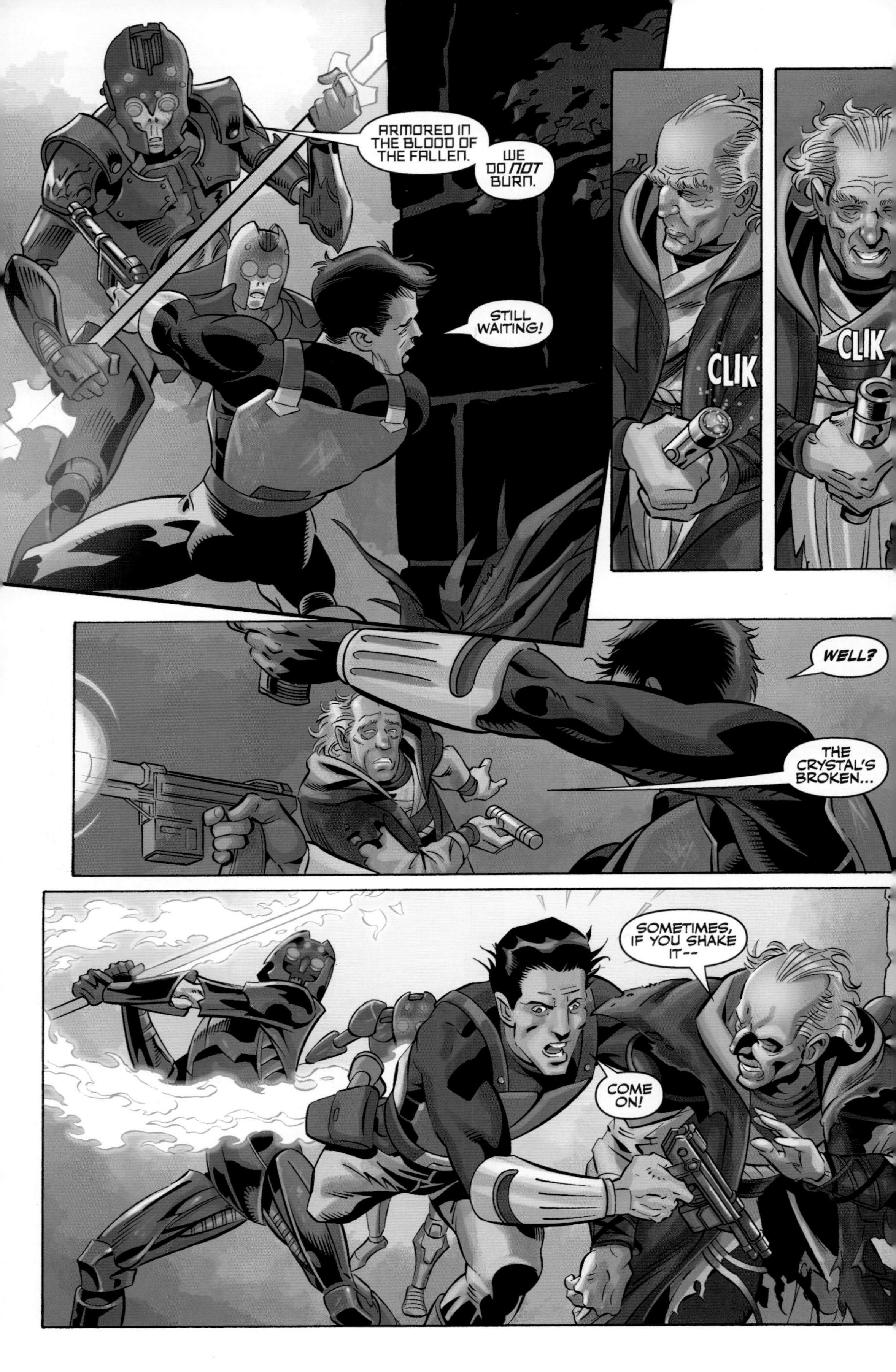
ARMORED IN THE BLOOD OF THE FALLEN.
WE DO NOT BURN.
STILL WAITING!
CLIK
CLIK
WELL?
THE CRYSTAL'S BROKEN...
SOMETIMES, IF YOU SHAKE IT--
COME ON!

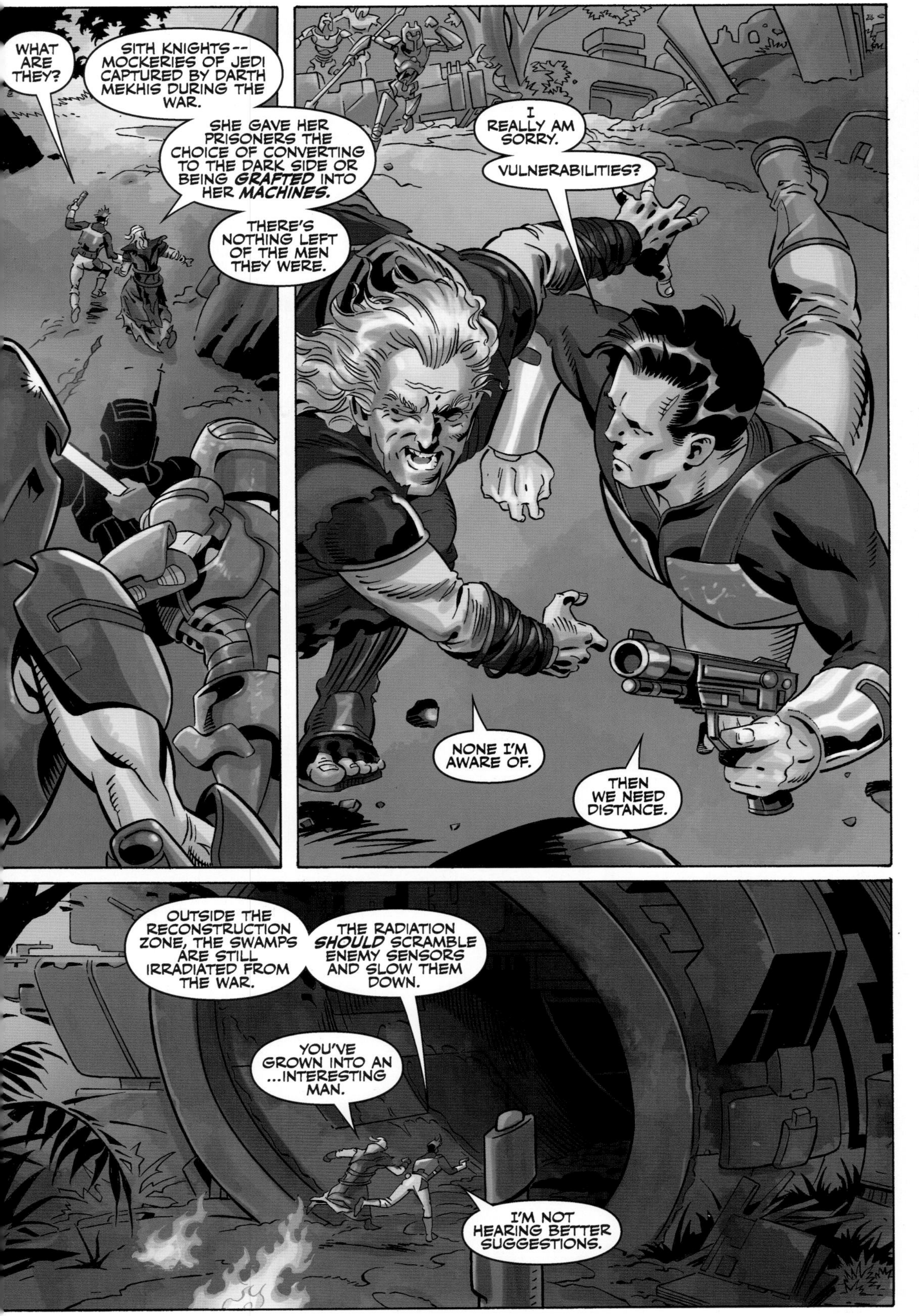
WHAT ARE THEY?
SITH KNIGHTS-- MOCKERIES OF JEDI CAPTURED BY DARTH MEKHIS DURING THE WAR.
SHE GAVE HER PRISONERS THE CHOICE OF CONVERTING TO THE DARK SIDE OR BEING GRAFTED INTO HER MACHINES.
THERE'S NOTHING LEFT OF THE MEN THEY WERE.
I REALLY AM SORRY.
VULNERABILITIES?
NONE I'M AWARE OF.
THEN WE NEED DISTANCE.
OUTSIDE THE RECONSTRUCTION ZONE, THE SWAMPS ARE STILL IRRADIATED FROM THE WAR.
THE RADIATION SHOULD SCRAMBLE ENEMY SENSORS AND SLOW THEM DOWN.
YOU'VE GROWN INTO AN ...INTERESTING MAN.
I'M NOT HEARING BETTER SUGGESTIONS.

I'VE SIGNALED THE SHIP FOR PICKUP--THERE'S A CLEARING NOT FAR FROM HERE.

NOW WHAT WERE YOU *DOING* IN IMPERIAL SPACE THAT CAUGHT THE ATTENTION OF THE DARK COUNCIL?

I WAS THERE ALMOST...TEN YEARS? WHAT *DIDN'T* I DO? *HA!*

MASTER--

I *TOLD* YOU, I'VE BEEN TO THE VESLA SYSTEM-- SACRIFICED BY OUR GOVERNMENT TO DARTH MEKHIS!

AND WHAT WAS DARTH MEKHIS *DOING* THERE? *WHAT* DID YOU SEE?

I SAW THE SITH KNIGHTS!

THAT'S NOT--

TZZN

RAAARRRGHR

--BLAST. THAT'S OUR PURSUERS MOWING THROUGH THE WILDLIFE.

THERON TO M-6--I HAVE ADDITIONAL ORDERS.

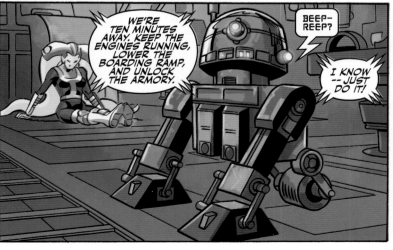

WE'RE TEN MINUTES AWAY. KEEP THE ENGINES RUNNING, LOWER THE BOARDING RAMP, AND UNLOCK THE ARMORY.

BEEP-- REEP?

I KNOW --JUST DO IT!

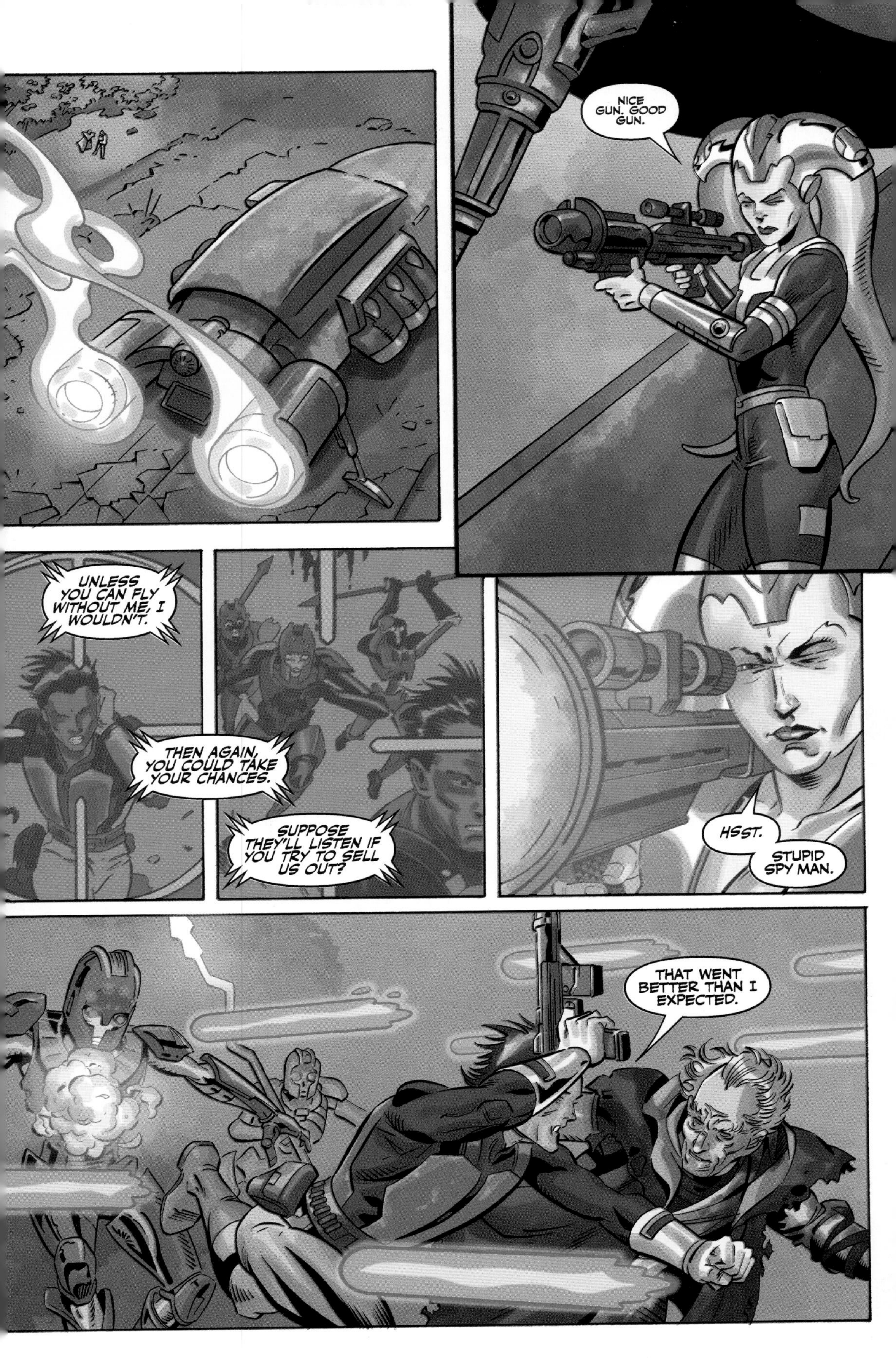
NICE GUN. GOOD GUN.
UNLESS YOU CAN FLY WITHOUT ME, I WOULDN'T.
THEN AGAIN, YOU COULD TAKE YOUR CHANCES.
SUPPOSE THEY'LL LISTEN IF YOU TRY TO SELL US OUT?
HSST.
STUPID SPY MAN.
THAT WENT BETTER THAN I EXPECTED.

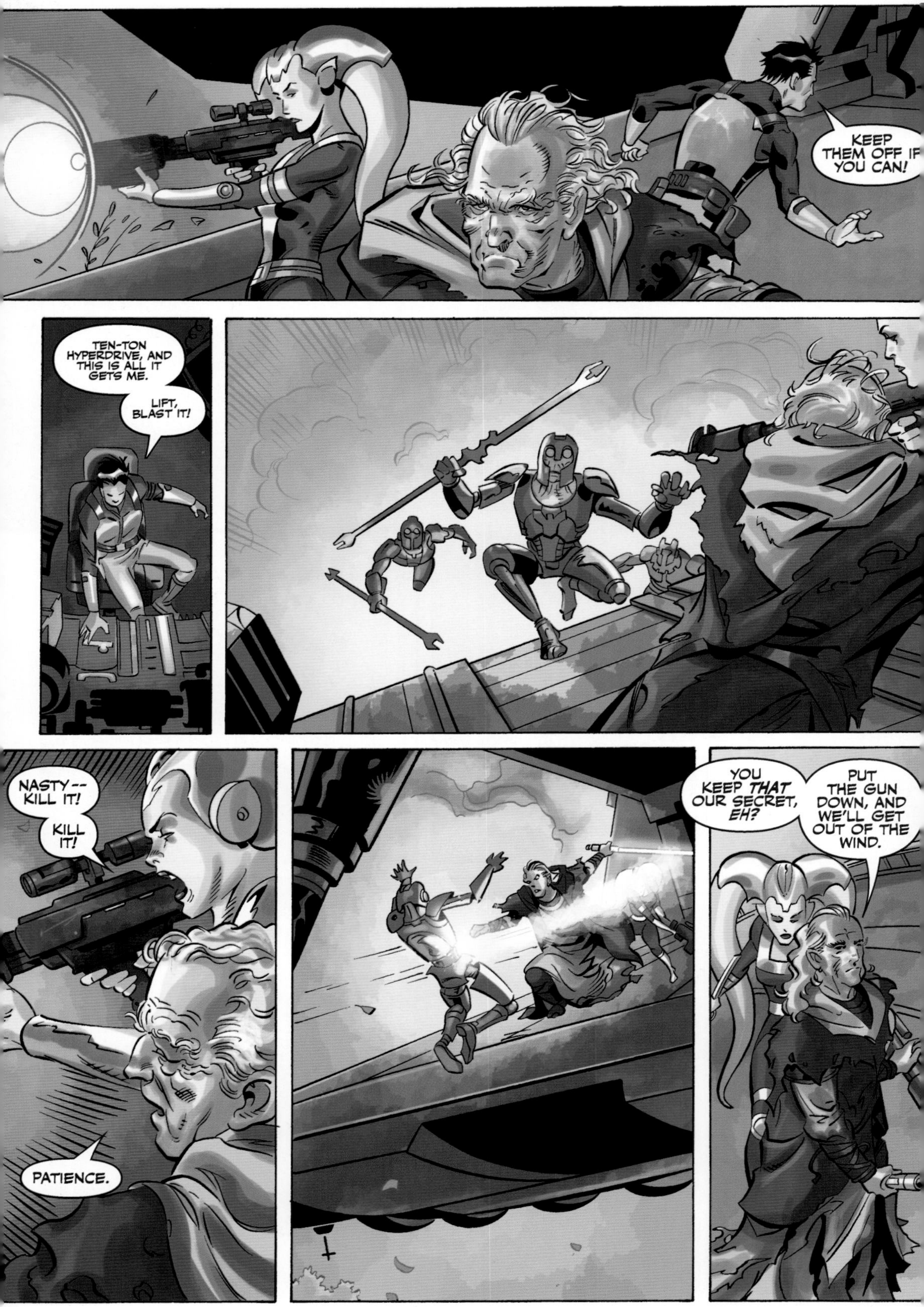
KEEP THEM OFF IF YOU CAN!
TEN-TON HYPERDRIVE, AND THIS IS ALL IT GETS ME.
LIFT, BLAST IT!
NASTY-- KILL IT!
KILL IT!
PATIENCE.
YOU KEEP *THAT* OUR SECRET, *EH?*
PUT THE GUN DOWN, AND WE'LL GET OUT OF THE WIND.

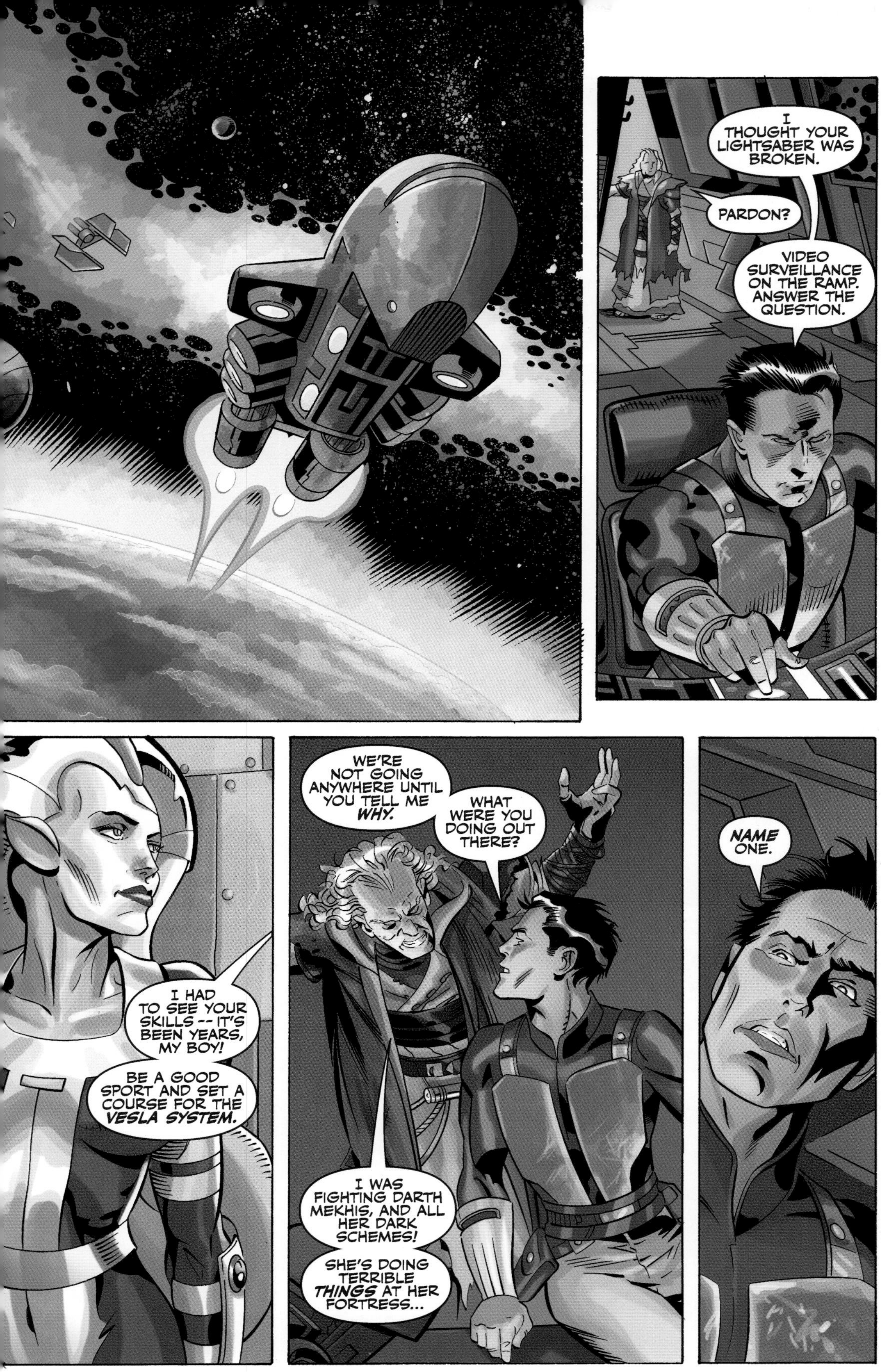
I THOUGHT YOUR LIGHTSABER WAS BROKEN.
PARDON?
VIDEO SURVEILLANCE ON THE RAMP. ANSWER THE QUESTION.
I HAD TO SEE YOUR SKILLS -- IT'S BEEN YEARS, MY BOY!
BE A GOOD SPORT AND SET A COURSE FOR THE *VESLA SYSTEM.*
WE'RE NOT GOING ANYWHERE UNTIL YOU TELL ME *WHY.*
WHAT WERE YOU DOING OUT THERE?
I WAS FIGHTING DARTH MEKHIS, AND ALL HER DARK SCHEMES!
SHE'S DOING TERRIBLE *THINGS* AT HER FORTRESS...
NAME ONE.

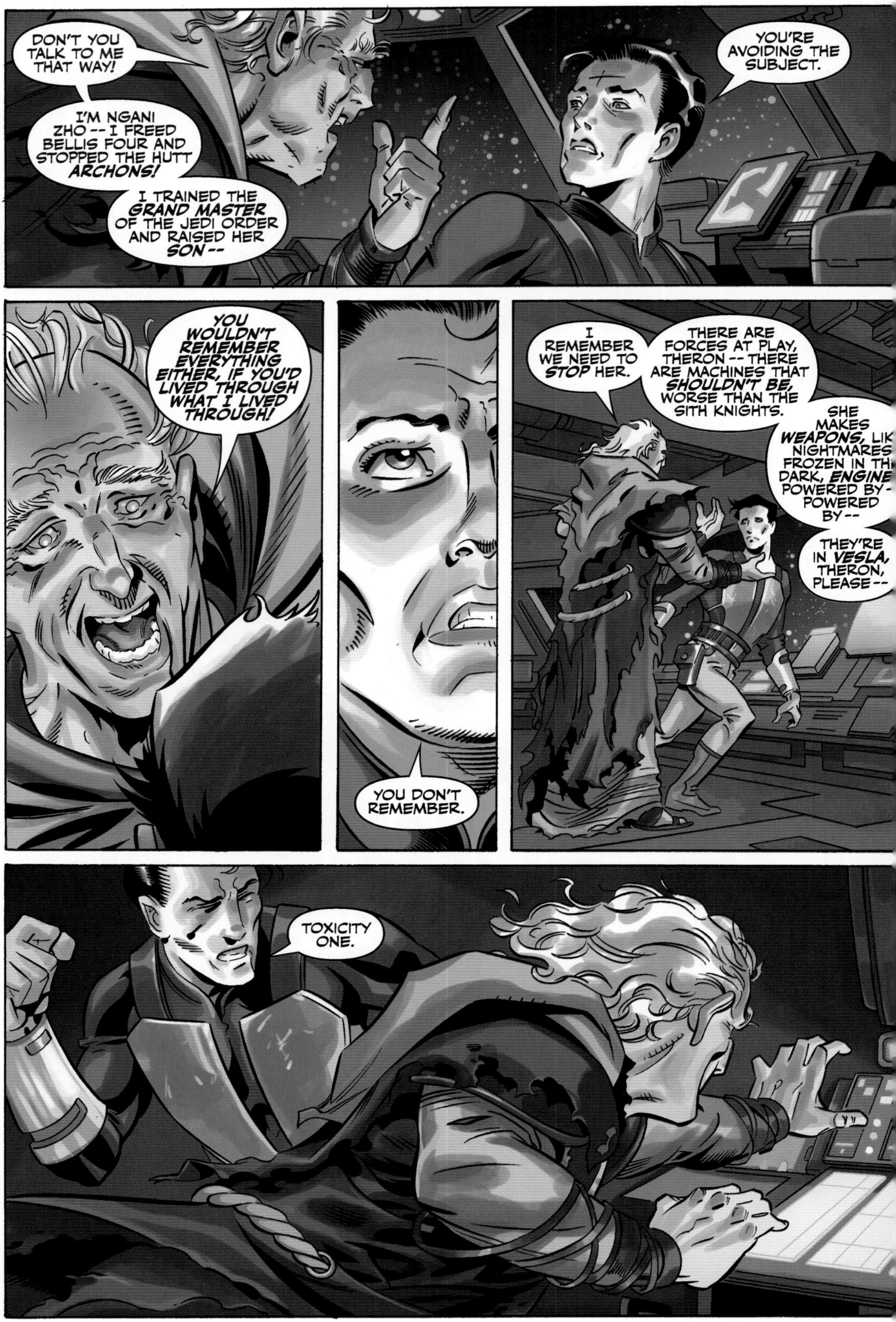
DON'T YOU TALK TO ME THAT WAY!
I'M NGANI ZHO -- I FREED BELLIS FOUR AND STOPPED THE HUTT ARCHONS!
I TRAINED THE GRAND MASTER OF THE JEDI ORDER AND RAISED HER SON --
YOU'RE AVOIDING THE SUBJECT.
YOU WOULDN'T REMEMBER EVERYTHING EITHER, IF YOU'D LIVED THROUGH WHAT I LIVED THROUGH!
YOU DON'T REMEMBER.
I REMEMBER WE NEED TO STOP HER.
THERE ARE FORCES AT PLAY, THERON -- THERE ARE MACHINES THAT SHOULDN'T BE, WORSE THAN THE SITH KNIGHTS.
SHE MAKES WEAPONS, LIK NIGHTMARES FROZEN IN TH DARK, ENGINE POWERED BY-- POWERED BY--
THEY'RE IN VESLA, THERON, PLEASE--
TOXICITY ONE.

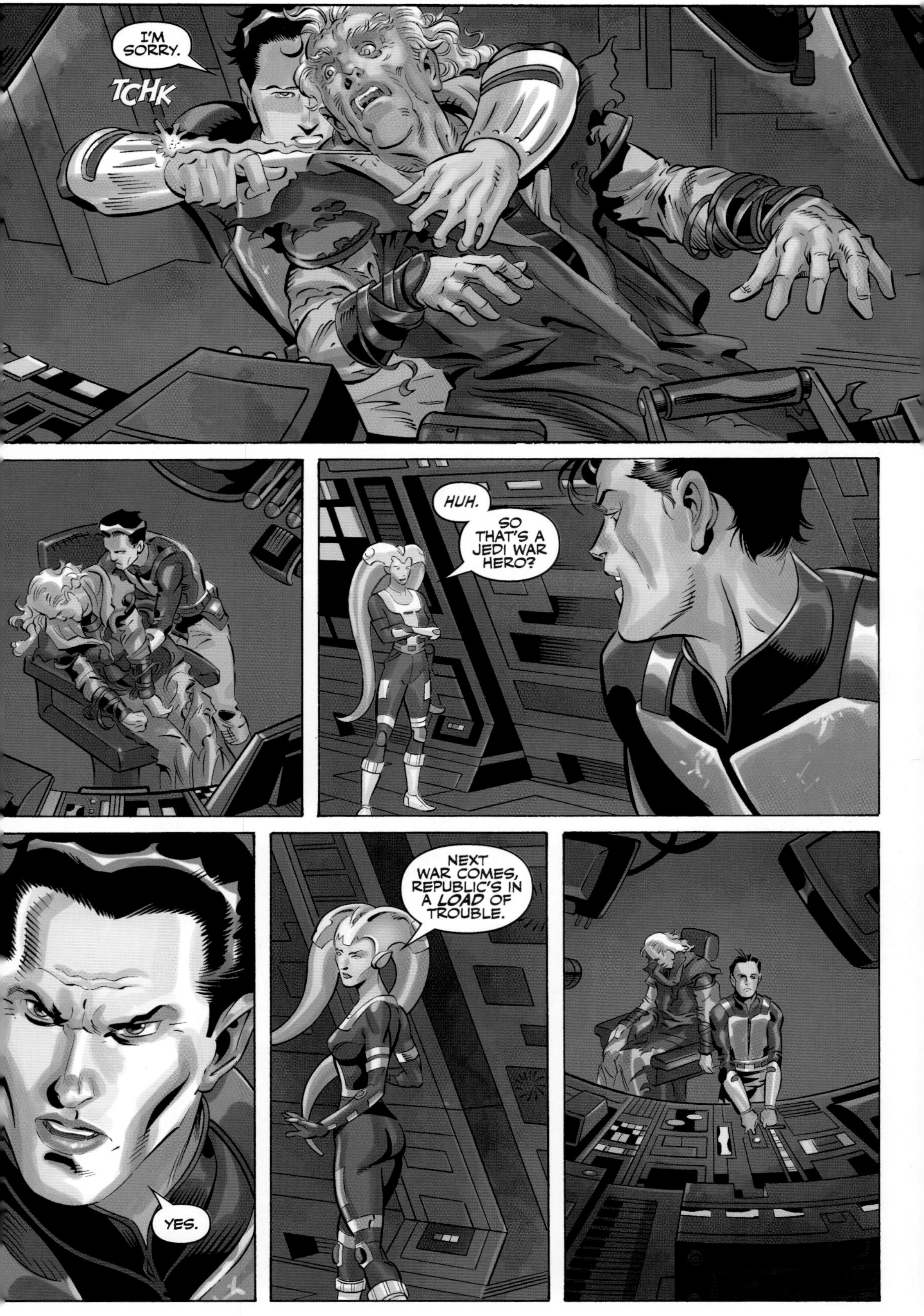
I'M SORRY.
TCHK
HUH.
SO THAT'S A JEDI WAR HERO?
YES.
NEXT WAR COMES, REPUBLIC'S IN A *LOAD* OF TROUBLE.

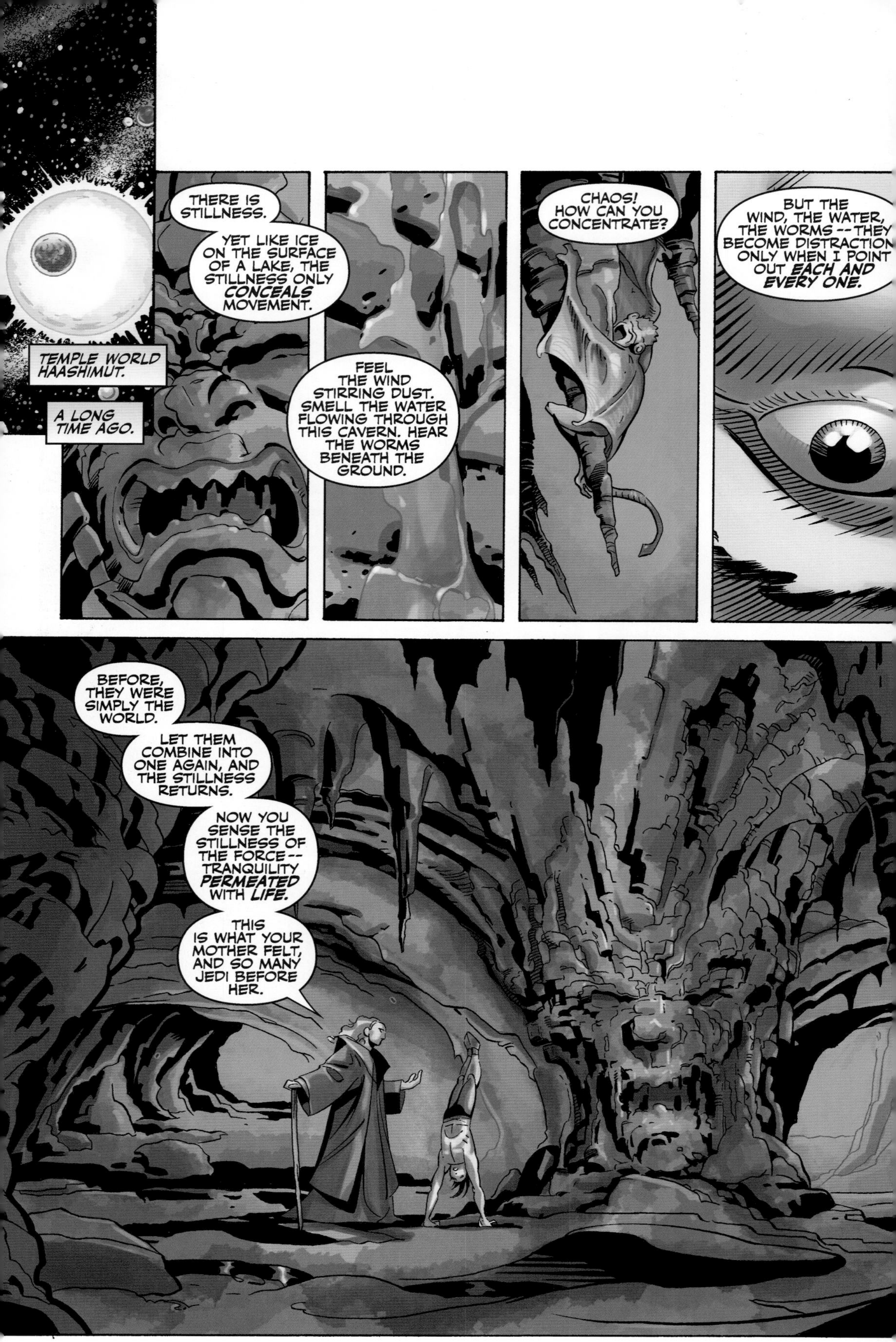
TEMPLE WORLD HAASHIMUT.
A LONG TIME AGO.
THERE IS STILLNESS.
YET LIKE ICE ON THE SURFACE OF A LAKE, THE STILLNESS ONLY CONCEALS MOVEMENT.
FEEL THE WIND STIRRING DUST. SMELL THE WATER FLOWING THROUGH THIS CAVERN. HEAR THE WORMS BENEATH THE GROUND.
CHAOS! HOW CAN YOU CONCENTRATE?
BUT THE WIND, THE WATER, THE WORMS--THEY BECOME DISTRACTION ONLY WHEN I POINT OUT EACH AND EVERY ONE.
BEFORE, THEY WERE SIMPLY THE WORLD.
LET THEM COMBINE INTO ONE AGAIN, AND THE STILLNESS RETURNS.
NOW YOU SENSE THE STILLNESS OF THE FORCE--TRANQUILITY PERMEATED WITH LIFE.
THIS IS WHAT YOUR MOTHER FELT, AND SO MANY JEDI BEFORE HER.

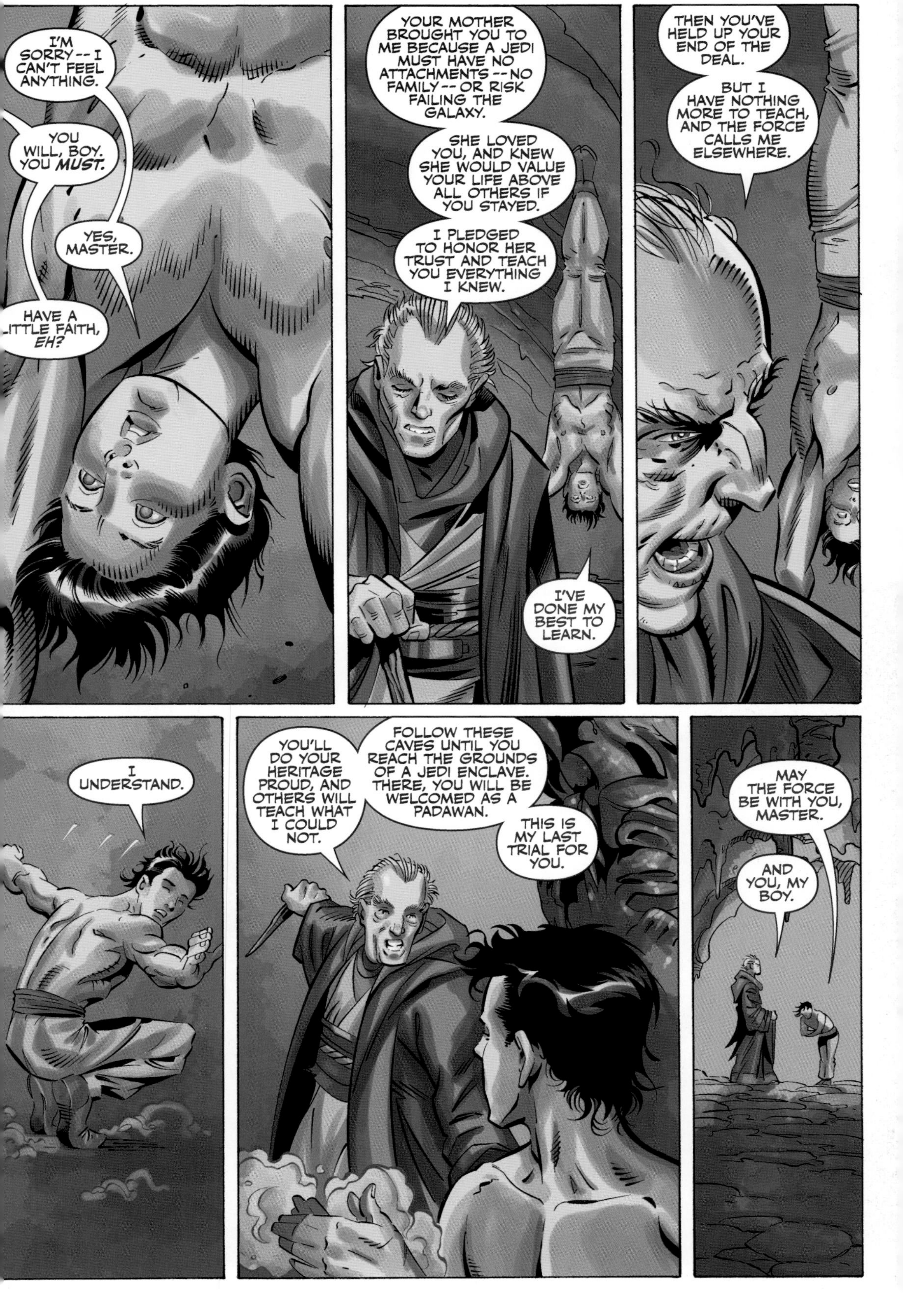

I'M SORRY -- I CAN'T FEEL ANYTHING.
YOU WILL, BOY. YOU *MUST.*
YES, MASTER.
HAVE A LITTLE FAITH, *EH?*
YOUR MOTHER BROUGHT YOU TO ME BECAUSE A JEDI MUST HAVE NO ATTACHMENTS -- NO FAMILY -- OR RISK FAILING THE GALAXY.
SHE LOVED YOU, AND KNEW SHE WOULD VALUE YOUR LIFE ABOVE ALL OTHERS IF YOU STAYED.
I PLEDGED TO HONOR HER TRUST AND TEACH YOU EVERYTHING I KNEW.
I'VE DONE MY BEST TO LEARN.
THEN YOU'VE HELD UP YOUR END OF THE DEAL.
BUT I HAVE NOTHING MORE TO TEACH, AND THE FORCE CALLS ME ELSEWHERE.
I UNDERSTAND.
FOLLOW THESE CAVES UNTIL YOU REACH THE GROUNDS OF A JEDI ENCLAVE. THERE, YOU WILL BE WELCOMED AS A PADAWAN.
YOU'LL DO YOUR HERITAGE PROUD, AND OTHERS WILL TEACH WHAT I COULD NOT.
THIS IS MY LAST TRIAL FOR YOU.
MAY THE FORCE BE WITH YOU, MASTER.
AND YOU, MY BOY.

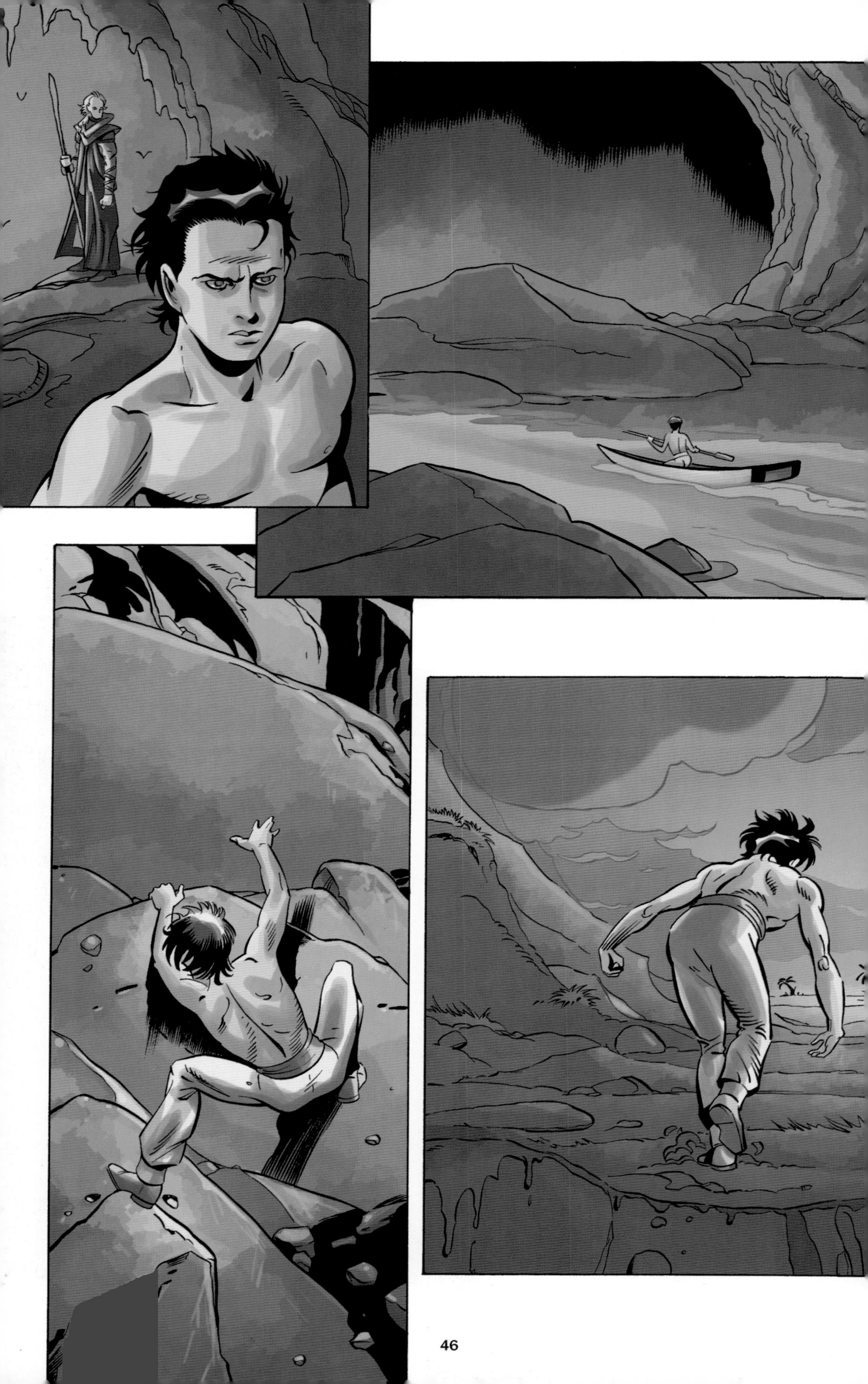

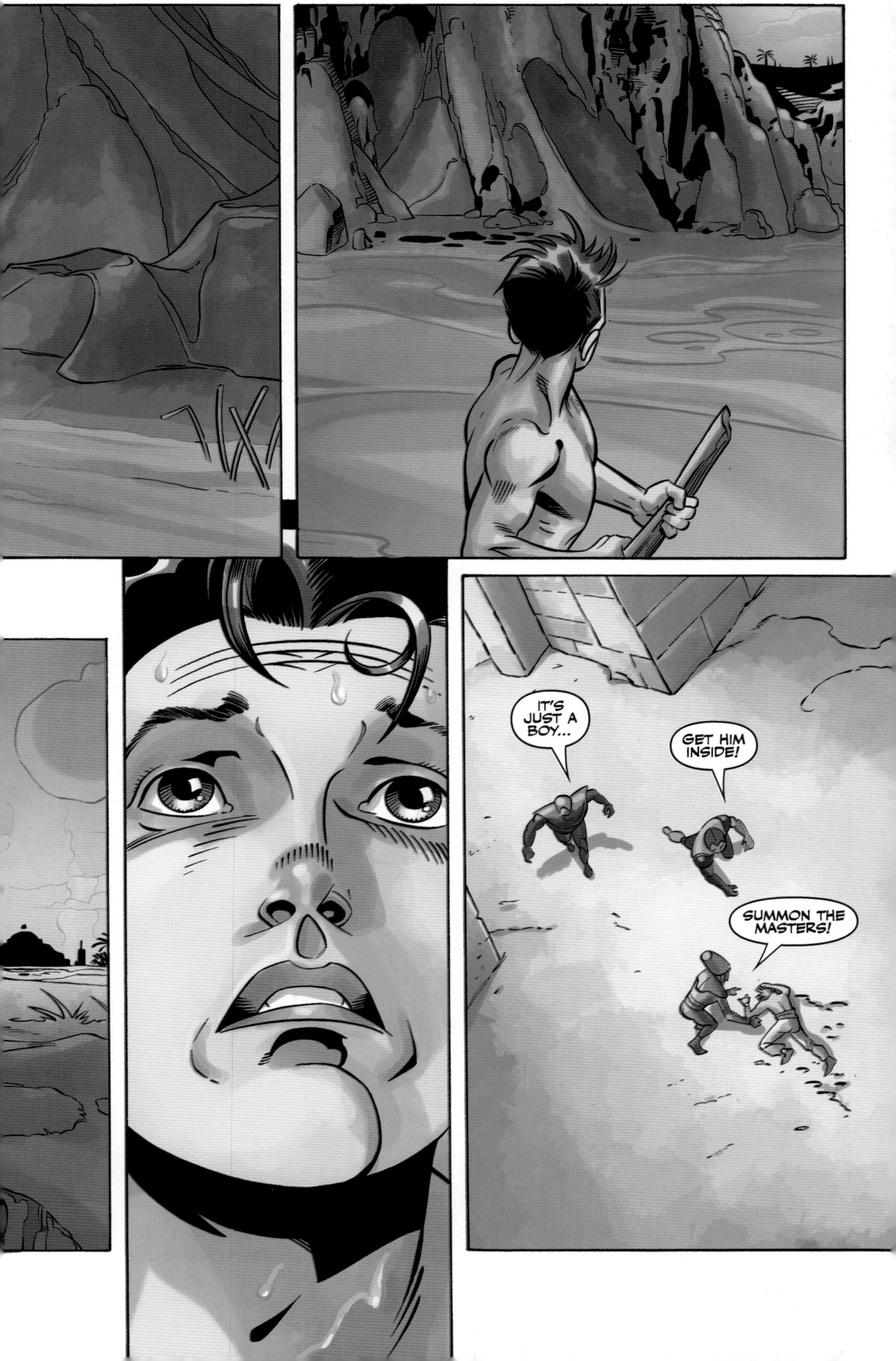
IT'S JUST A BOY...
GET HIM INSIDE!
SUMMON THE MASTERS!

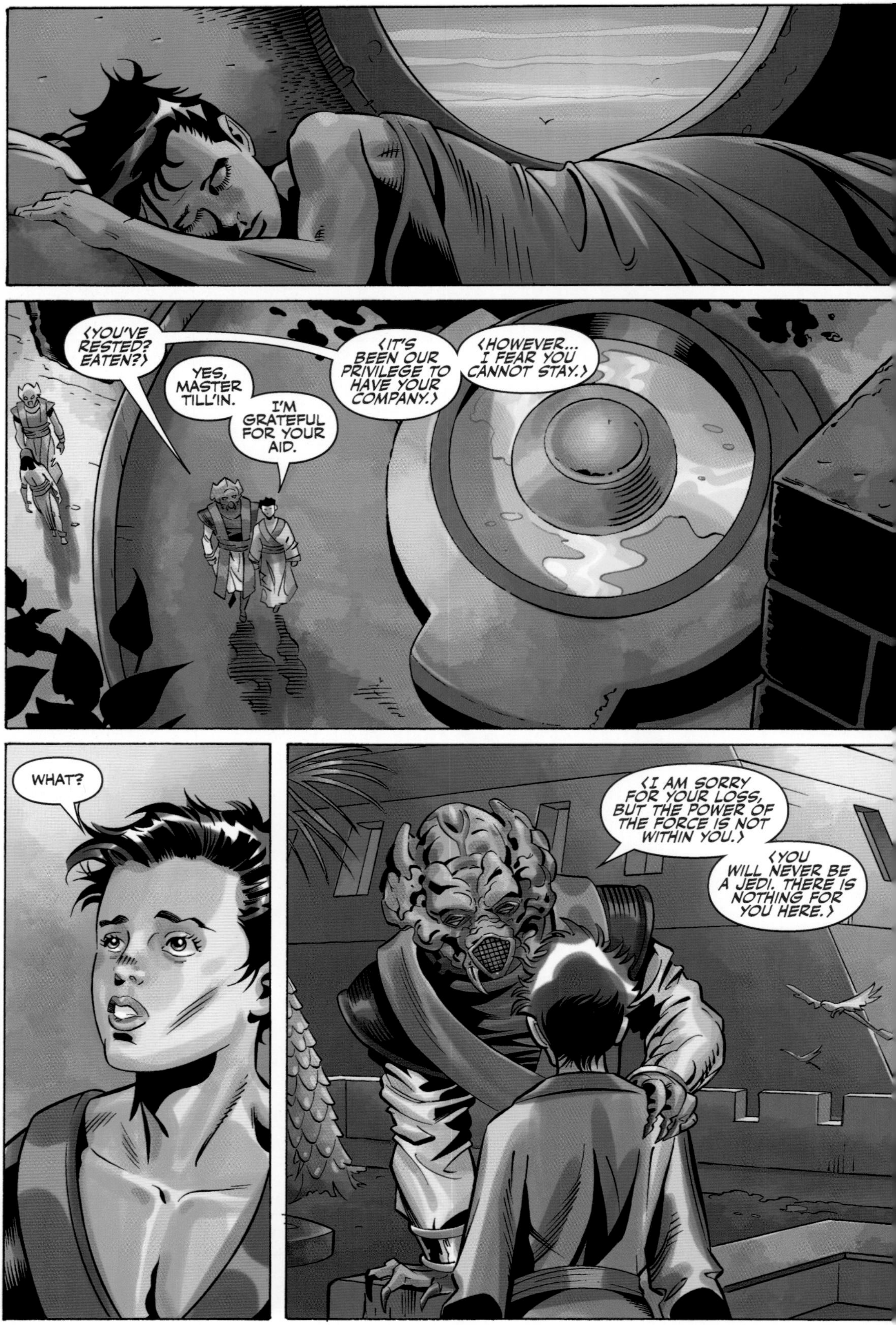

<YOU'VE RESTED? EATEN?>
YES, MASTER TILL'IN.
I'M GRATEFUL FOR YOUR AID.
<IT'S BEEN OUR PRIVILEGE TO HAVE YOUR COMPANY.>
<HOWEVER... I FEAR YOU CANNOT STAY.>
WHAT?
<I AM SORRY FOR YOUR LOSS, BUT THE POWER OF THE FORCE IS NOT WITHIN YOU.>
<YOU WILL NEVER BE A JEDI. THERE IS NOTHING FOR YOU HERE.>

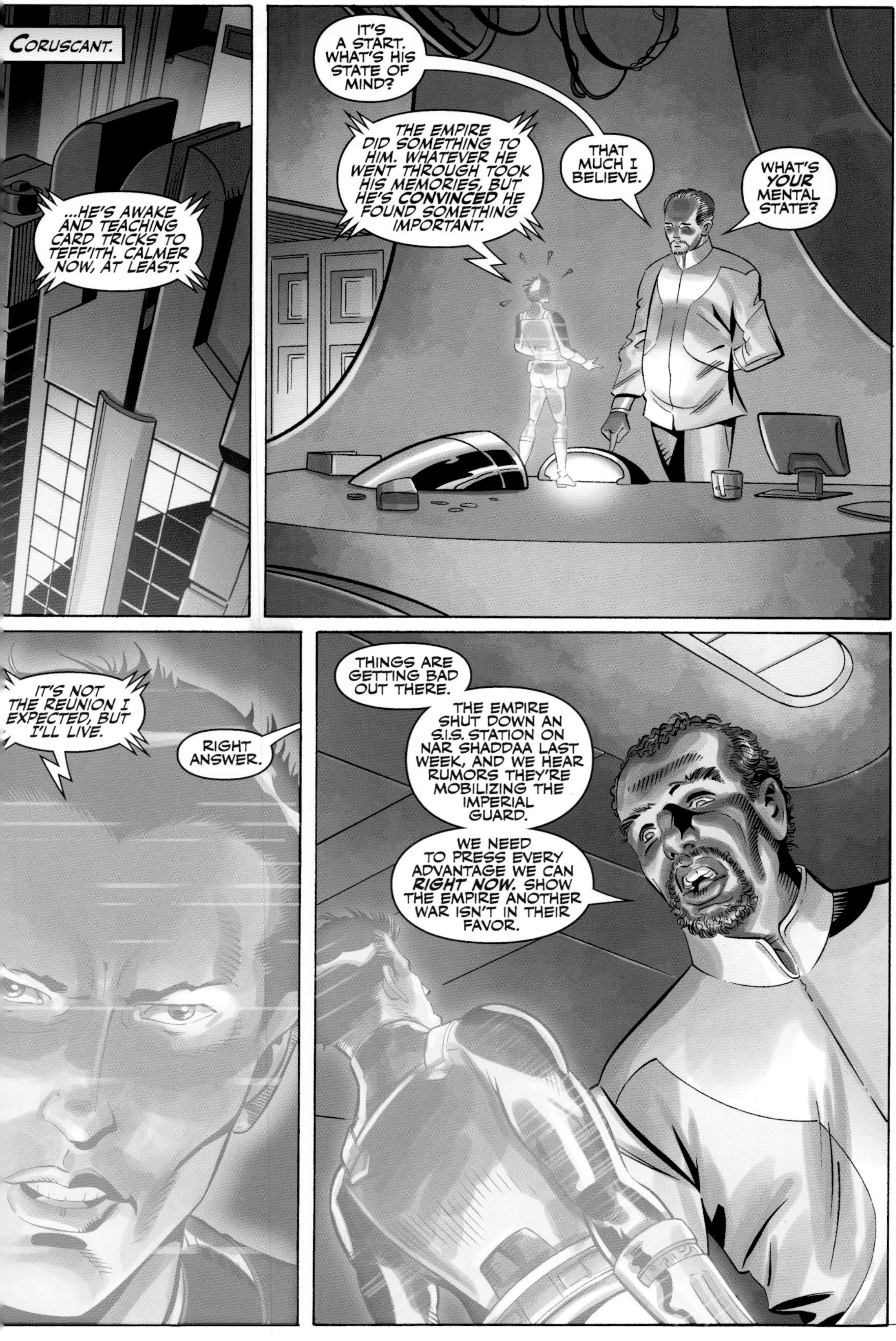
CORUSCANT.
...HE'S AWAKE AND TEACHING CARD TRICKS TO TEFF'ITH. CALMER NOW, AT LEAST.
IT'S A START. WHAT'S HIS STATE OF MIND?
THE EMPIRE DID SOMETHING TO HIM. WHATEVER HE WENT THROUGH TOOK HIS MEMORIES, BUT HE'S CONVINCED HE FOUND SOMETHING IMPORTANT.
THAT MUCH I BELIEVE.
WHAT'S YOUR MENTAL STATE?
IT'S NOT THE REUNION I EXPECTED, BUT I'LL LIVE.
RIGHT ANSWER.
THINGS ARE GETTING BAD OUT THERE.
THE EMPIRE SHUT DOWN AN S.I.S. STATION ON NAR SHADDAA LAST WEEK, AND WE HEAR RUMORS THEY'RE MOBILIZING THE IMPERIAL GUARD.
WE NEED TO PRESS EVERY ADVANTAGE WE CAN RIGHT NOW. SHOW THE EMPIRE ANOTHER WAR ISN'T IN THEIR FAVOR.

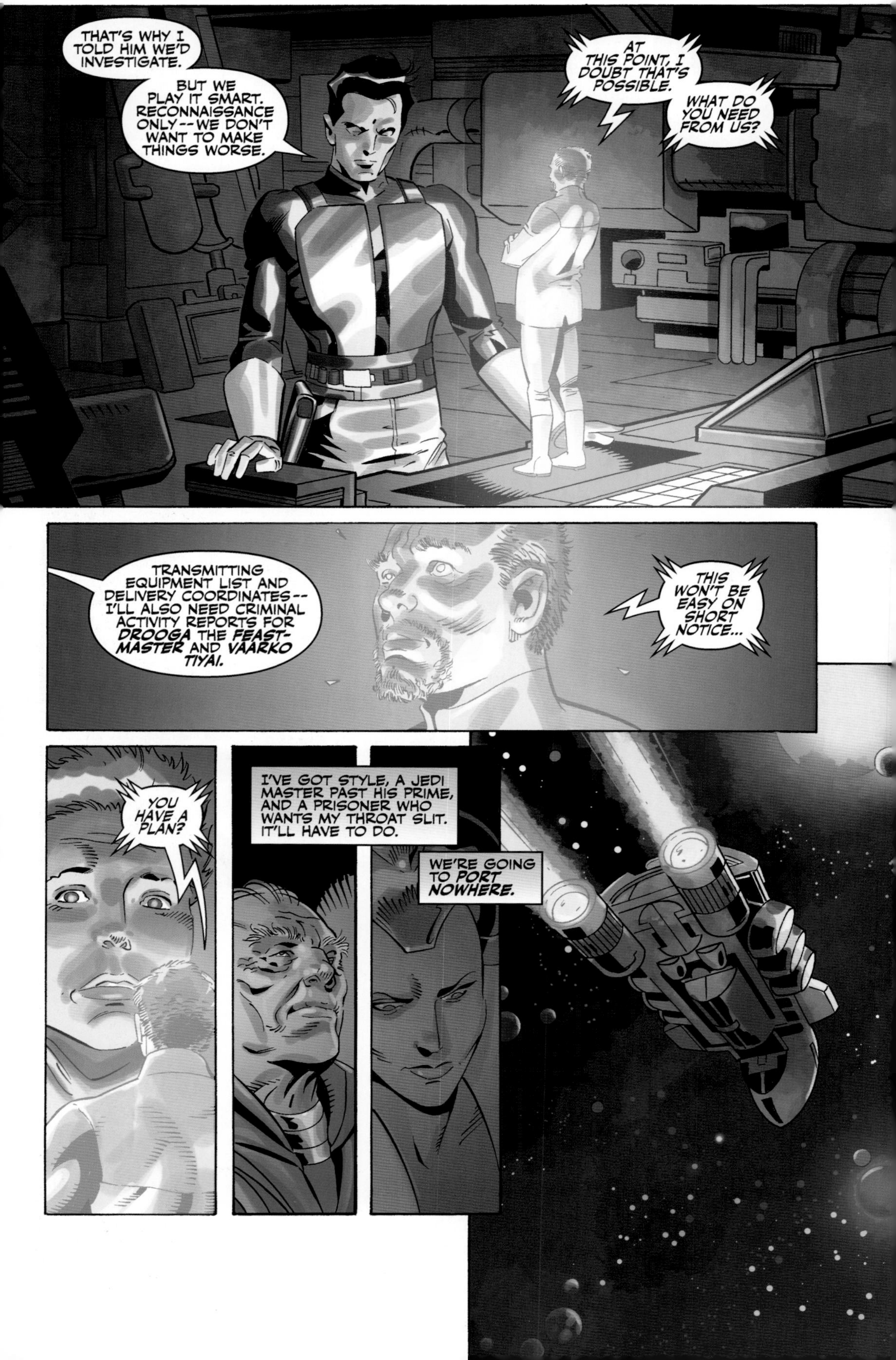
THAT'S WHY I TOLD HIM WE'D INVESTIGATE.
BUT WE PLAY IT SMART. RECONNAISSANCE ONLY--WE DON'T WANT TO MAKE THINGS WORSE.
AT THIS POINT, I DOUBT THAT'S POSSIBLE.
WHAT DO YOU NEED FROM US?
TRANSMITTING EQUIPMENT LIST AND DELIVERY COORDINATES--I'LL ALSO NEED CRIMINAL ACTIVITY REPORTS FOR *DROOGA* THE *FEAST-MASTER* AND *VAARKO TIYAI.*
THIS WON'T BE EASY ON SHORT NOTICE...
YOU HAVE A PLAN?
I'VE GOT STYLE, A JEDI MASTER PAST HIS PRIME, AND A PRISONER WHO WANTS MY THROAT SLIT. IT'LL HAVE TO DO.
WE'RE GOING TO *PORT NOWHERE.*

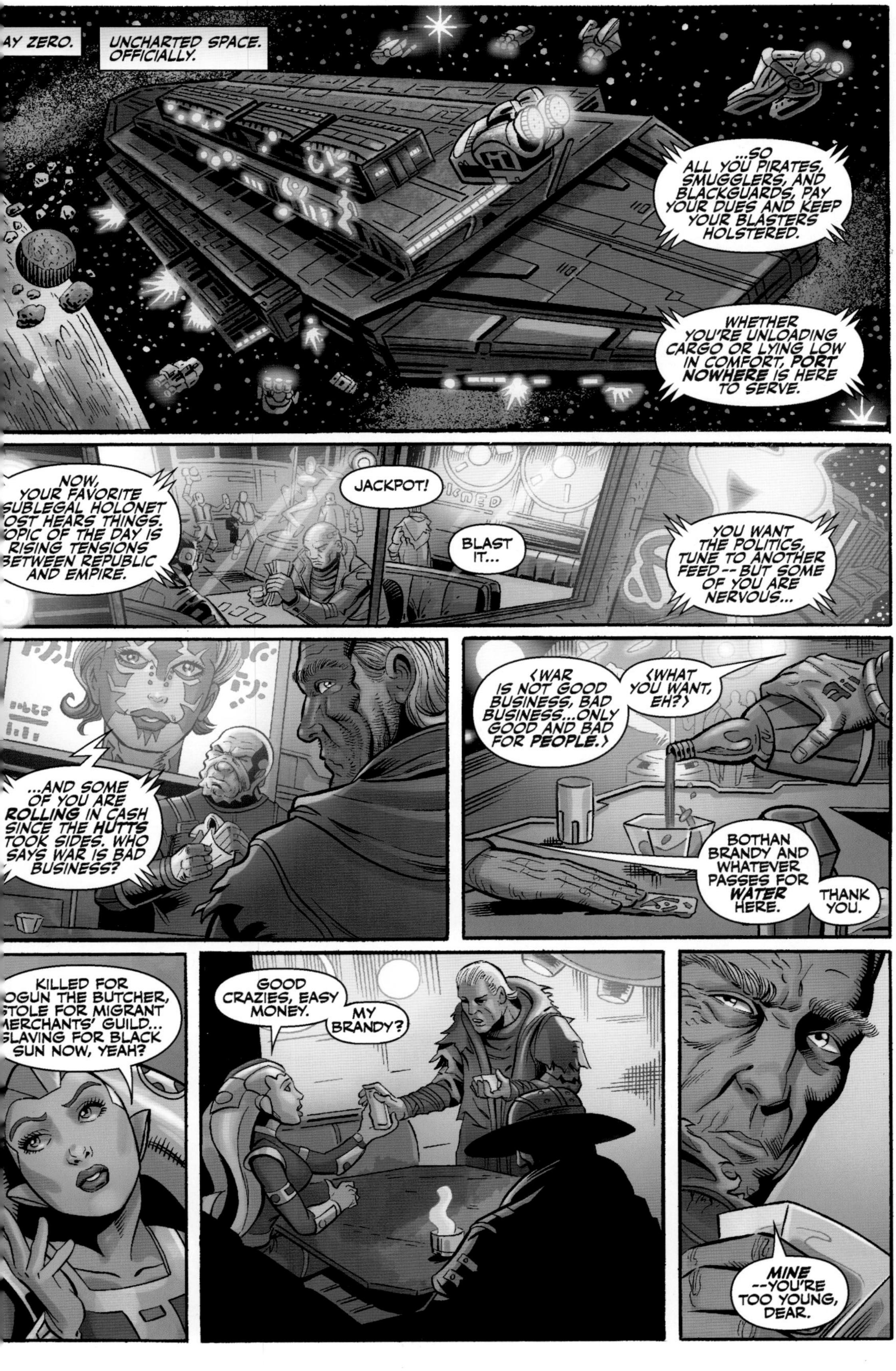
AY ZERO.
UNCHARTED SPACE. OFFICIALLY.
...SO ALL YOU PIRATES, SMUGGLERS, AND BLACKGUARDS, PAY YOUR DUES AND KEEP YOUR BLASTERS HOLSTERED.
WHETHER YOU'RE UNLOADING CARGO OR LYING LOW IN COMFORT, PORT NOWHERE IS HERE TO SERVE.
NOW, YOUR FAVORITE SUBLEGAL HOLONET OST HEARS THINGS. OPIC OF THE DAY IS RISING TENSIONS BETWEEN REPUBLIC AND EMPIRE.
JACKPOT!
BLAST IT...
YOU WANT THE POLITICS, TUNE TO ANOTHER FEED--BUT SOME OF YOU ARE NERVOUS...
...AND SOME OF YOU ARE ROLLING IN CASH SINCE THE HUTTS TOOK SIDES. WHO SAYS WAR IS BAD BUSINESS?
‹WAR IS NOT GOOD BUSINESS, BAD BUSINESS...ONLY GOOD AND BAD FOR PEOPLE.›
‹WHAT YOU WANT, EH?›
BOTHAN BRANDY AND WHATEVER PASSES FOR WATER HERE.
THANK YOU.
KILLED FOR OGUN THE BUTCHER, STOLE FOR MIGRANT MERCHANTS' GUILD... SLAVING FOR BLACK SUN NOW, YEAH?
GOOD CRAZIES, EASY MONEY.
MY BRANDY?
MINE --YOU'RE TOO YOUNG, DEAR.

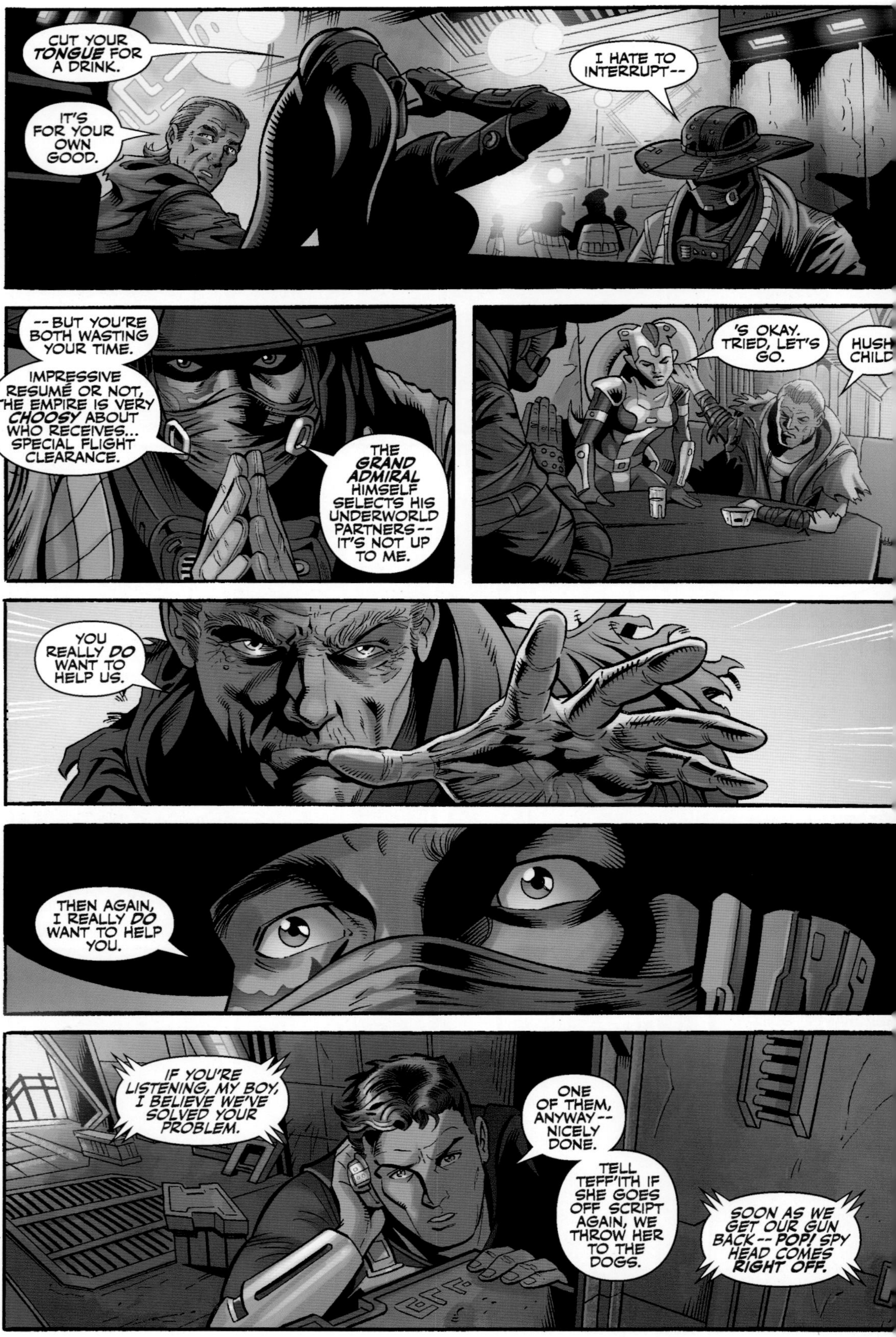
CUT YOUR TONGUE FOR A DRINK.
IT'S FOR YOUR OWN GOOD.
I HATE TO INTERRUPT--
--BUT YOU'RE BOTH WASTING YOUR TIME.
IMPRESSIVE RESUMÉ OR NOT, THE EMPIRE IS VERY CHOOSY ABOUT WHO RECEIVES... SPECIAL FLIGHT CLEARANCE.
THE GRAND ADMIRAL HIMSELF SELECTS HIS UNDERWORLD PARTNERS-- IT'S NOT UP TO ME.
'S OKAY. TRIED, LET'S GO.
HUSH CHILD
YOU REALLY DO WANT TO HELP US.
THEN AGAIN, I REALLY DO WANT TO HELP YOU.
IF YOU'RE LISTENING, MY BOY, I BELIEVE WE'VE SOLVED YOUR PROBLEM.
ONE OF THEM, ANYWAY-- NICELY DONE.
TELL TEFF'ITH IF SHE GOES OFF SCRIPT AGAIN, WE THROW HER TO THE DOGS.
SOON AS WE GET OUR GUN BACK-- POP! SPY HEAD COMES RIGHT OFF.

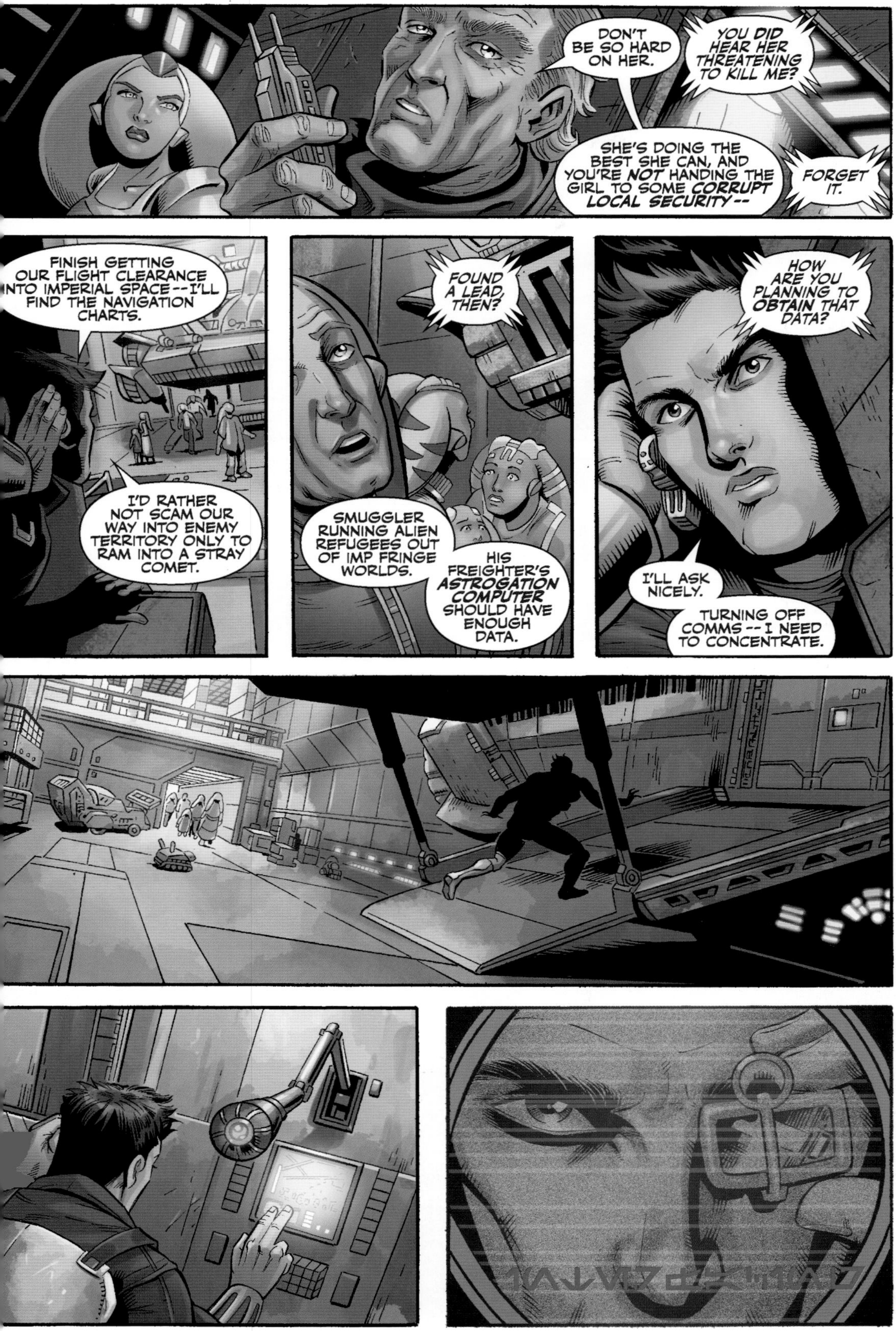
DON'T BE SO HARD ON HER.
YOU DID HEAR HER THREATENING TO KILL ME?
SHE'S DOING THE BEST SHE CAN, AND YOU'RE NOT HANDING THE GIRL TO SOME CORRUPT LOCAL SECURITY--
FORGET IT.
FINISH GETTING OUR FLIGHT CLEARANCE INTO IMPERIAL SPACE--I'LL FIND THE NAVIGATION CHARTS.
I'D RATHER NOT SCAM OUR WAY INTO ENEMY TERRITORY ONLY TO RAM INTO A STRAY COMET.
FOUND A LEAD, THEN?
SMUGGLER RUNNING ALIEN REFUGEES OUT OF IMP FRINGE WORLDS.
HIS FREIGHTER'S ASTROGATION COMPUTER SHOULD HAVE ENOUGH DATA.
HOW ARE YOU PLANNING TO OBTAIN THAT DATA?
I'LL ASK NICELY.
TURNING OFF COMMS--I NEED TO CONCENTRATE.

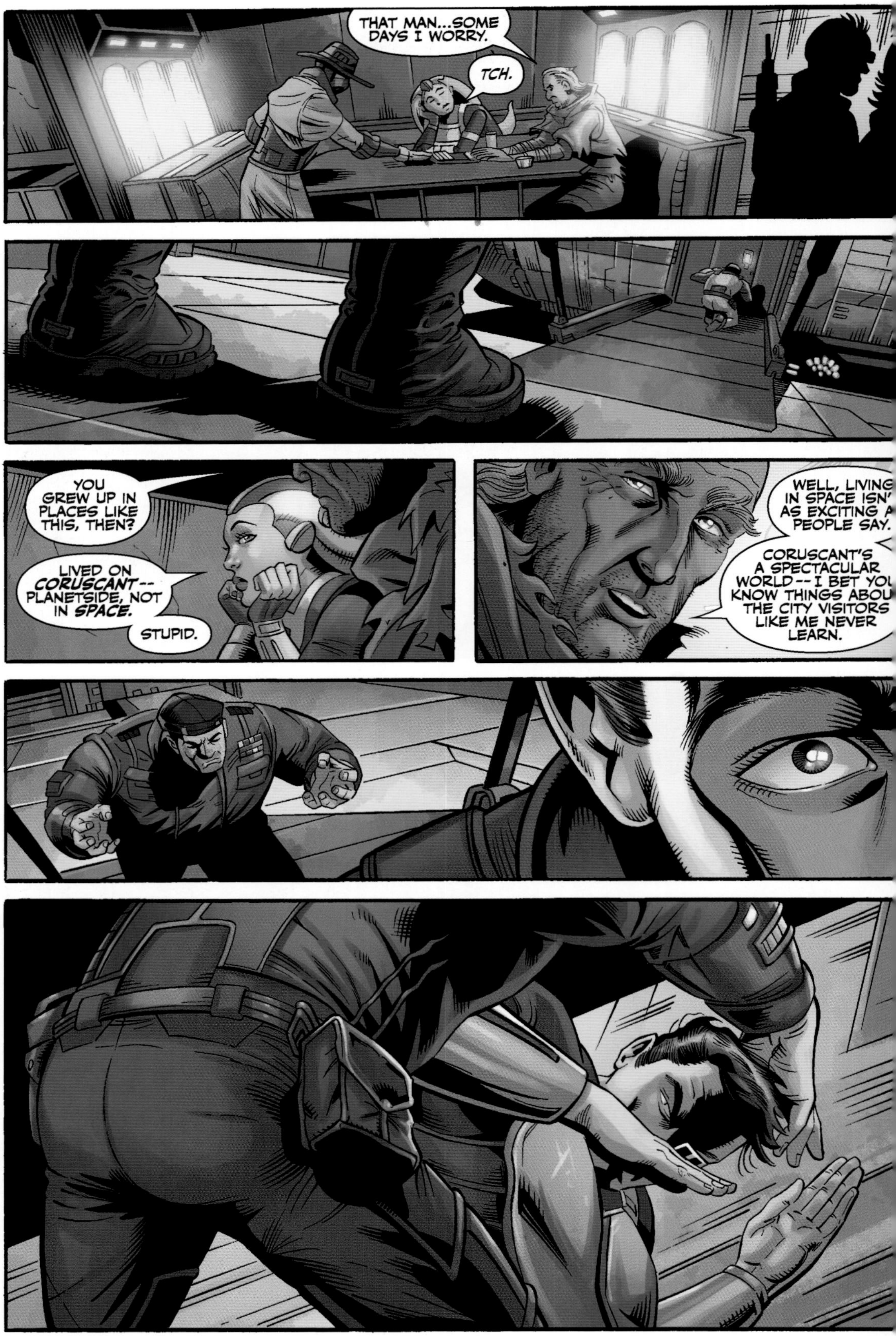
THAT MAN...SOME DAYS I WORRY.
TCH.
YOU GREW UP IN PLACES LIKE THIS, THEN?
LIVED ON CORUSCANT-- PLANETSIDE, NOT IN SPACE.
STUPID.
WELL, LIVING IN SPACE ISN' AS EXCITING A PEOPLE SAY.
CORUSCANT'S A SPECTACULAR WORLD--I BET YOU KNOW THINGS ABOU THE CITY VISITORS LIKE ME NEVER LEARN.

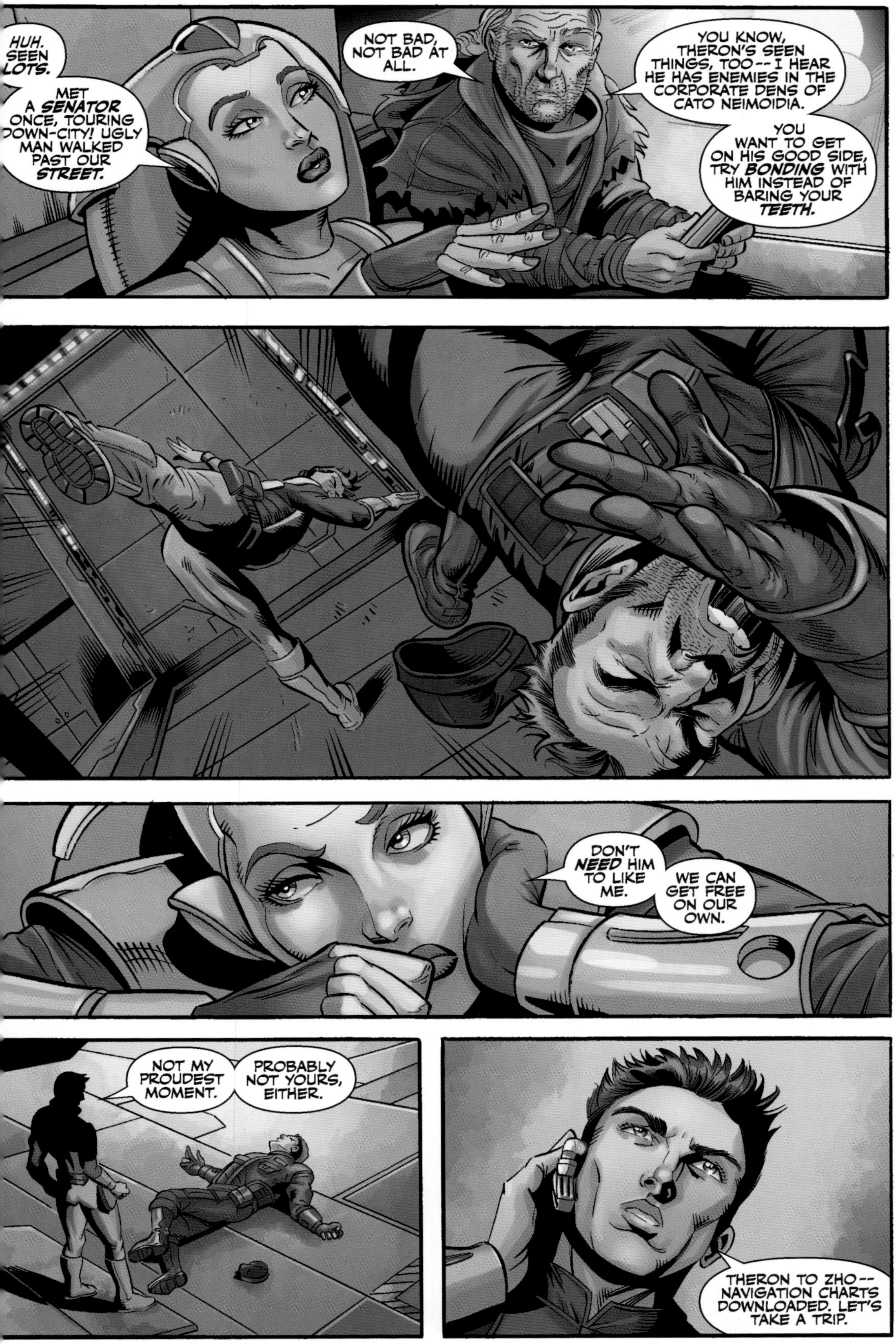
HUH. SEEN LOTS.
MET A SENATOR ONCE, TOURING DOWN-CITY! UGLY MAN WALKED PAST OUR STREET.
NOT BAD, NOT BAD AT ALL.
YOU KNOW, THERON'S SEEN THINGS, TOO-- I HEAR HE HAS ENEMIES IN THE CORPORATE DENS OF CATO NEIMOIDIA.
YOU WANT TO GET ON HIS GOOD SIDE, TRY BONDING WITH HIM INSTEAD OF BARING YOUR TEETH.
DON'T NEED HIM TO LIKE ME.
WE CAN GET FREE ON OUR OWN.
NOT MY PROUDEST MOMENT.
PROBABLY NOT YOURS, EITHER.
THERON TO ZHO-- NAVIGATION CHARTS DOWNLOADED. LET'S TAKE A TRIP.

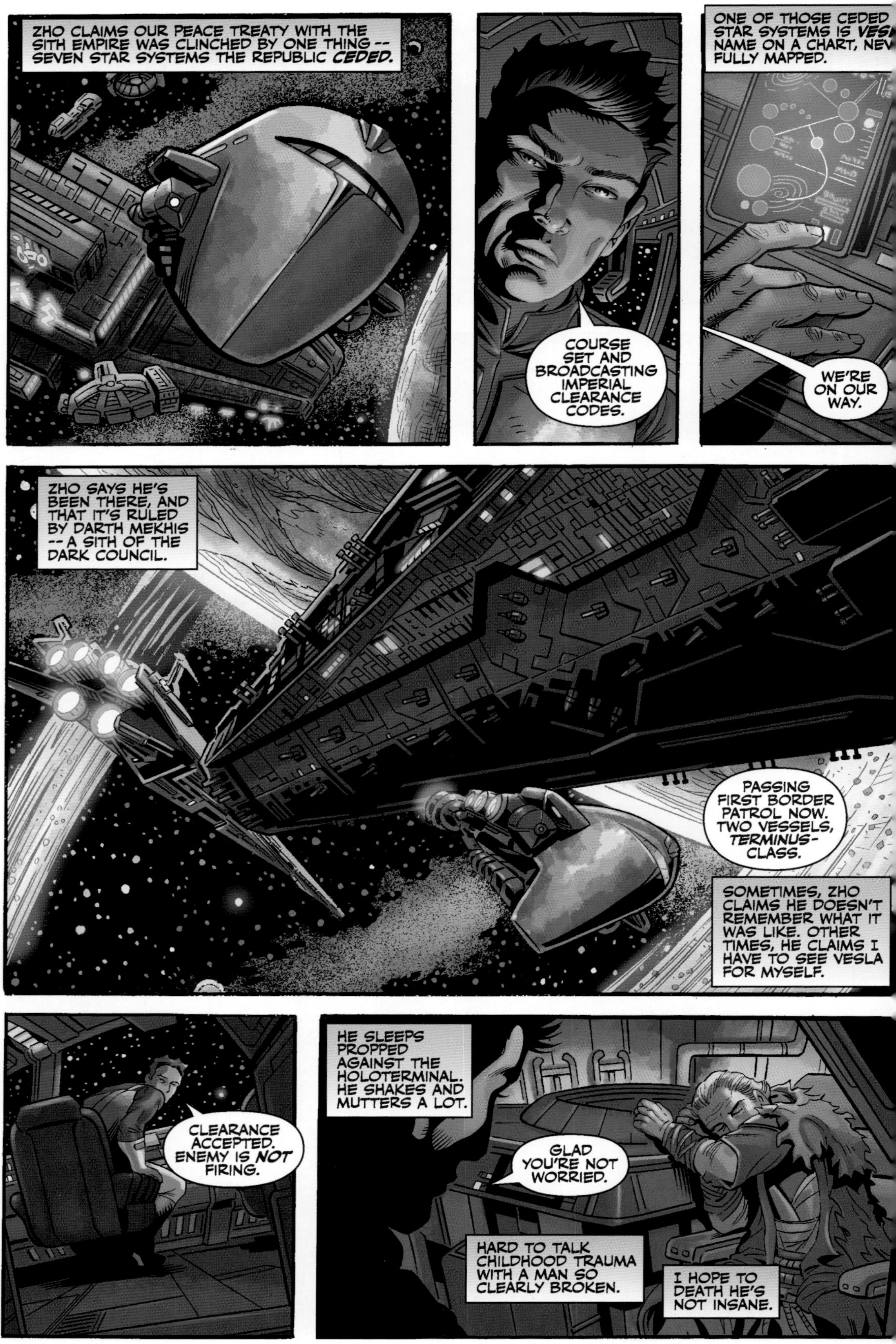
ZHO CLAIMS OUR PEACE TREATY WITH THE SITH EMPIRE WAS CLINCHED BY ONE THING -- SEVEN STAR SYSTEMS THE REPUBLIC *CEDED.*
COURSE SET AND BROADCASTING IMPERIAL CLEARANCE CODES.
ONE OF THOSE CEDED STAR SYSTEMS IS *VES* NAME ON A CHART, NEV FULLY MAPPED.
WE'RE ON OUR WAY.
ZHO SAYS HE'S BEEN THERE, AND THAT IT'S RULED BY DARTH MEKHIS -- A SITH OF THE DARK COUNCIL.
PASSING FIRST BORDER PATROL NOW. TWO VESSELS, *TERMINUS*-CLASS.
SOMETIMES, ZHO CLAIMS HE DOESN'T REMEMBER WHAT IT WAS LIKE. OTHER TIMES, HE CLAIMS I HAVE TO SEE VESLA FOR MYSELF.
CLEARANCE ACCEPTED. ENEMY IS *NOT* FIRING.
HE SLEEPS PROPPED AGAINST THE HOLOTERMINAL. HE SHAKES AND MUTTERS A LOT.
GLAD YOU'RE NOT WORRIED.
HARD TO TALK CHILDHOOD TRAUMA WITH A MAN SO CLEARLY BROKEN.
I HOPE TO DEATH HE'S NOT INSANE.

PAY ONE.

BEE—REEOOP.

JUMPING OUT OF HYPERSPACE.

WE SHOULD BE INSYSTEM, BUT SENSORS ARE A MESS...

SHE'S BLINDING US!

DARTH MEKHIS STRIKES!

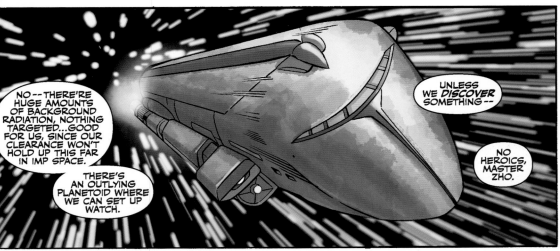

NO--THERE'RE HUGE AMOUNTS OF BACKGROUND RADIATION, NOTHING TARGETED...GOOD FOR US, SINCE OUR CLEARANCE WON'T HOLD UP THIS FAR IN IMP SPACE.

THERE'S AN OUTLYING PLANETOID WHERE WE CAN SET UP WATCH.

UNLESS WE DISCOVER SOMETHING --

NO HEROICS, MASTER ZHO.

SCATTERED LIFE SIGNS ON THE SURFACE, BUT NO ENERGY SIGNATURES.

THAT RIDGE SHOULD SERVE AS A BASE OF OPERATIONS -- UNLESS YOU OBJECT?

WHAT?

NO, NO -- THAT WILL DO.

THEN I'M BRINGING US IN.

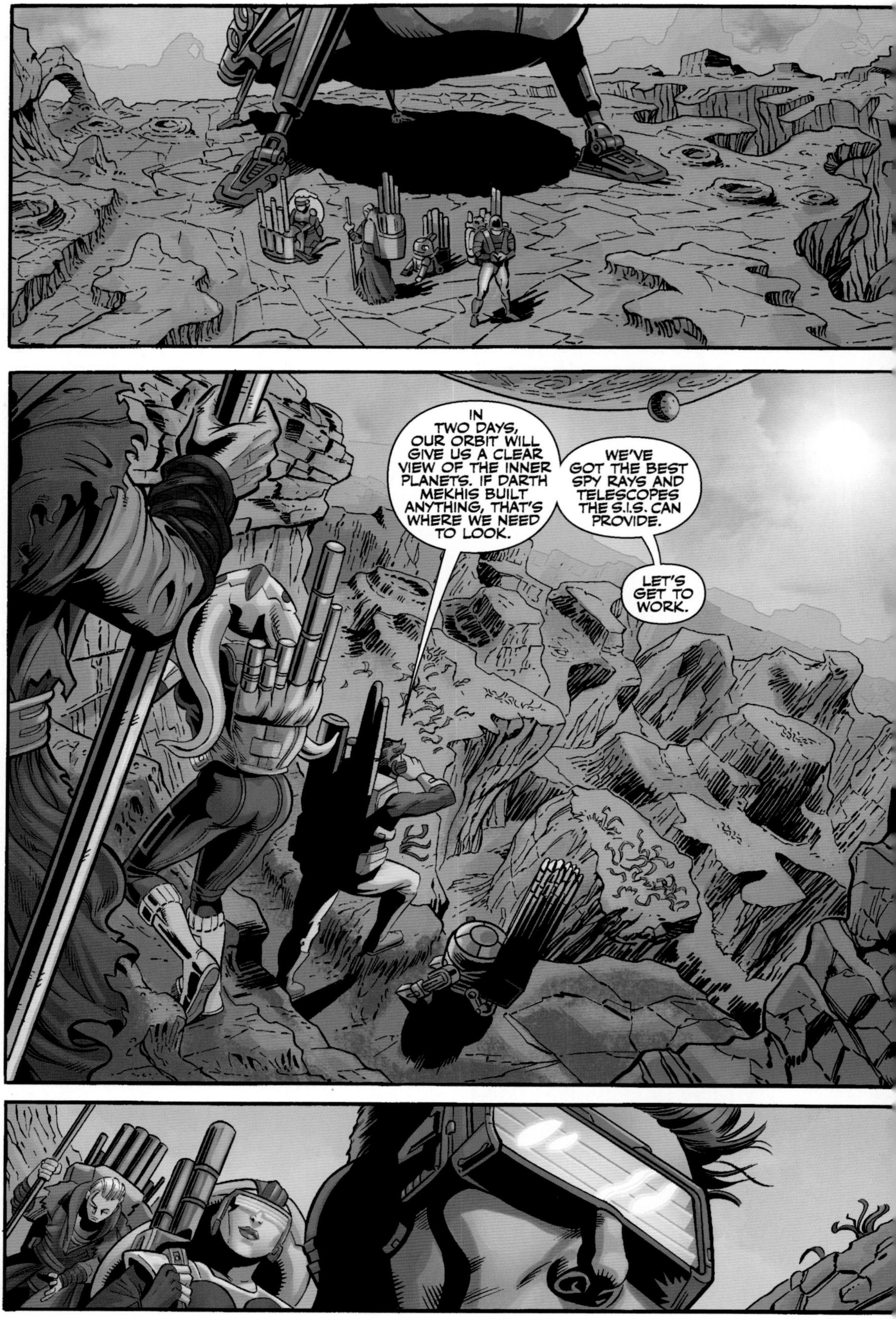
IN TWO DAYS, OUR ORBIT WILL GIVE US A CLEAR VIEW OF THE INNER PLANETS. IF DARTH MEKHIS BUILT ANYTHING, THAT'S WHERE WE NEED TO LOOK.
WE'VE GOT THE BEST SPY RAYS AND TELESCOPES THE S.I.S. CAN PROVIDE.
LET'S GET TO WORK.

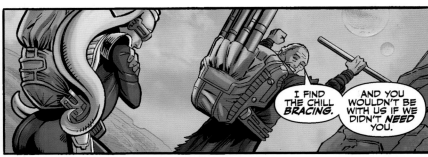

COLD.
WANT TO **STAY** ON THE SHIP.

I FIND THE CHILL **BRACING.**

AND YOU WOULDN'T BE WITH US IF WE DIDN'T **NEED** YOU.

BEE-REEP?

I'VE NOTICED THE WILDLIFE, AND I DON'T SEE THE POINT IN **WORRYING** ANYONE.

JUST KEEP YOUR SCANNERS RUNNING.

BEE-ROO.

I'M NOT ARGUING WITH A DROID.

STEP ONE, STEP TWO -- HEAD UP, GIRL!

YOU'LL FREEZE TO DEATH IF YOU DON'T GET THAT BLOOD PUMPING!

WE'LL SET UP HERE -- HIGH ALTITUDE, MINIMAL DISTURBANCES.

HAVE YOU BUILT ONE OF THESE BEFORE?

I EXPECTED BETTER OF YOU, MASTER ZHO...

...YOU'RE ASKING FOR CLASSIFIED BACKGROUND ON S.I.S. PERSONNEL?

PASSING THE TIME, IS ALL!

I'LL GET OUT THE LENSES, YOU ASSEMBLE THE SCOPE, AND WE CAN REMINISCE ABOUT THE VALLEY OF THE DEATHDROIDS...

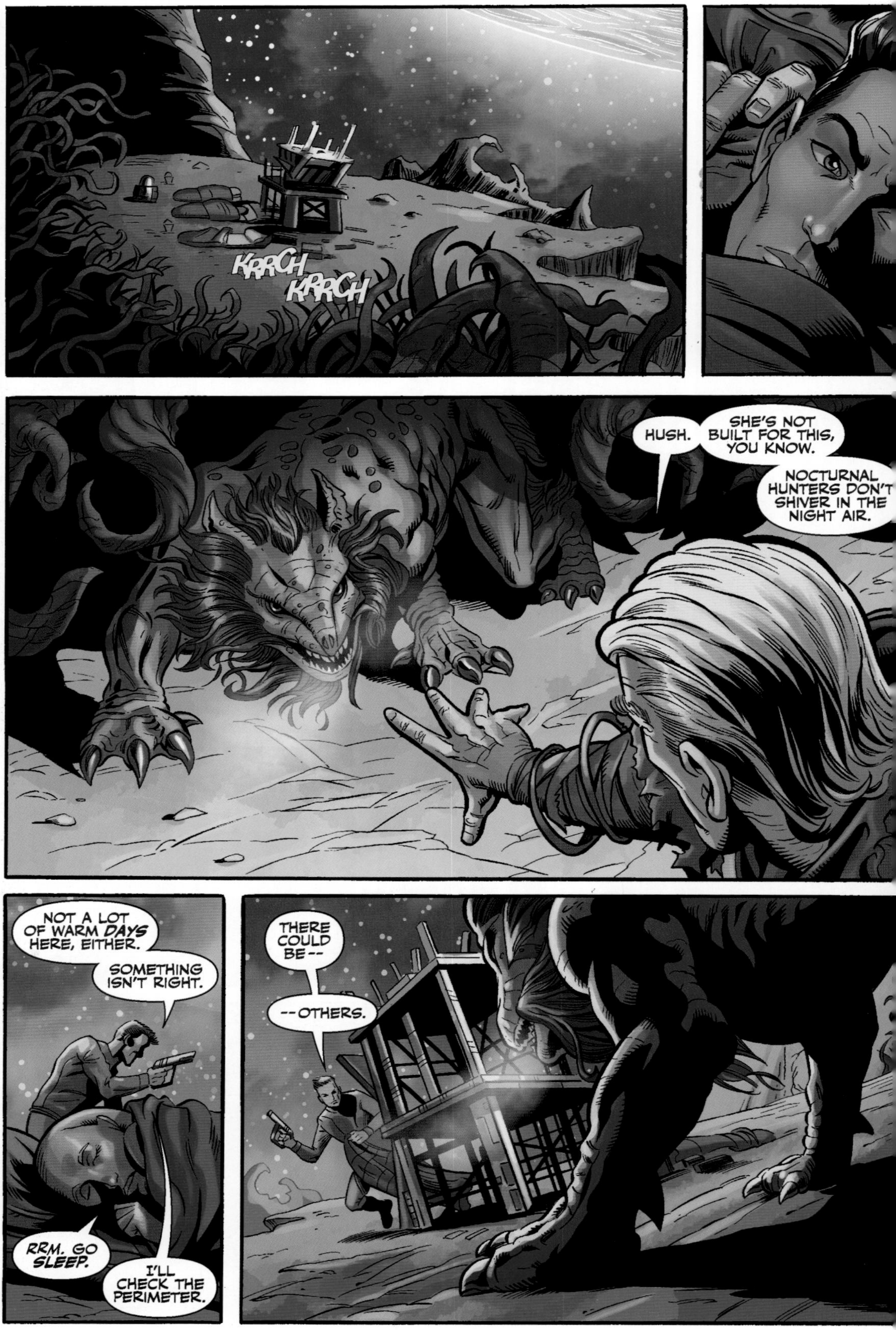
KRRCH KRRCH
HUSH.
SHE'S NOT BUILT FOR THIS, YOU KNOW.
NOCTURNAL HUNTERS DON'T SHIVER IN THE NIGHT AIR.
NOT A LOT OF WARM *DAYS* HERE, EITHER.
SOMETHING ISN'T RIGHT.
RRM. GO *SLEEP*.
I'LL CHECK THE PERIMETER.
THERE COULD BE--
--OTHERS.

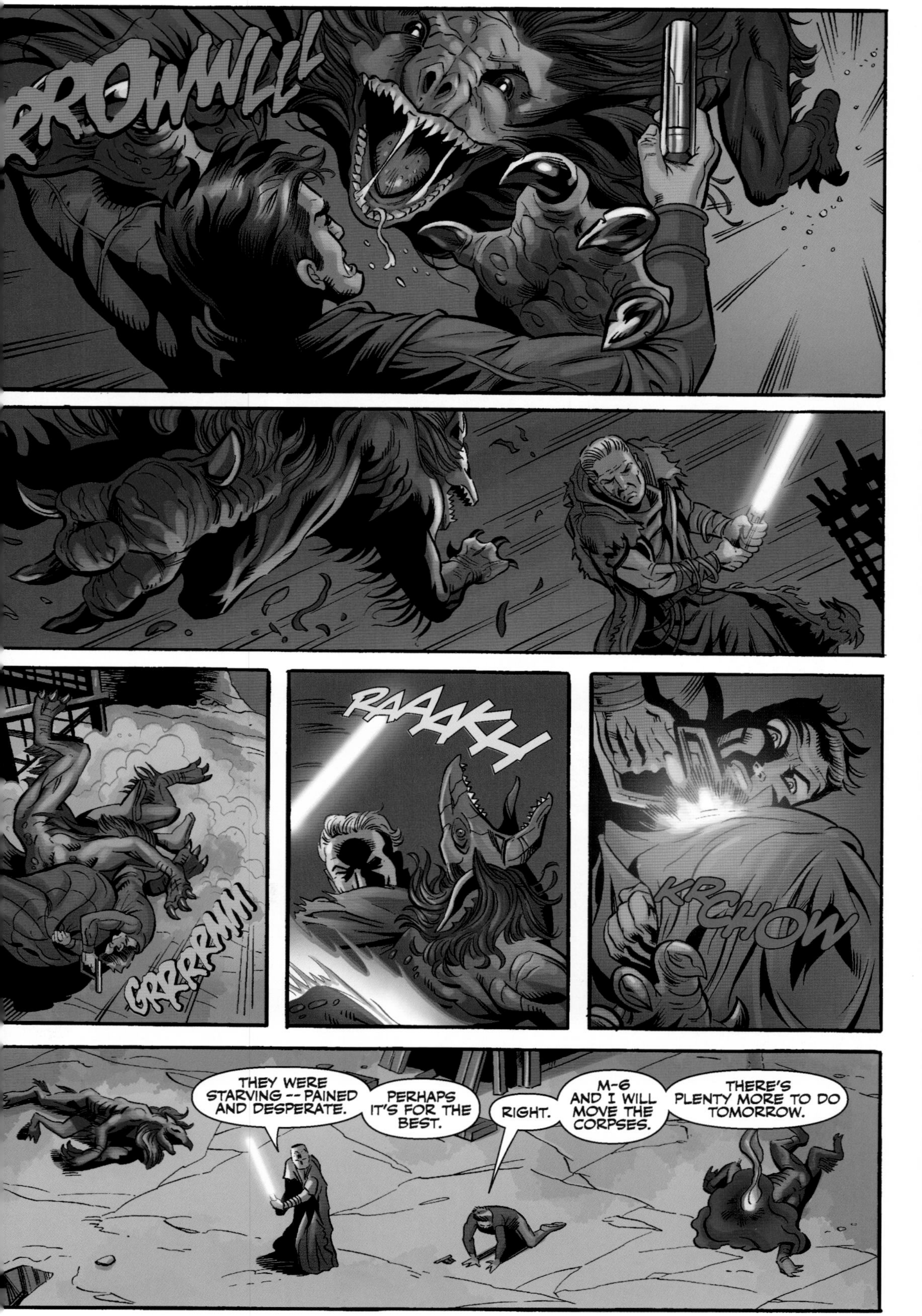
PROWLL!
GRRRMM
RAAAKH
KRCHOW
THEY WERE STARVING -- PAINED AND DESPERATE.
PERHAPS IT'S FOR THE BEST.
RIGHT.
M-6 AND I WILL MOVE THE CORPSES.
THERE'S PLENTY MORE TO DO TOMORROW.

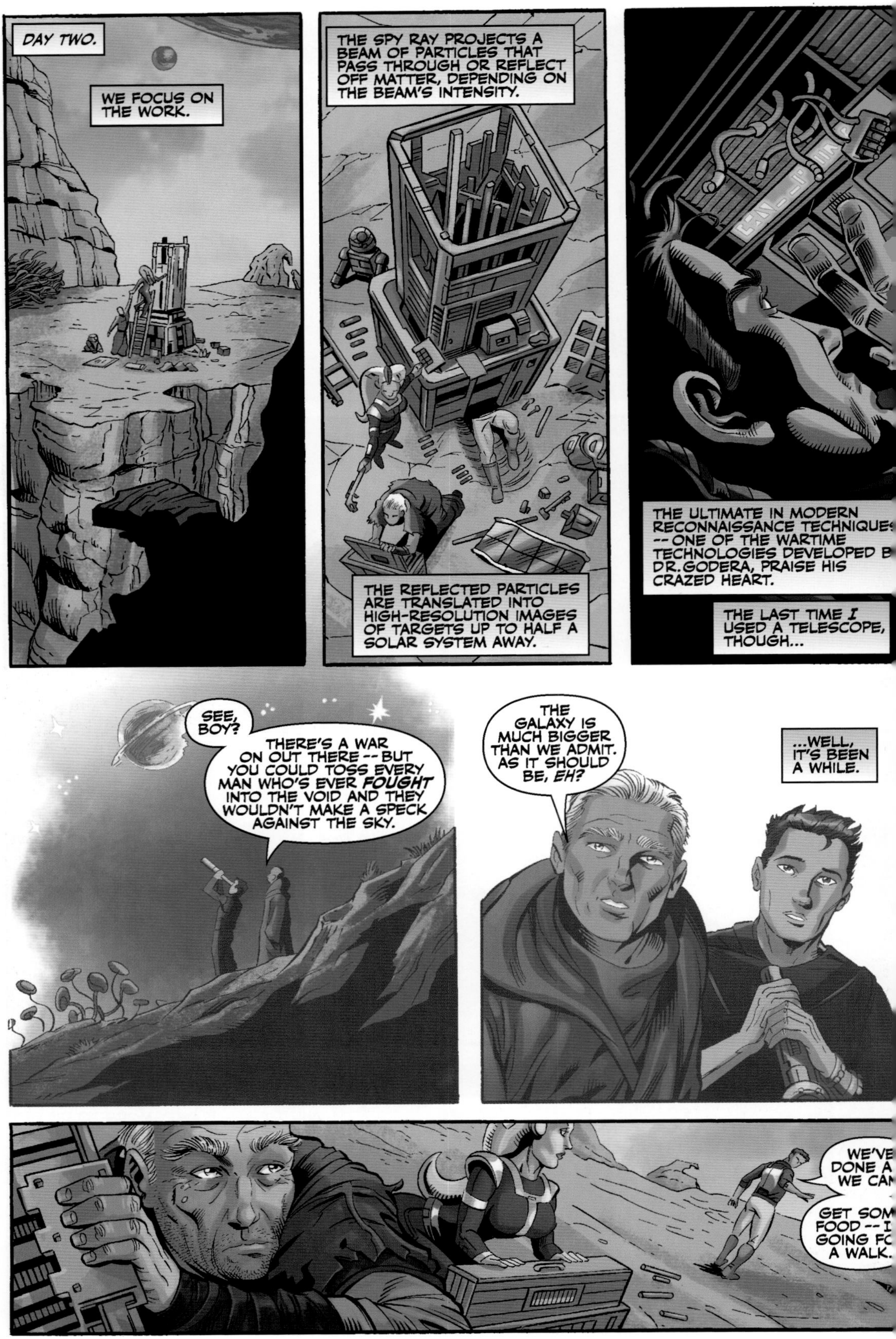

DAY TWO.
WE FOCUS ON THE WORK.
THE SPY RAY PROJECTS A BEAM OF PARTICLES THAT PASS THROUGH OR REFLECT OFF MATTER, DEPENDING ON THE BEAM'S INTENSITY.
THE REFLECTED PARTICLES ARE TRANSLATED INTO HIGH-RESOLUTION IMAGES OF TARGETS UP TO HALF A SOLAR SYSTEM AWAY.
THE ULTIMATE IN MODERN RECONNAISSANCE TECHNIQUES --ONE OF THE WARTIME TECHNOLOGIES DEVELOPED B DR.GODERA, PRAISE HIS CRAZED HEART.
THE LAST TIME *I* USED A TELESCOPE, THOUGH...
SEE, BOY?
THERE'S A WAR ON OUT THERE -- BUT YOU COULD TOSS EVERY MAN WHO'S EVER *FOUGHT* INTO THE VOID AND THEY WOULDN'T MAKE A SPECK AGAINST THE SKY.
THE GALAXY IS MUCH BIGGER THAN WE ADMIT. AS IT SHOULD BE, *EH*?
...WELL, IT'S BEEN A WHILE.
WE'VE DONE A WE CAN
GET SOM FOOD -- I GOING FO A WALK.

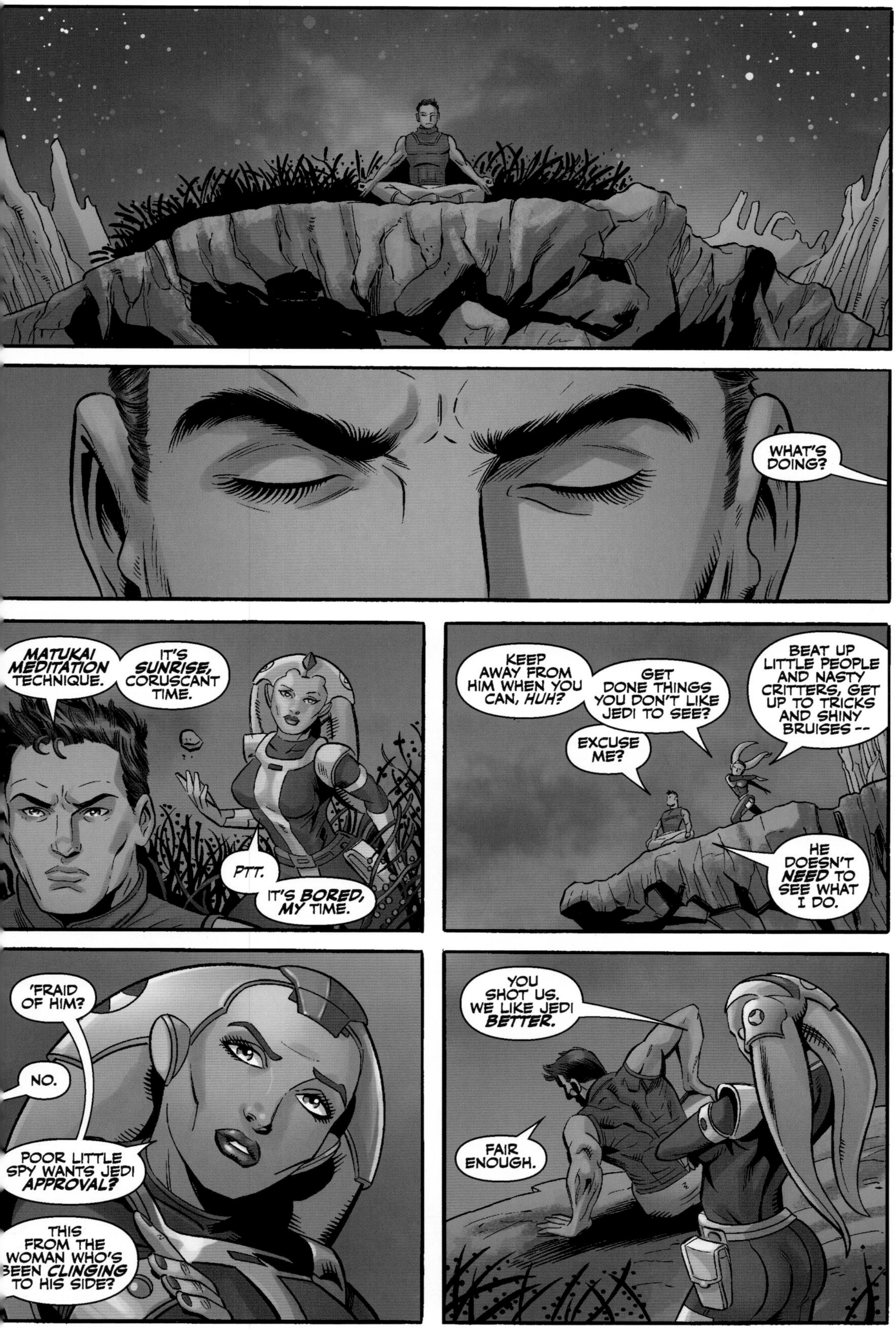
WHAT'S DOING?
MATUKAI MEDITATION TECHNIQUE.
IT'S SUNRISE, CORUSCANT TIME.
PTT.
IT'S BORED, MY TIME.
KEEP AWAY FROM HIM WHEN YOU CAN, HUH?
GET DONE THINGS YOU DON'T LIKE JEDI TO SEE?
EXCUSE ME?
BEAT UP LITTLE PEOPLE AND NASTY CRITTERS, GET UP TO TRICKS AND SHINY BRUISES --
HE DOESN'T NEED TO SEE WHAT I DO.
'FRAID OF HIM?
NO.
POOR LITTLE SPY WANTS JEDI APPROVAL?
THIS FROM THE WOMAN WHO'S BEEN CLINGING TO HIS SIDE?
YOU SHOT US. WE LIKE JEDI BETTER.
FAIR ENOUGH.

YOU REALLY WANT TO KNOW?

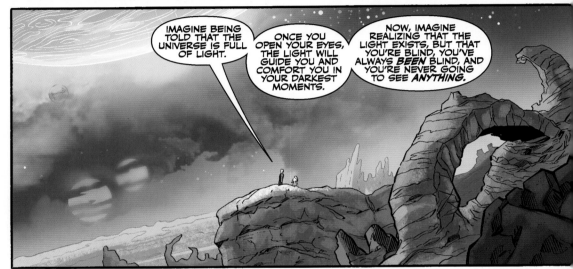

IMAGINE BEING TOLD THAT THE UNIVERSE IS FULL OF LIGHT.

ONCE YOU OPEN YOUR EYES, THE LIGHT WILL GUIDE YOU AND COMFORT YOU IN YOUR DARKEST MOMENTS.

NOW, IMAGINE REALIZING THAT THE LIGHT EXISTS, BUT THAT YOU'RE BLIND, YOU'VE ALWAYS *BEEN* BLIND, AND YOU'RE NEVER GOING TO SEE *ANYTHING*.

I DON'T RESENT THE JEDI -- I JUST DON'T NEED REMINDERS OF WHAT I'M NOT.

HA!

THERE'S NOTHING LIKE THE TINGLING OF FROSTBITTEN TOES!

NOW WE'VE BONDED, YOU LET ME FREE?

ABSOLUTELY NOT.

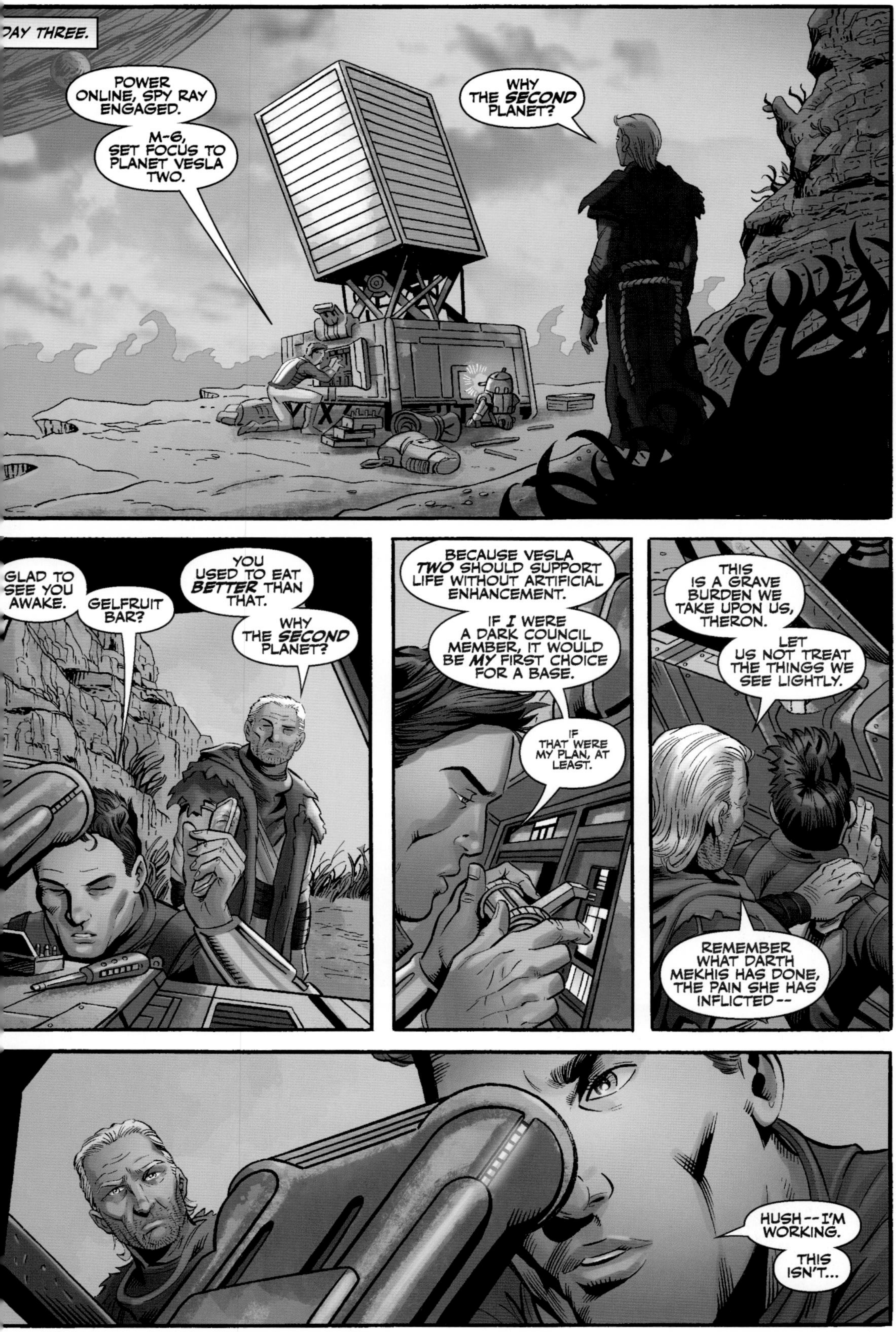
DAY THREE.
POWER ONLINE, SPY RAY ENGAGED.
M-6, SET FOCUS TO PLANET VESLA TWO.
WHY THE SECOND PLANET?
GLAD TO SEE YOU AWAKE.
GELFRUIT BAR?
YOU USED TO EAT BETTER THAN THAT.
WHY THE SECOND PLANET?
BECAUSE VESLA TWO SHOULD SUPPORT LIFE WITHOUT ARTIFICIAL ENHANCEMENT.
IF I WERE A DARK COUNCIL MEMBER, IT WOULD BE MY FIRST CHOICE FOR A BASE.
IF THAT WERE MY PLAN, AT LEAST.
THIS IS A GRAVE BURDEN WE TAKE UPON US, THERON.
LET US NOT TREAT THE THINGS WE SEE LIGHTLY.
REMEMBER WHAT DARTH MEKHIS HAS DONE, THE PAIN SHE HAS INFLICTED--
HUSH--I'M WORKING.
THIS ISN'T...

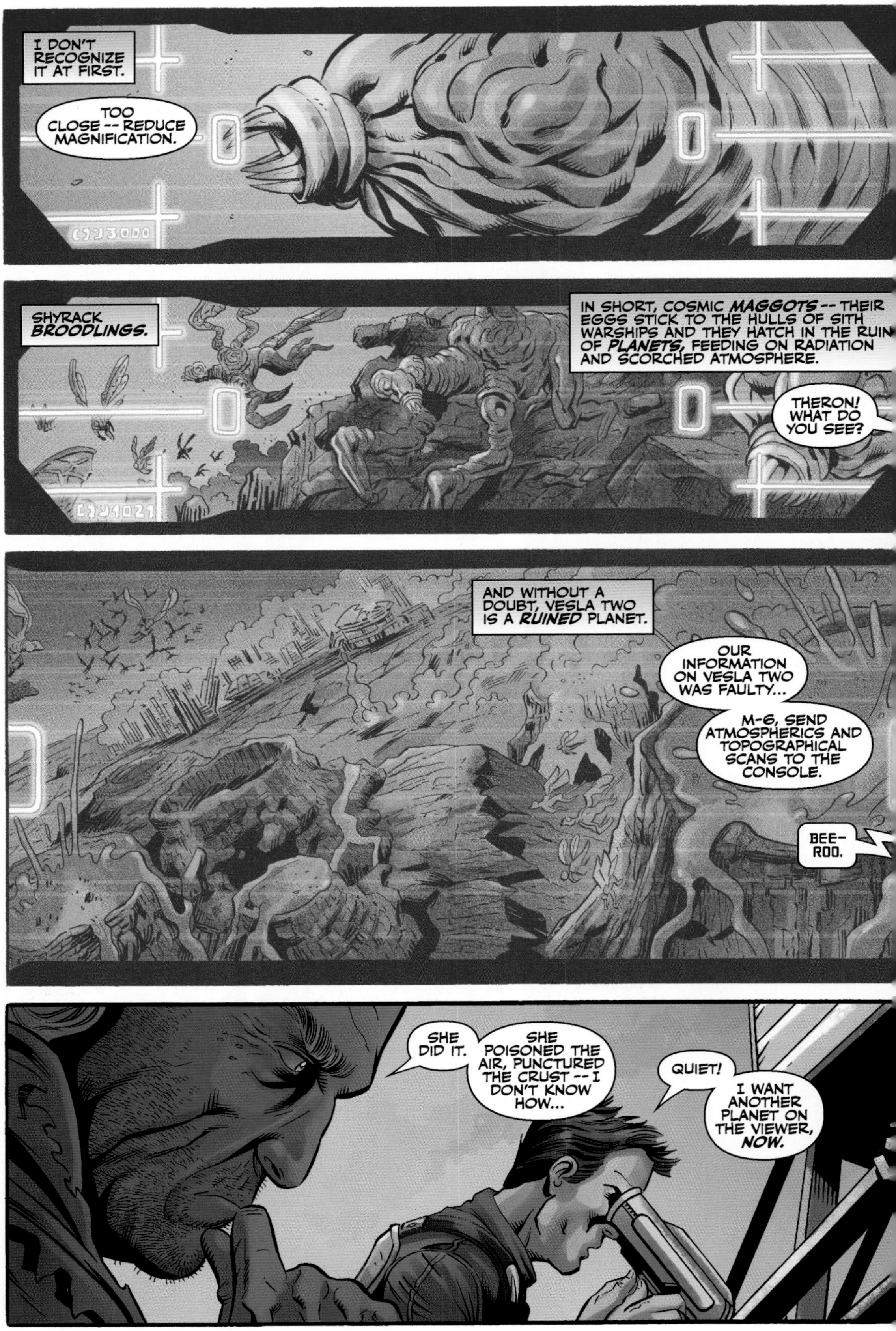
I DON'T RECOGNIZE IT AT FIRST.
TOO CLOSE -- REDUCE MAGNIFICATION.
SHYRACK BROODLINGS.
IN SHORT, COSMIC MAGGOTS -- THEIR EGGS STICK TO THE HULLS OF SITH WARSHIPS AND THEY HATCH IN THE RUIN OF PLANETS, FEEDING ON RADIATION AND SCORCHED ATMOSPHERE.
THERON! WHAT DO YOU SEE?
AND WITHOUT A DOUBT, VESLA TWO IS A RUINED PLANET.
OUR INFORMATION ON VESLA TWO WAS FAULTY...
M-6, SEND ATMOSPHERICS AND TOPOGRAPHICAL SCANS TO THE CONSOLE.
BEE-ROO.
SHE DID IT.
SHE POISONED THE AIR, PUNCTURED THE CRUST -- I DON'T KNOW HOW...
QUIET!
I WANT ANOTHER PLANET ON THE VIEWER, NOW.

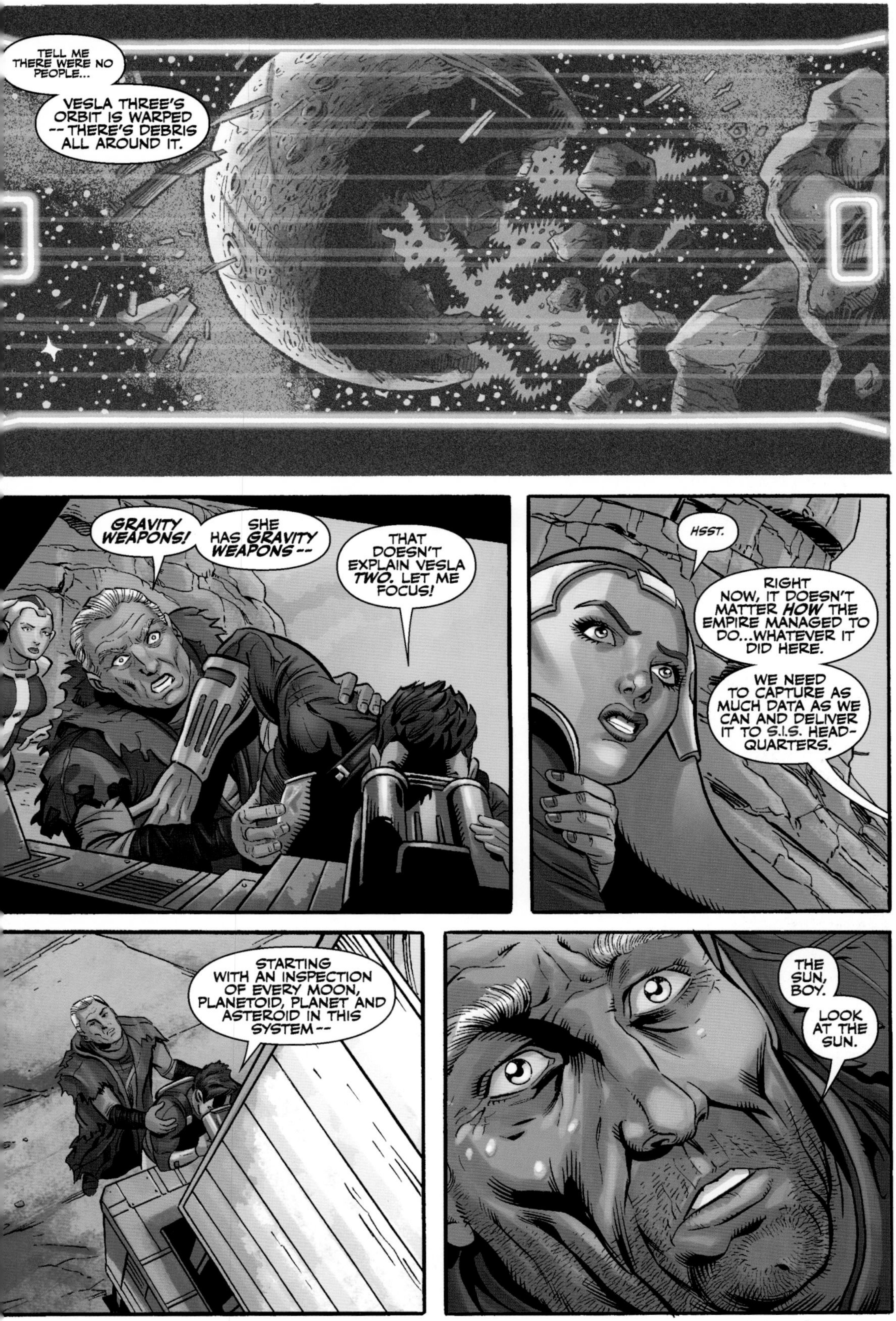
TELL ME THERE WERE NO PEOPLE...
VESLA THREE'S ORBIT IS WARPED -- THERE'S DEBRIS ALL AROUND IT.
GRAVITY WEAPONS!
SHE HAS GRAVITY WEAPONS --
THAT DOESN'T EXPLAIN VESLA TWO. LET ME FOCUS!
HSST.
RIGHT NOW, IT DOESN'T MATTER HOW THE EMPIRE MANAGED TO DO...WHATEVER IT DID HERE.
WE NEED TO CAPTURE AS MUCH DATA AS WE CAN AND DELIVER IT TO S.I.S. HEAD-QUARTERS.
STARTING WITH AN INSPECTION OF EVERY MOON, PLANETOID, PLANET AND ASTEROID IN THIS SYSTEM --
THE SUN, BOY.
LOOK AT THE SUN.

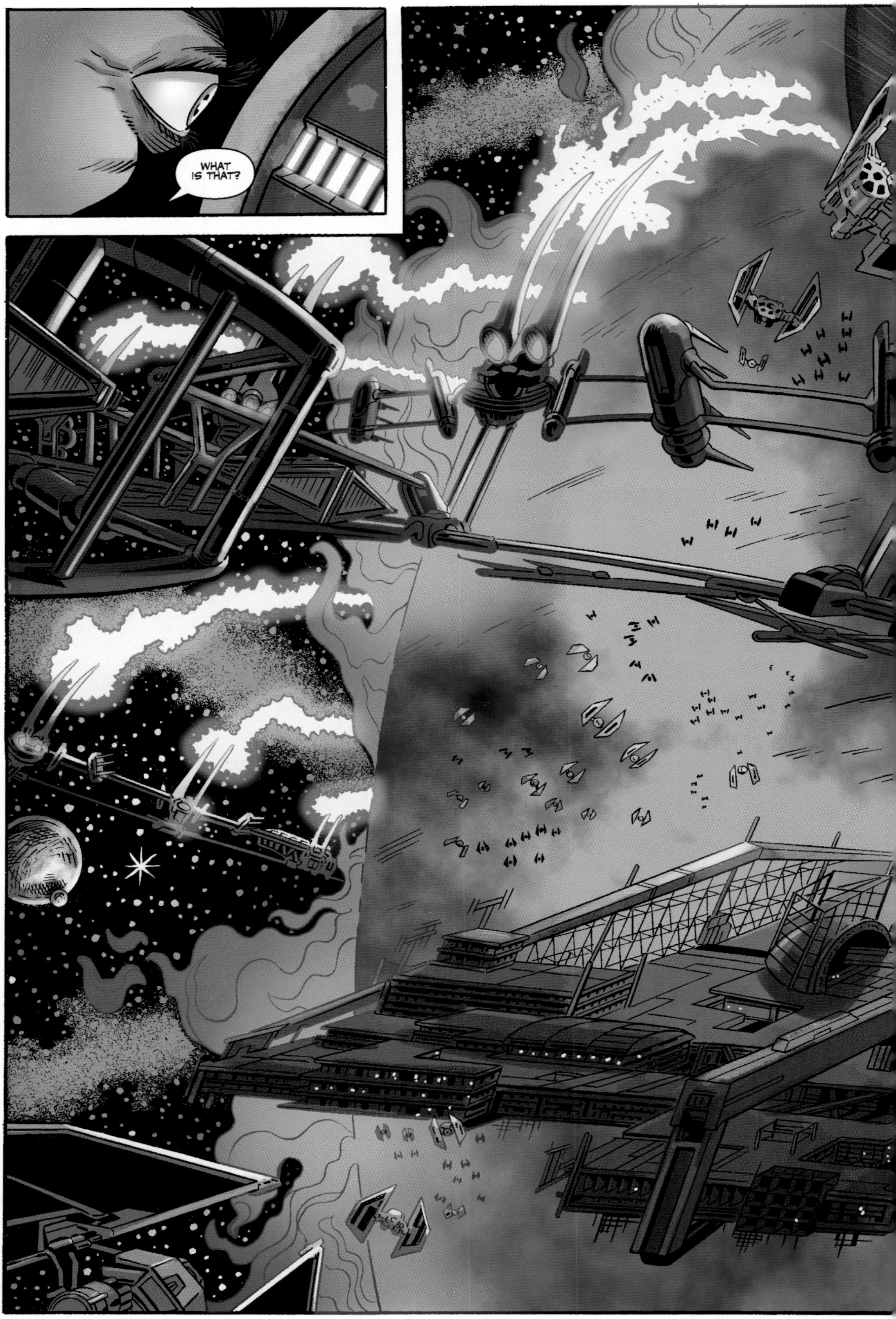
WHAT IS THAT?

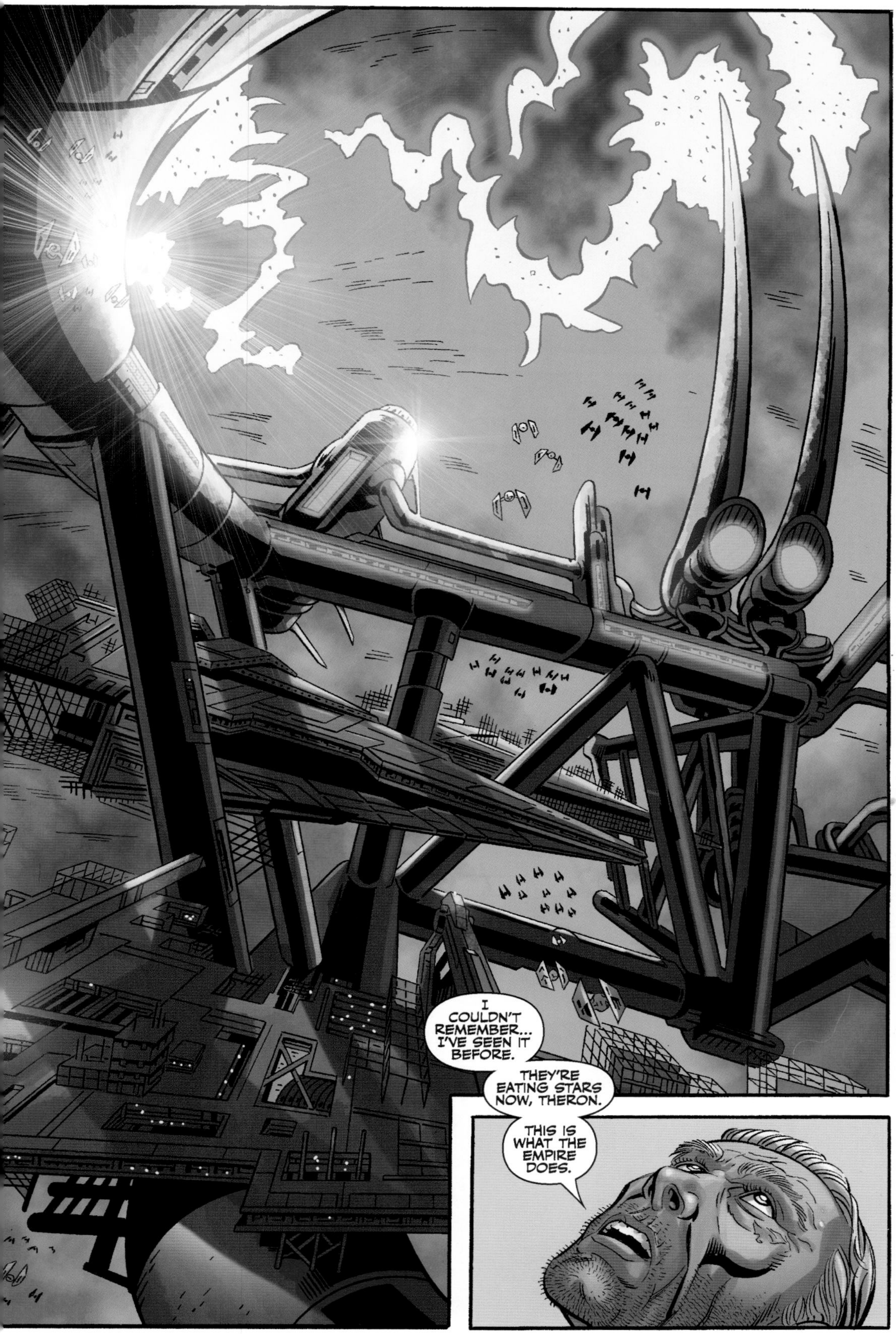
I COULDN'T REMEMBER... I'VE SEEN IT BEFORE.
THEY'RE EATING STARS NOW, THERON.
THIS IS WHAT THE EMPIRE DOES.

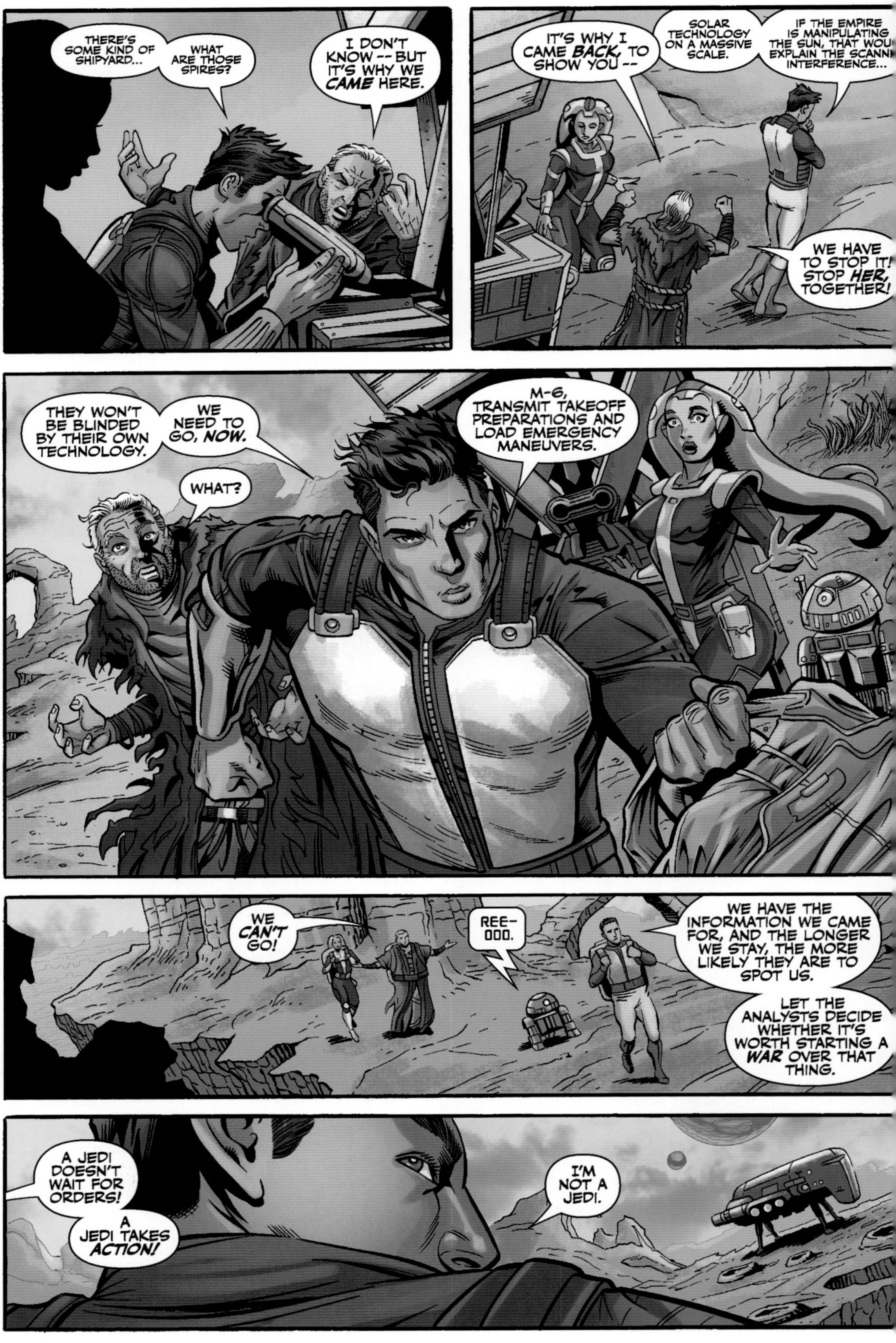
THERE'S SOME KIND OF SHIPYARD...
WHAT ARE THOSE SPIRES?
I DON'T KNOW -- BUT IT'S WHY WE CAME HERE.
IT'S WHY I CAME BACK, TO SHOW YOU --
SOLAR TECHNOLOGY ON A MASSIVE SCALE.
IF THE EMPIRE IS MANIPULATING THE SUN, THAT WOU EXPLAIN THE SCANN INTERFERENCE...
WE HAVE TO STOP IT! STOP HER, TOGETHER!
THEY WON'T BE BLINDED BY THEIR OWN TECHNOLOGY.
WE NEED TO GO, NOW.
M-6, TRANSMIT TAKEOFF PREPARATIONS AND LOAD EMERGENCY MANEUVERS.
WHAT?
WE CAN'T GO!
REE-OOO.
WE HAVE THE INFORMATION WE CAME FOR, AND THE LONGER WE STAY, THE MORE LIKELY THEY ARE TO SPOT US.
LET THE ANALYSTS DECIDE WHETHER IT'S WORTH STARTING A WAR OVER THAT THING.
A JEDI DOESN'T WAIT FOR ORDERS!
A JEDI TAKES ACTION!
I'M NOT A JEDI.

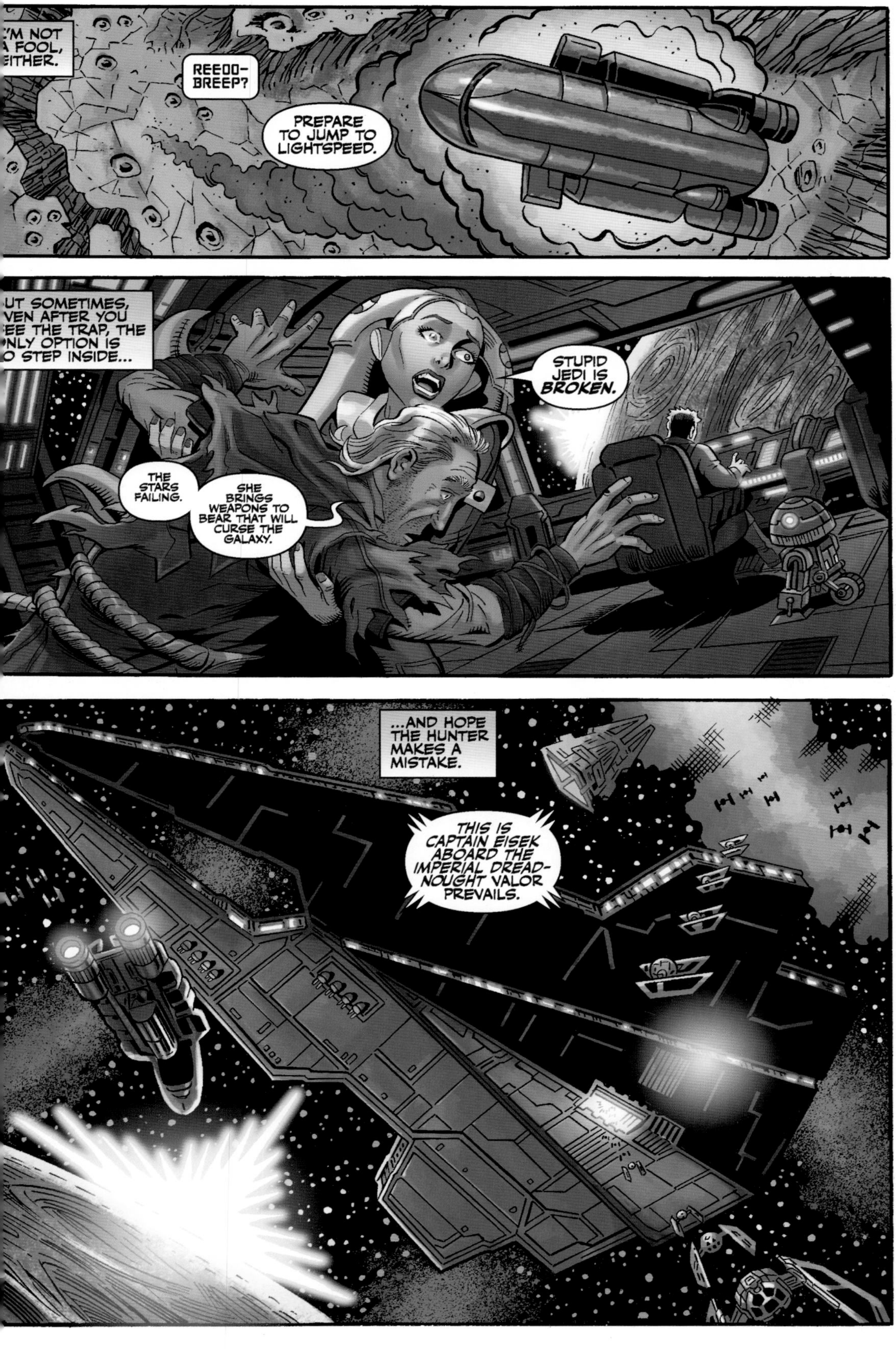
'M NOT
A FOOL,
EITHER.
REEOO-
BREEP?
PREPARE
TO JUMP TO
LIGHTSPEED.
UT SOMETIMES,
VEN AFTER YOU
EE THE TRAP, THE
NLY OPTION IS
O STEP INSIDE...
STUPID
JEDI IS
BROKEN.
THE
STARS
FAILING.
SHE
BRINGS
WEAPONS TO
BEAR THAT WILL
CURSE THE
GALAXY.
...AND HOPE
THE HUNTER
MAKES A
MISTAKE.
THIS IS
CAPTAIN EISEK
ABOARD THE
IMPERIAL DREAD-
NOUGHT VALOR
PREVAILS.

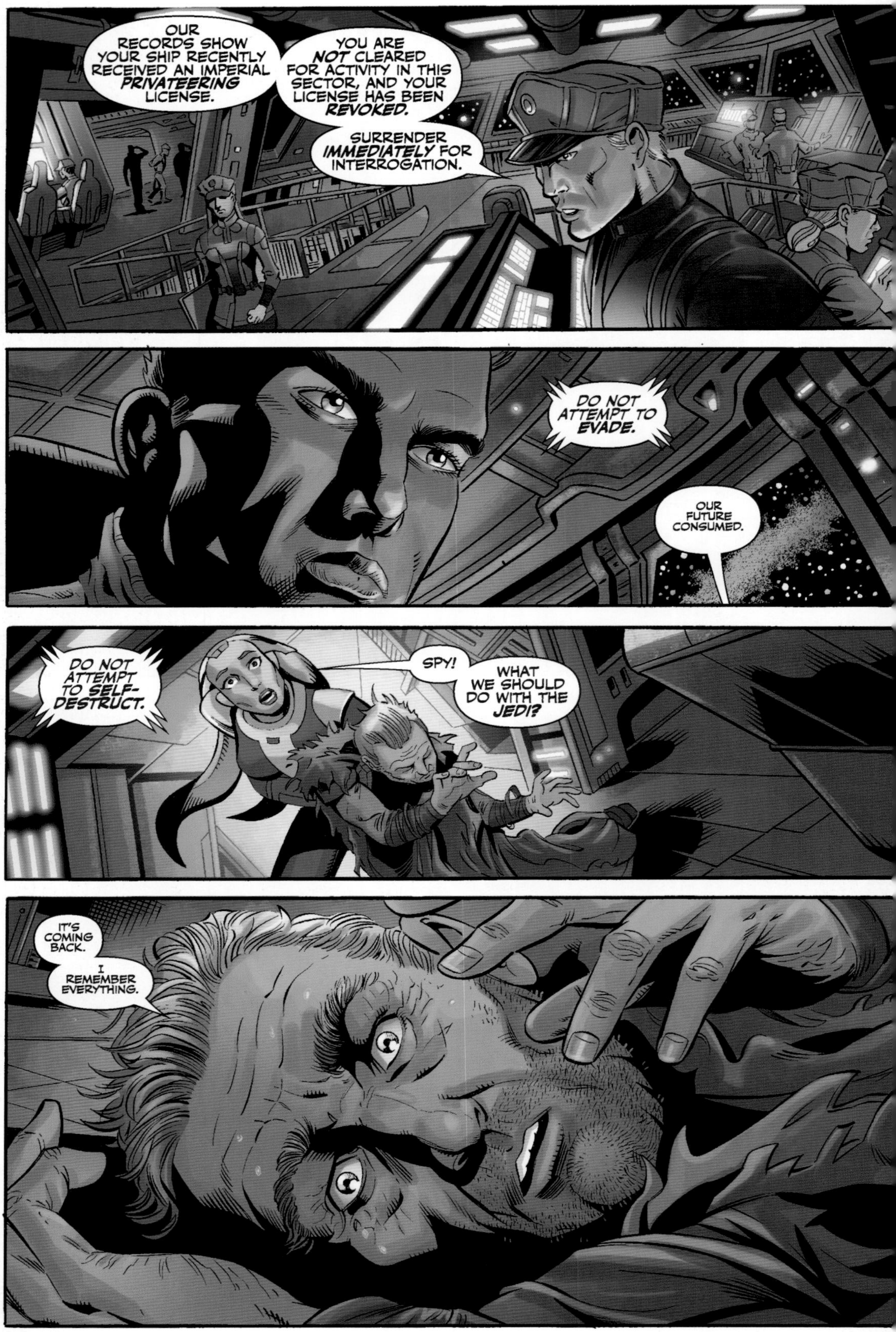
OUR RECORDS SHOW YOUR SHIP RECENTLY RECEIVED AN IMPERIAL PRIVATEERING LICENSE.
YOU ARE NOT CLEARED FOR ACTIVITY IN THIS SECTOR, AND YOUR LICENSE HAS BEEN REVOKED.
SURRENDER IMMEDIATELY FOR INTERROGATION.
DO NOT ATTEMPT TO EVADE.
OUR FUTURE CONSUMED.
DO NOT ATTEMPT TO SELF-DESTRUCT.
SPY!
WHAT WE SHOULD DO WITH THE JEDI?
IT'S COMING BACK.
I REMEMBER EVERYTHING.

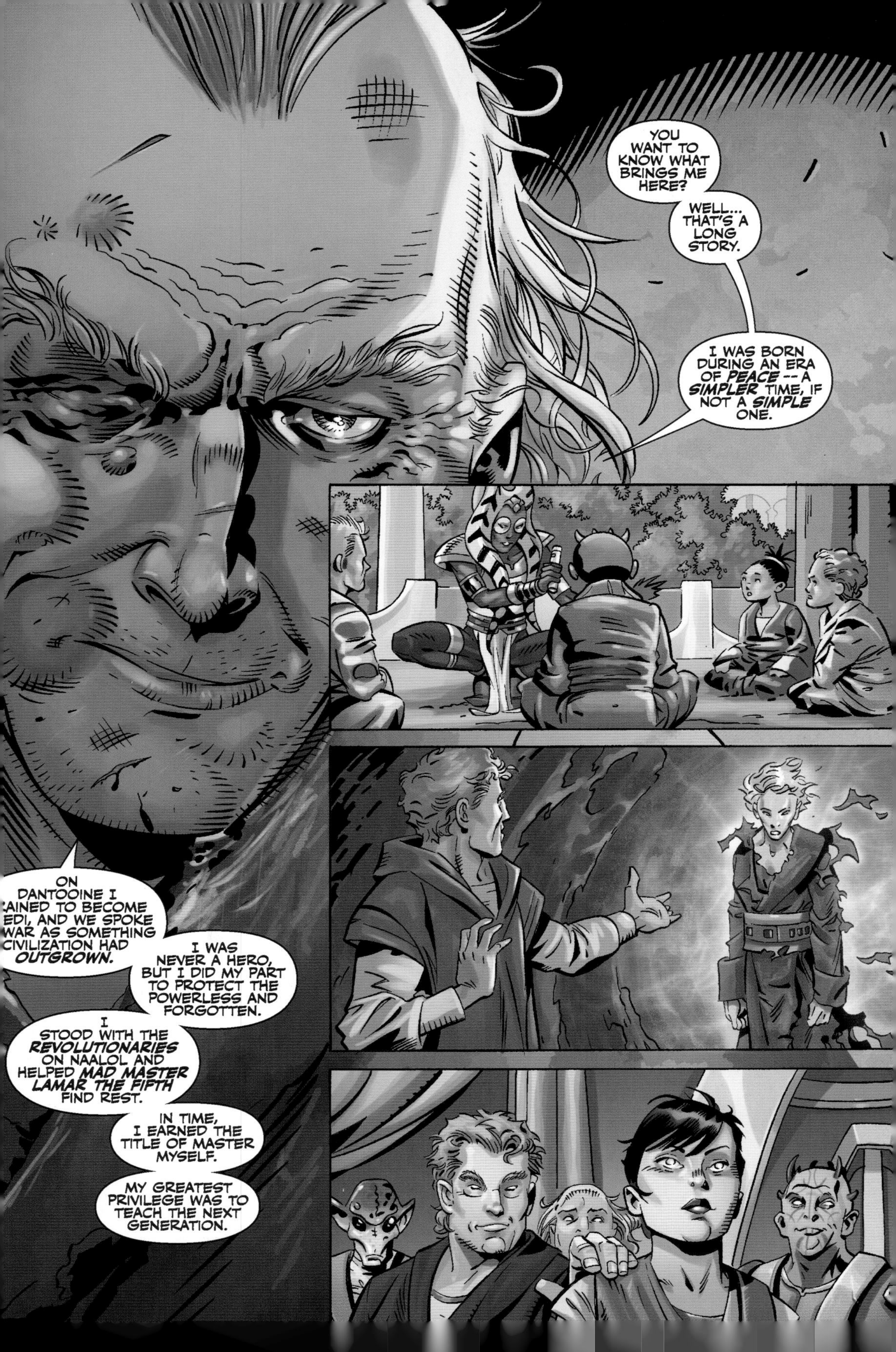
YOU WANT TO KNOW WHAT BRINGS ME HERE?
WELL... THAT'S A LONG STORY.
I WAS BORN DURING AN ERA OF *PEACE* -- A *SIMPLER* TIME, IF NOT A *SIMPLE* ONE.
ON DANTOOINE I RAINED TO BECOME EDI, AND WE SPOKE WAR AS SOMETHING CIVILIZATION HAD *OUTGROWN.*
I WAS NEVER A HERO, BUT I DID MY PART TO PROTECT THE POWERLESS AND FORGOTTEN.
I STOOD WITH THE *REVOLUTIONARIES* ON NAALOL AND HELPED *MAD MASTER LAMAR THE FIFTH* FIND REST.
IN TIME, I EARNED THE TITLE OF MASTER MYSELF.
MY GREATEST PRIVILEGE WAS TO TEACH THE NEXT GENERATION.

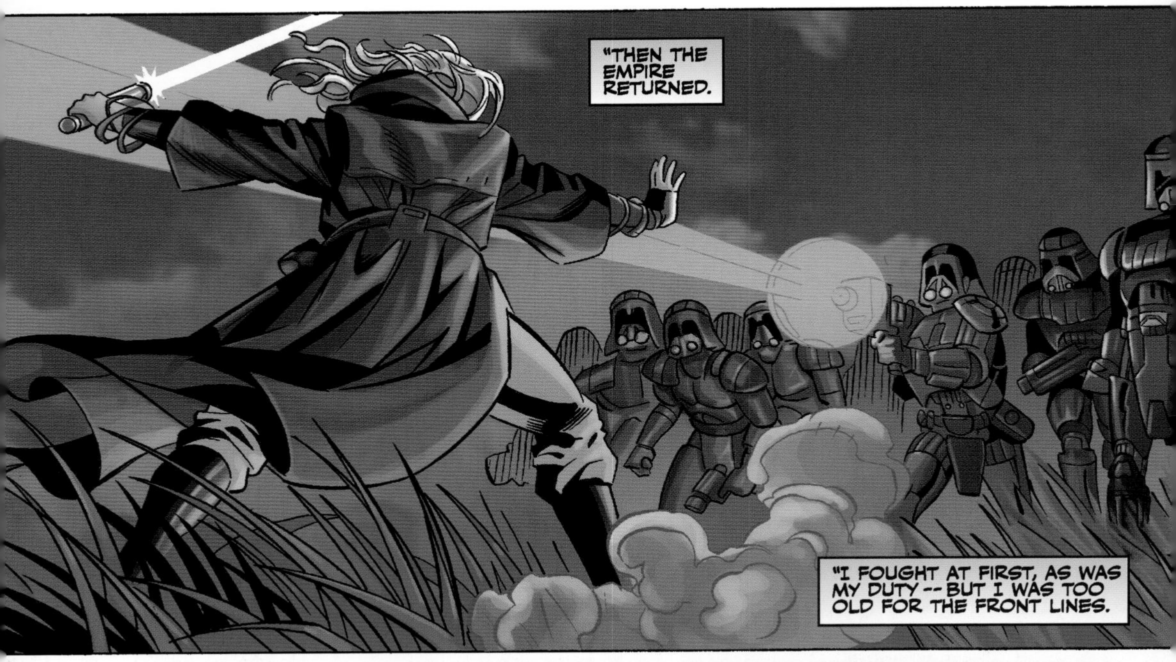
"THEN THE EMPIRE RETURNED.
"I FOUGHT AT FIRST, AS WAS MY DUTY -- BUT I WAS TOO OLD FOR THE FRONT LINES.

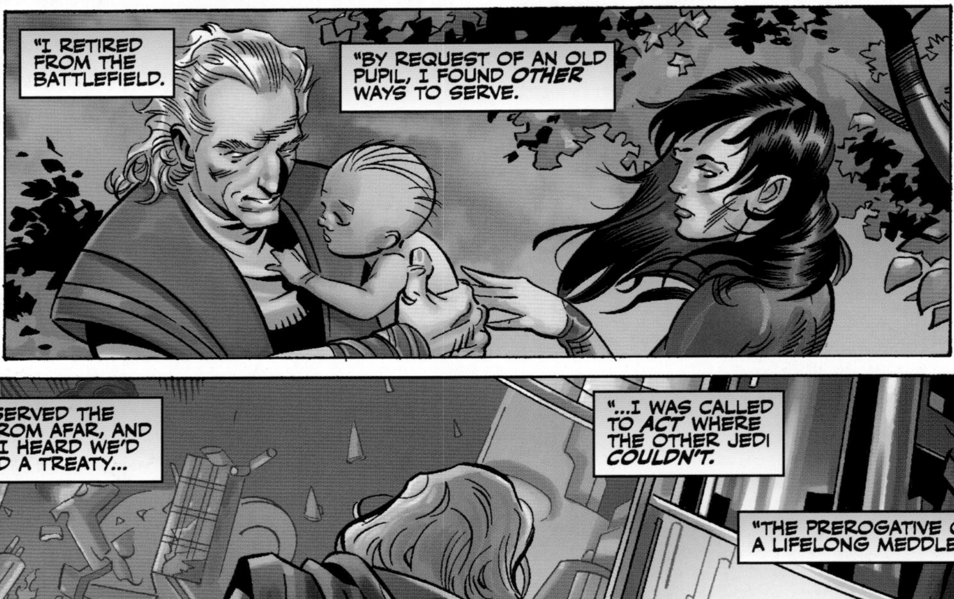
"I RETIRED FROM THE BATTLEFIELD.
"BY REQUEST OF AN OLD PUPIL, I FOUND OTHER WAYS TO SERVE.

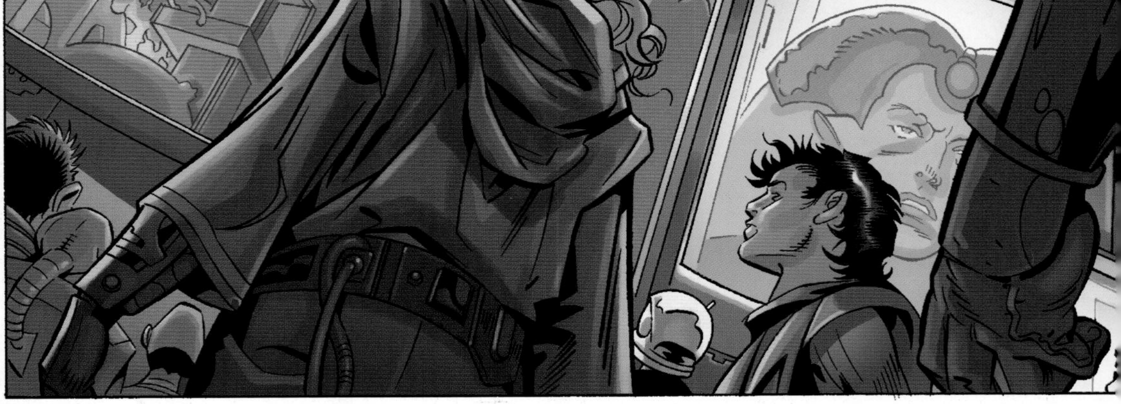
"I OBSERVED THE WAR FROM AFAR, AND WHEN I HEARD WE'D SIGNED A TREATY...
"...I WAS CALLED TO ACT WHERE THE OTHER JEDI COULDN'T.
"THE PREROGATIVE OF A LIFELONG MEDDLER.

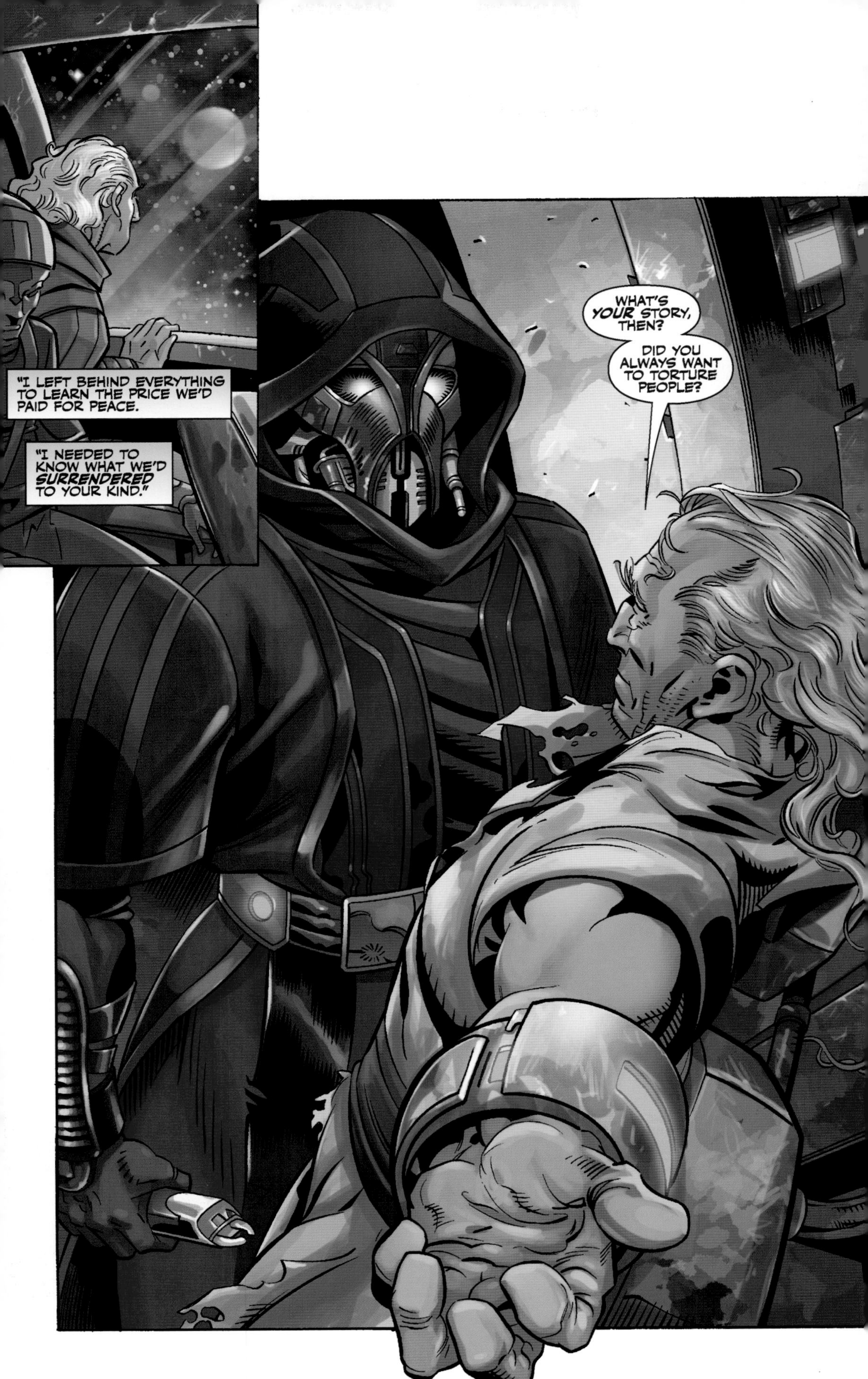
"I LEFT BEHIND EVERYTHING TO LEARN THE PRICE WE'D PAID FOR PEACE.
"I NEEDED TO KNOW WHAT WE'D SURRENDERED TO YOUR KIND."
WHAT'S YOUR STORY, THEN?
DID YOU ALWAYS WANT TO TORTURE PEOPLE?

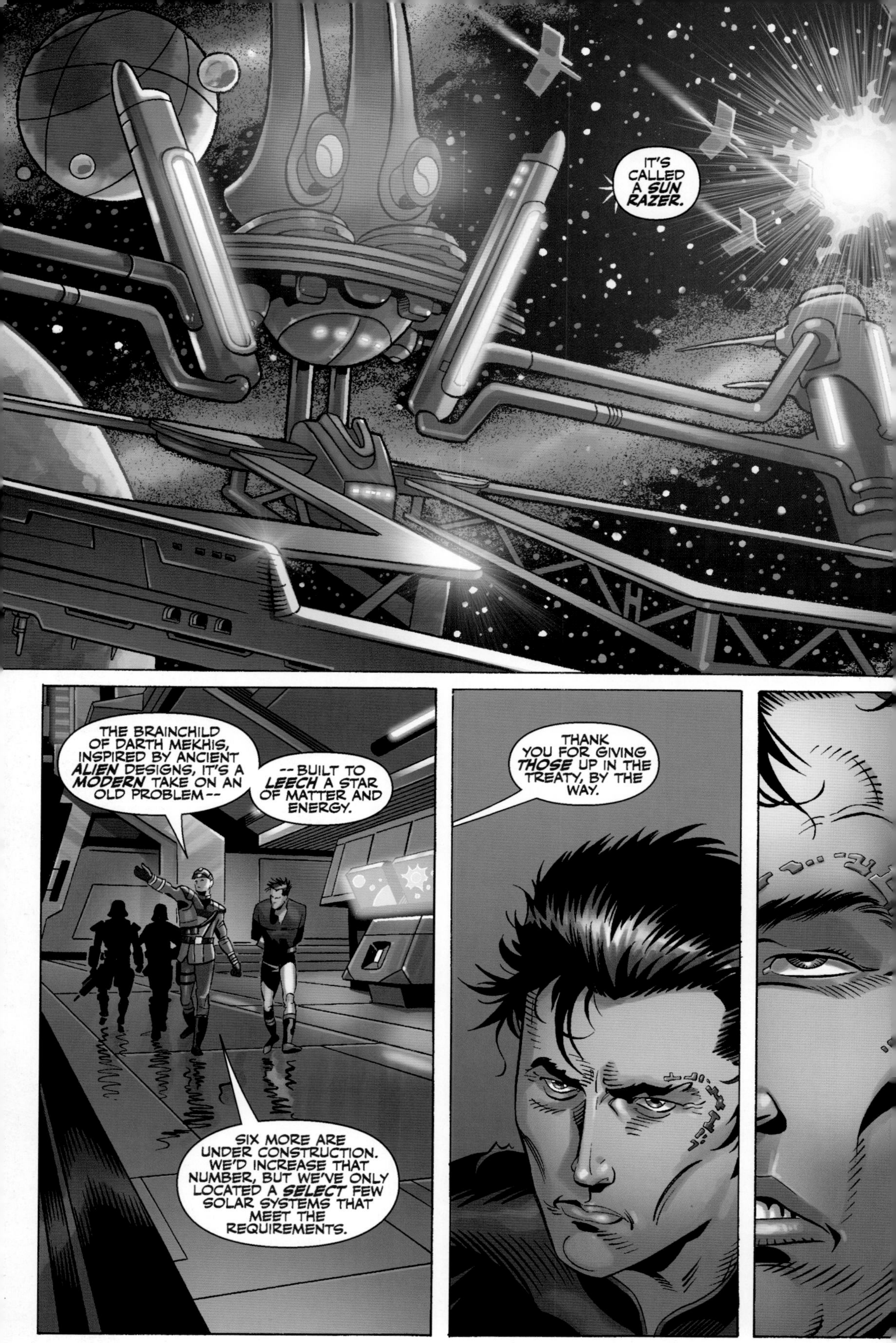
IT'S CALLED A SUN RAZER.
THE BRAINCHILD OF DARTH MEKHIS, INSPIRED BY ANCIENT ALIEN DESIGNS, IT'S A MODERN TAKE ON AN OLD PROBLEM--
--BUILT TO LEECH A STAR OF MATTER AND ENERGY.
SIX MORE ARE UNDER CONSTRUCTION. WE'D INCREASE THAT NUMBER, BUT WE'VE ONLY LOCATED A SELECT FEW SOLAR SYSTEMS THAT MEET THE REQUIREMENTS.
THANK YOU FOR GIVING THOSE UP IN THE TREATY, BY THE WAY.

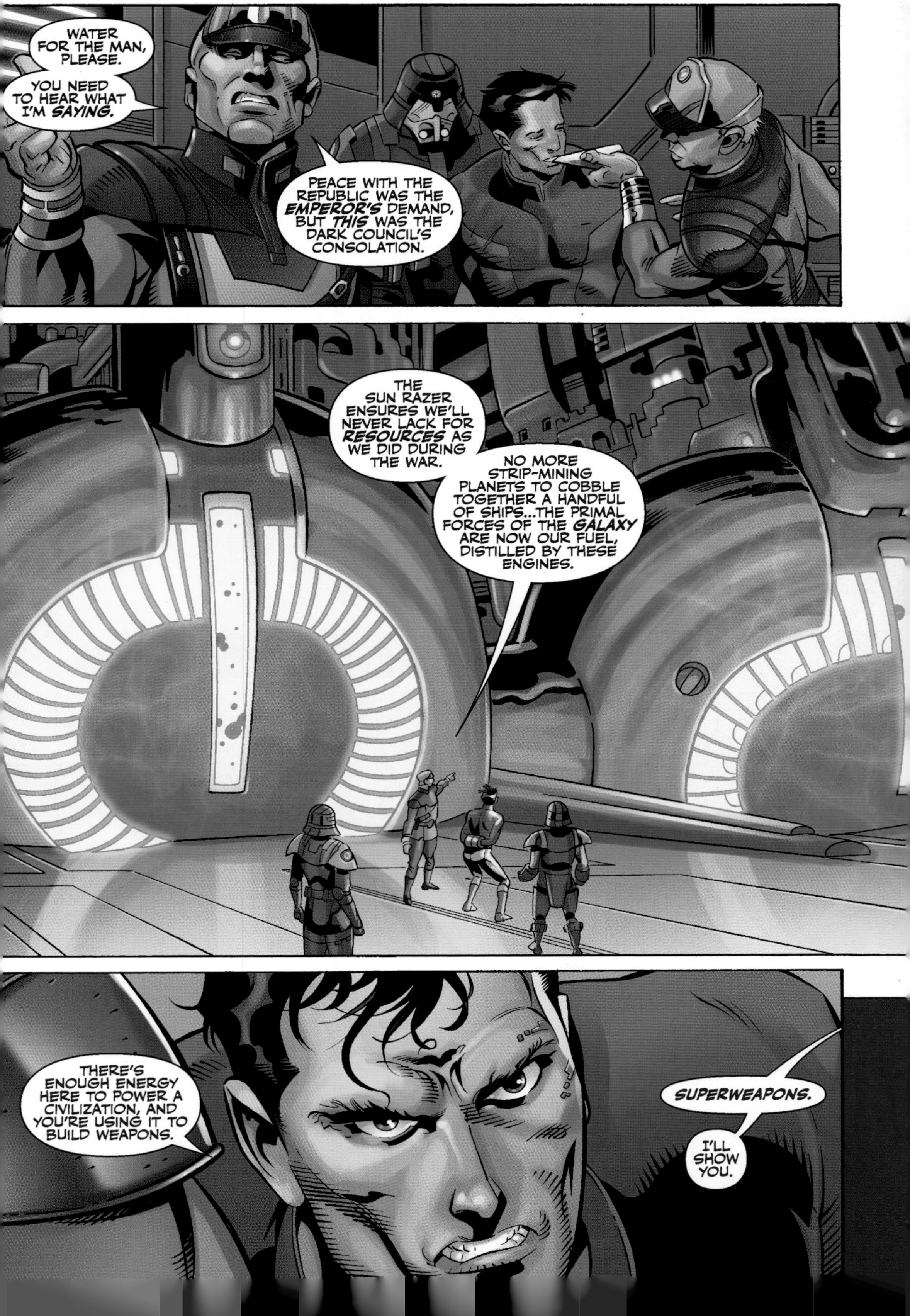
WATER FOR THE MAN, PLEASE.
YOU NEED TO HEAR WHAT I'M *SAYING.*
PEACE WITH THE REPUBLIC WAS THE *EMPEROR'S* DEMAND, BUT *THIS* WAS THE DARK COUNCIL'S CONSOLATION.
THE SUN RAZER ENSURES WE'LL NEVER LACK FOR *RESOURCES* AS WE DID DURING THE WAR.
NO MORE STRIP-MINING PLANETS TO COBBLE TOGETHER A HANDFUL OF SHIPS...THE PRIMAL FORCES OF THE *GALAXY* ARE NOW OUR FUEL, DISTILLED BY THESE ENGINES.
THERE'S ENOUGH ENERGY HERE TO POWER A CIVILIZATION, AND YOU'RE USING IT TO BUILD WEAPONS.
SUPERWEAPONS.
I'LL SHOW YOU.

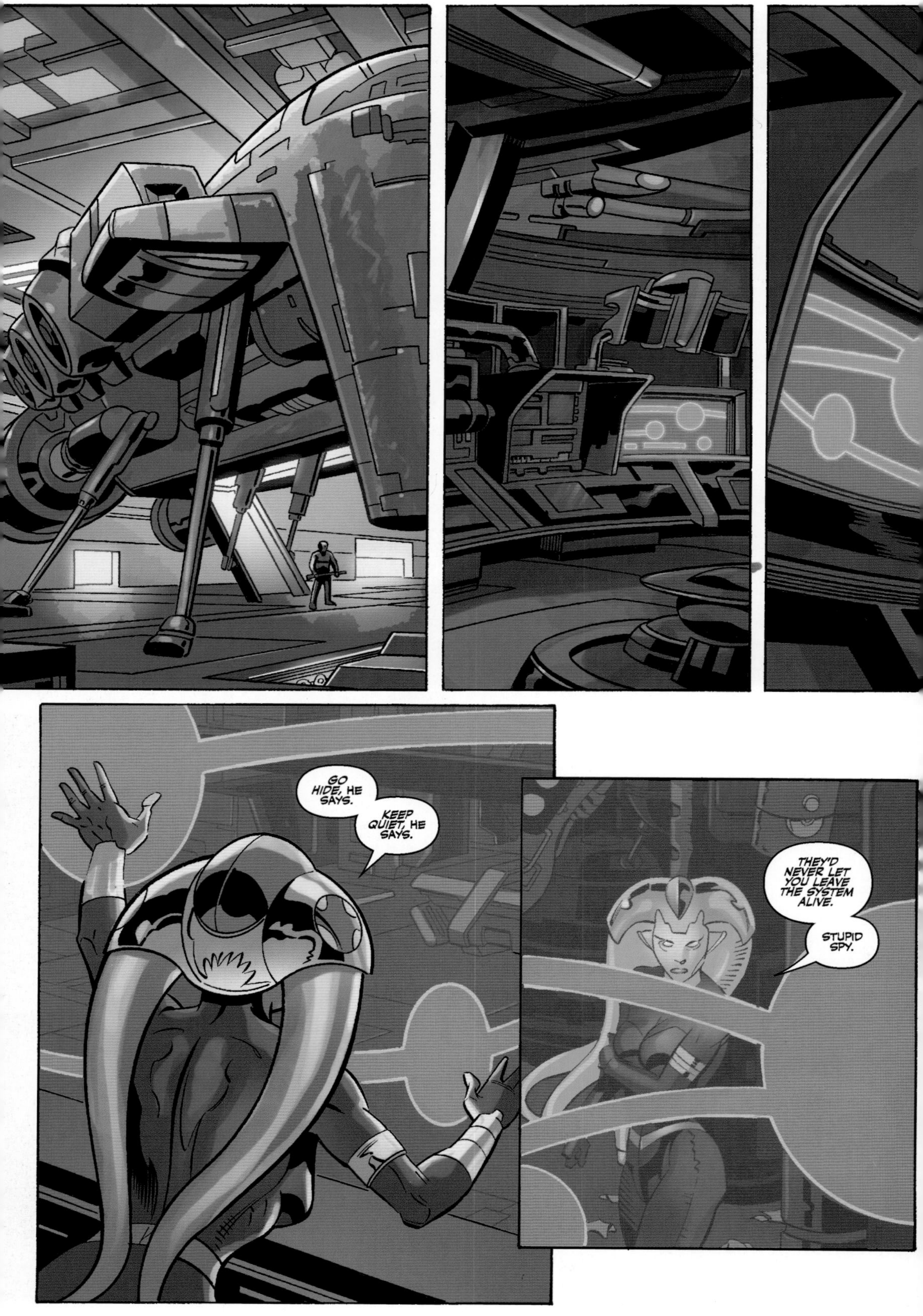
GO HIDE, HE SAYS.
KEEP QUIET, HE SAYS.
THEY'D NEVER LET YOU LEAVE THE SYSTEM ALIVE.
STUPID SPY.

IT MUST BE GETTING LATE. YOU SHOULD GO HOME TO YOUR FAMILY-- THEY'LL BE WORRIED.

EVEN IF YOUR WIFE UNDERSTANDS, THE CHILDREN --

GET ON WITH IT.

GLADLY, SIR, GLADLY.

DO YOU REMEMBER WHEN YOU STARTED BUILDING THIS SUN-EATING ABOMINATION...?

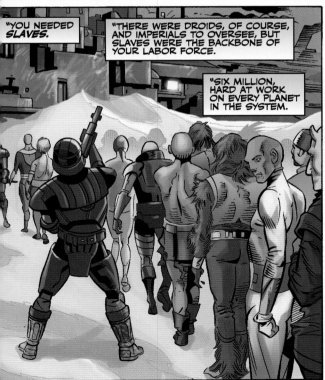

"YOU NEEDED SLAVES.

"THERE WERE DROIDS, OF COURSE, AND IMPERIALS TO OVERSEE, BUT SLAVES WERE THE BACKBONE OF YOUR LABOR FORCE.

"SIX MILLION, HARD AT WORK ON EVERY PLANET IN THE SYSTEM.

"BY THE FOURTH SHIPMENT, I WAS AMONG THEM -- WHAT BETTER WAY FOR AN OLD MAN TO SLIP PAST THE BORDER, *EH?*

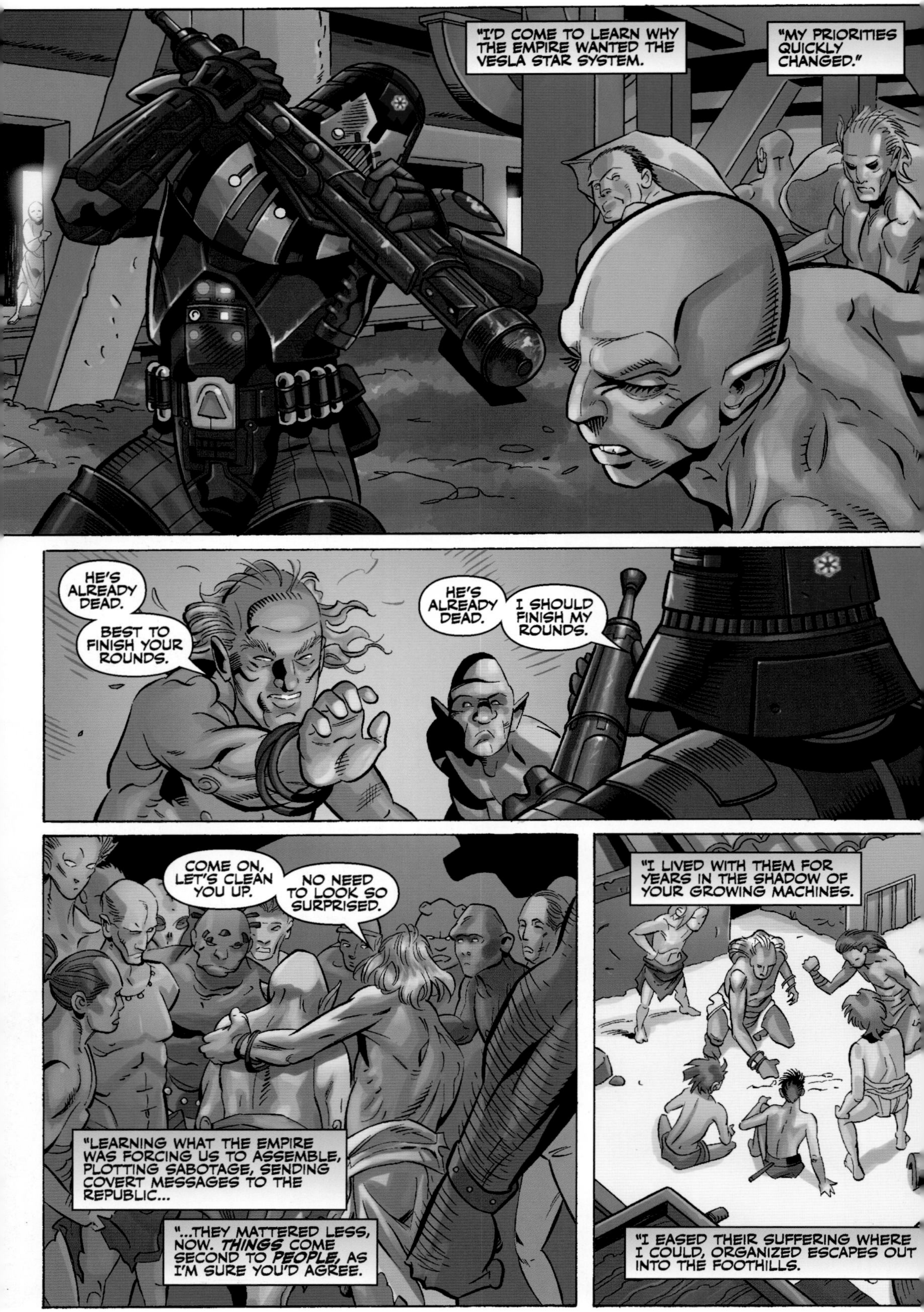
"I'D COME TO LEARN WHY THE EMPIRE WANTED THE VESLA STAR SYSTEM.
"MY PRIORITIES QUICKLY CHANGED."
HE'S ALREADY DEAD.
BEST TO FINISH YOUR ROUNDS.
HE'S ALREADY DEAD.
I SHOULD FINISH MY ROUNDS.
COME ON, LET'S CLEAN YOU UP.
NO NEED TO LOOK SO SURPRISED.
"LEARNING WHAT THE EMPIRE WAS FORCING US TO ASSEMBLE, PLOTTING SABOTAGE, SENDING COVERT MESSAGES TO THE REPUBLIC...
"...THEY MATTERED LESS, NOW. *THINGS* COME SECOND TO *PEOPLE,* AS I'M SURE YOU'D AGREE.
"I LIVED WITH THEM FOR YEARS IN THE SHADOW OF YOUR GROWING MACHINES.
"I EASED THEIR SUFFERING WHERE I COULD, ORGANIZED ESCAPES OUT INTO THE FOOTHILLS.

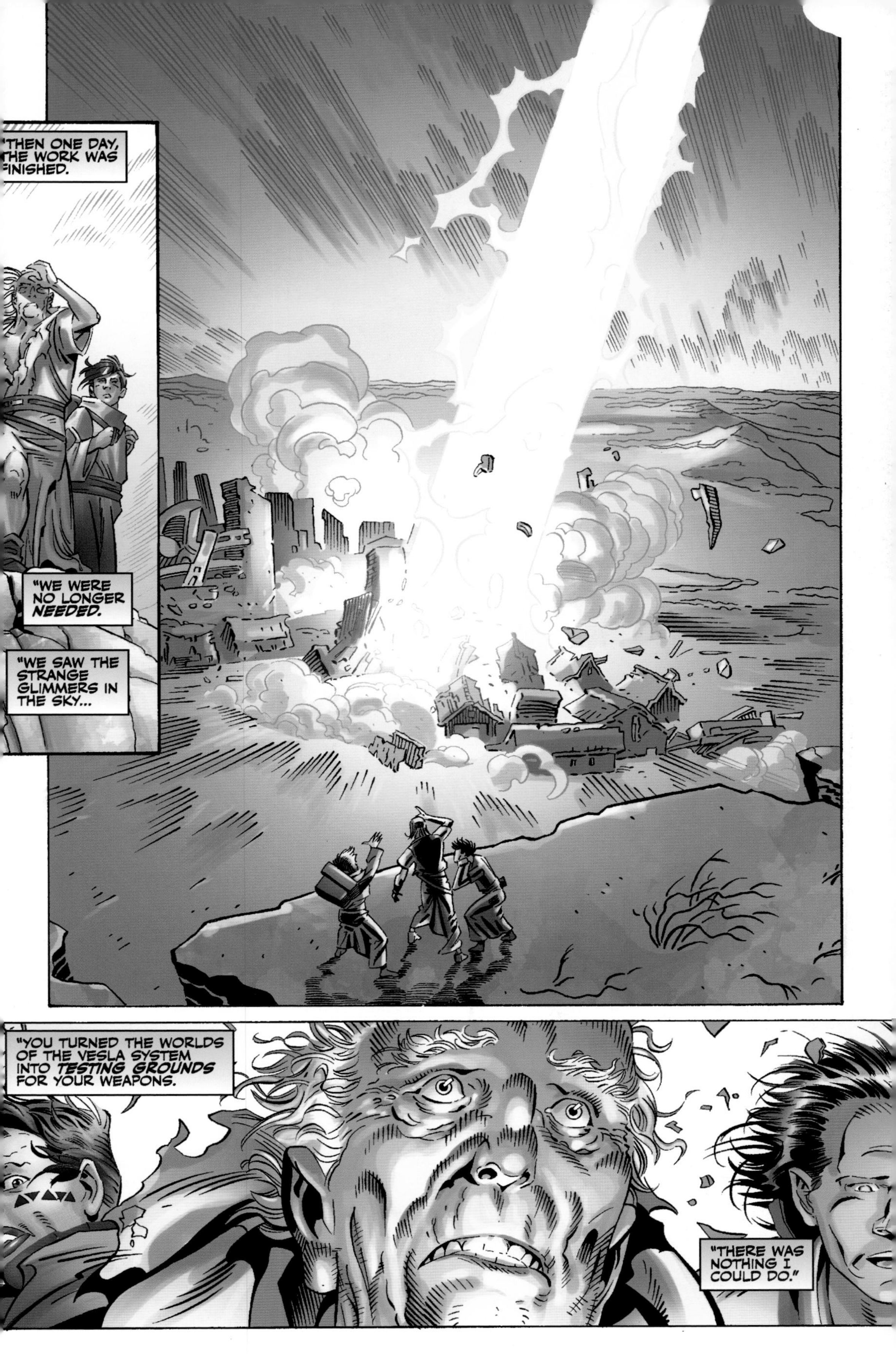
"THEN ONE DAY, THE WORK WAS FINISHED.
"WE WERE NO LONGER *NEEDED*.
"WE SAW THE STRANGE GLIMMERS IN THE SKY...
"YOU TURNED THE WORLDS OF THE VESLA SYSTEM INTO *TESTING GROUNDS* FOR YOUR WEAPONS.
"THERE WAS NOTHING I COULD DO."

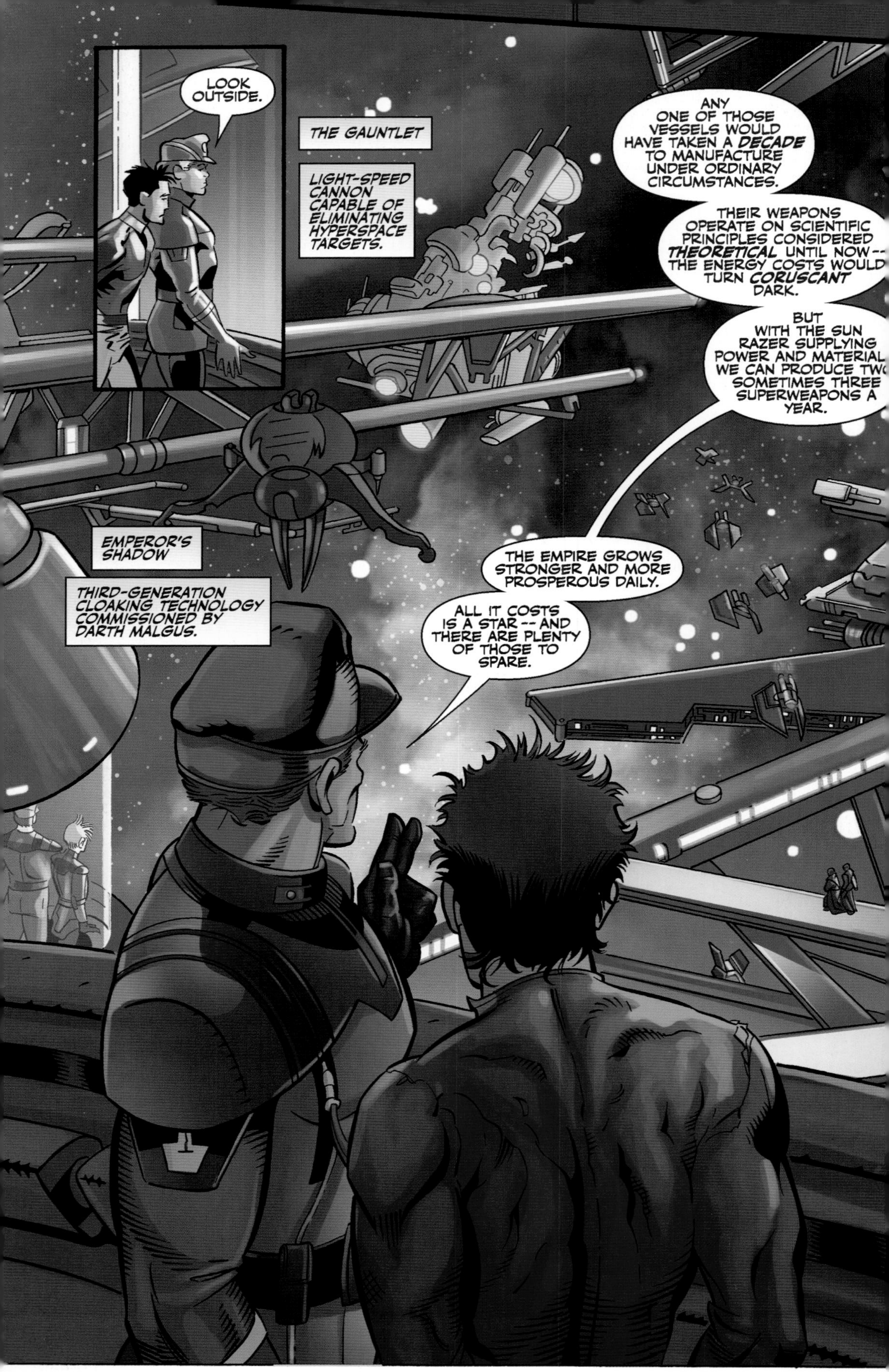
LOOK OUTSIDE.
THE GAUNTLET
LIGHT-SPEED CANNON CAPABLE OF ELIMINATING HYPERSPACE TARGETS.
ANY ONE OF THOSE VESSELS WOULD HAVE TAKEN A *DECADE* TO MANUFACTURE UNDER ORDINARY CIRCUMSTANCES.
THEIR WEAPONS OPERATE ON SCIENTIFIC PRINCIPLES CONSIDERED *THEORETICAL* UNTIL NOW-- THE ENERGY COSTS WOULD TURN *CORUSCANT* DARK.
BUT WITH THE SUN RAZER SUPPLYING POWER AND MATERIAL WE CAN PRODUCE TWO SOMETIMES THREE SUPERWEAPONS A YEAR.
EMPEROR'S SHADOW
THIRD-GENERATION CLOAKING TECHNOLOGY COMMISSIONED BY DARTH MALGUS.
THE EMPIRE GROWS STRONGER AND MORE PROSPEROUS DAILY.
ALL IT COSTS IS A STAR--AND THERE ARE PLENTY OF THOSE TO SPARE.

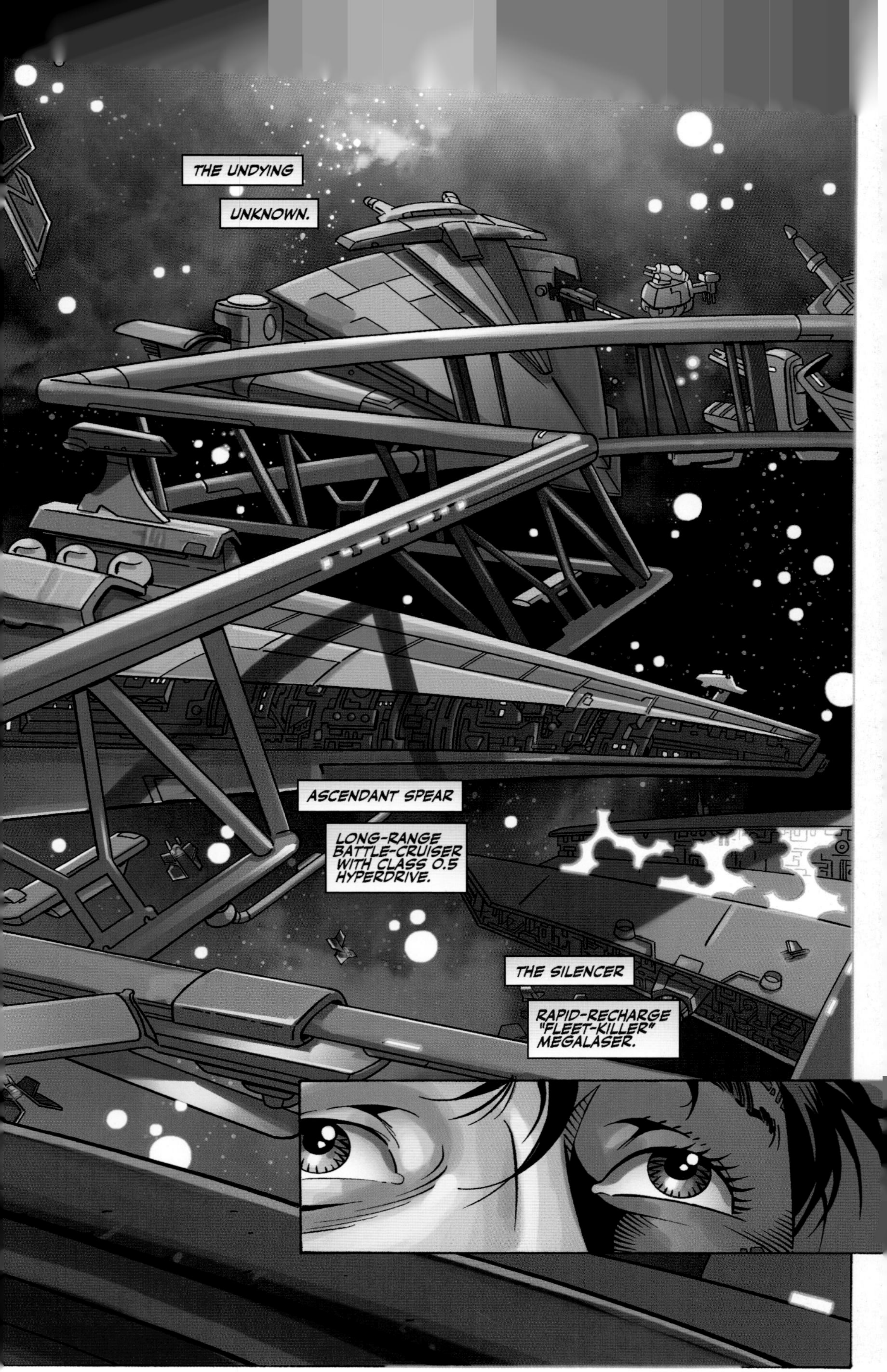
THE UNDYING
UNKNOWN.
ASCENDANT SPEAR
LONG-RANGE BATTLE-CRUISER WITH CLASS 0.5 HYPERDRIVE.
THE SILENCER
RAPID-RECHARGE "FLEET-KILLER" MEGALASER.

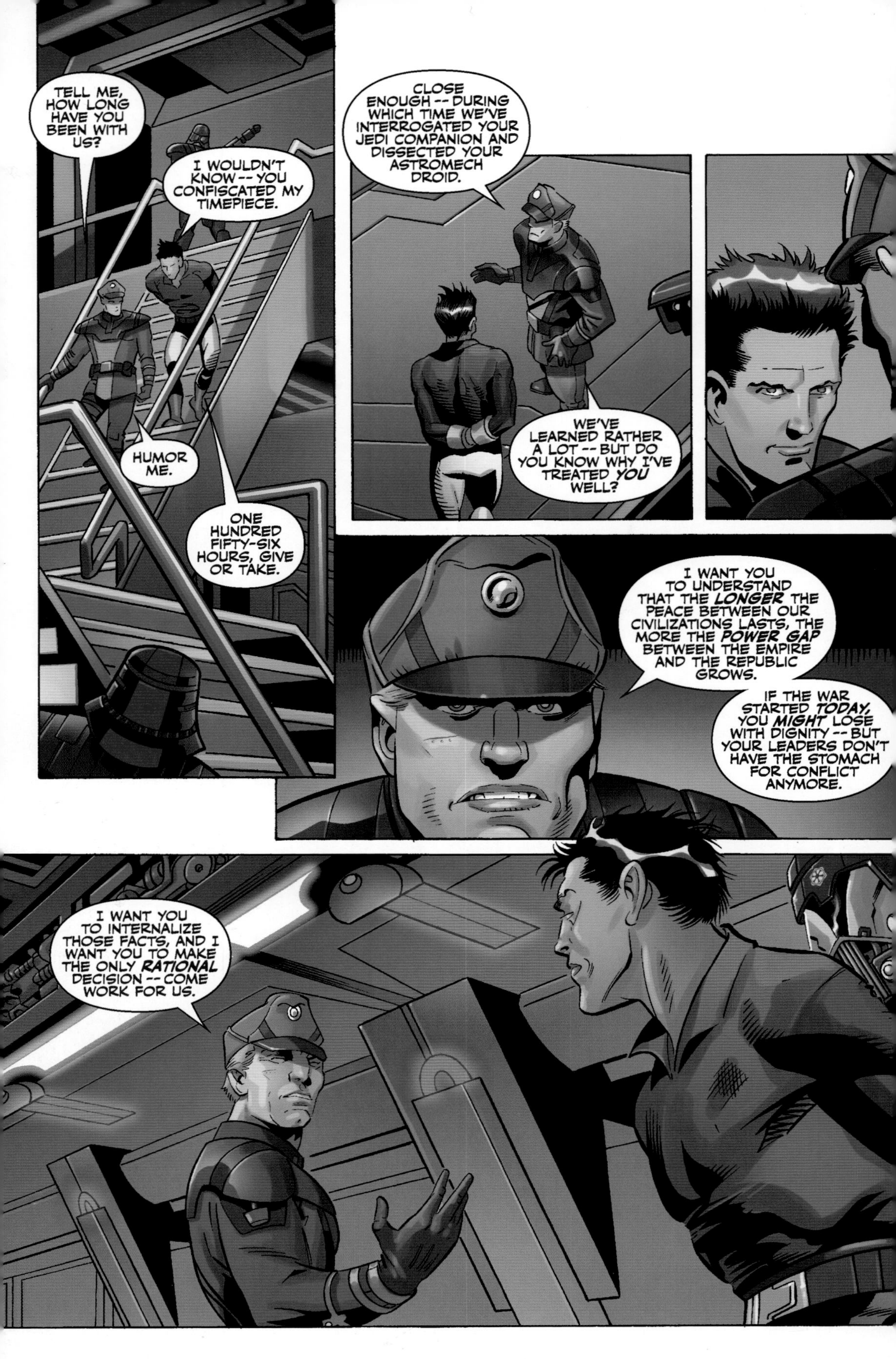
TELL ME, HOW LONG HAVE YOU BEEN WITH US?
I WOULDN'T KNOW -- YOU CONFISCATED MY TIMEPIECE.
HUMOR ME.
ONE HUNDRED FIFTY-SIX HOURS, GIVE OR TAKE.
CLOSE ENOUGH -- DURING WHICH TIME WE'VE INTERROGATED YOUR JEDI COMPANION AND DISSECTED YOUR ASTROMECH DROID.
WE'VE LEARNED RATHER A LOT -- BUT DO YOU KNOW WHY I'VE TREATED YOU WELL?
I WANT YOU TO UNDERSTAND THAT THE LONGER THE PEACE BETWEEN OUR CIVILIZATIONS LASTS, THE MORE THE POWER GAP BETWEEN THE EMPIRE AND THE REPUBLIC GROWS.
IF THE WAR STARTED TODAY, YOU MIGHT LOSE WITH DIGNITY -- BUT YOUR LEADERS DON'T HAVE THE STOMACH FOR CONFLICT ANYMORE.
I WANT YOU TO INTERNALIZE THOSE FACTS, AND I WANT YOU TO MAKE THE ONLY RATIONAL DECISION -- COME WORK FOR US.

WHAT PLACE IS THERE FOR ME IN THE EMPIRE?

WE KNOW YOU'RE A STRATEGIC INFORMATION SERVICE OPERATIVE -- THAT ALONE MAKES YOU VALUABLE.

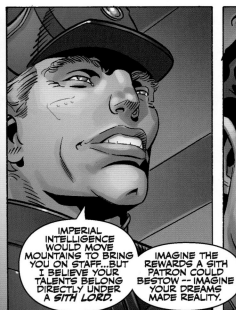

IMPERIAL INTELLIGENCE WOULD MOVE MOUNTAINS TO BRING YOU ON STAFF...BUT I BELIEVE YOUR TALENTS BELONG DIRECTLY UNDER A *SITH LORD.*

THERE IS ONE DREAM I'D LIKE FULFILLED.

CAN I HAVE A SLAVE BRAND LIKE YOURS?

IMAGINE THE REWARDS A SITH PATRON COULD BESTOW -- IMAGINE YOUR DREAMS MADE REALITY.

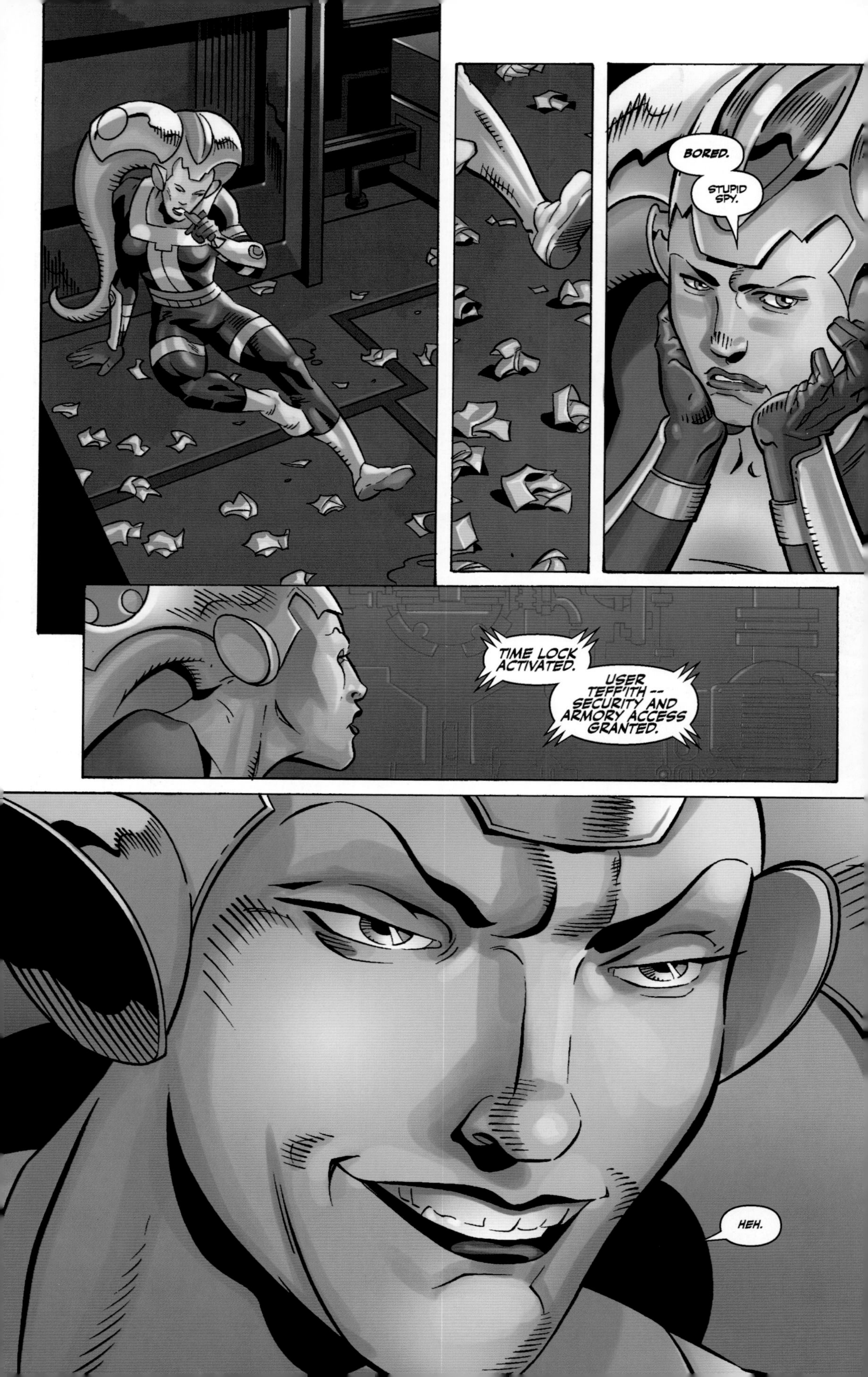
BORED.
STUPID SPY.
TIME LOCK ACTIVATED.
USER TEFF'ITH -- SECURITY AND ARMORY ACCESS GRANTED.
HEH.

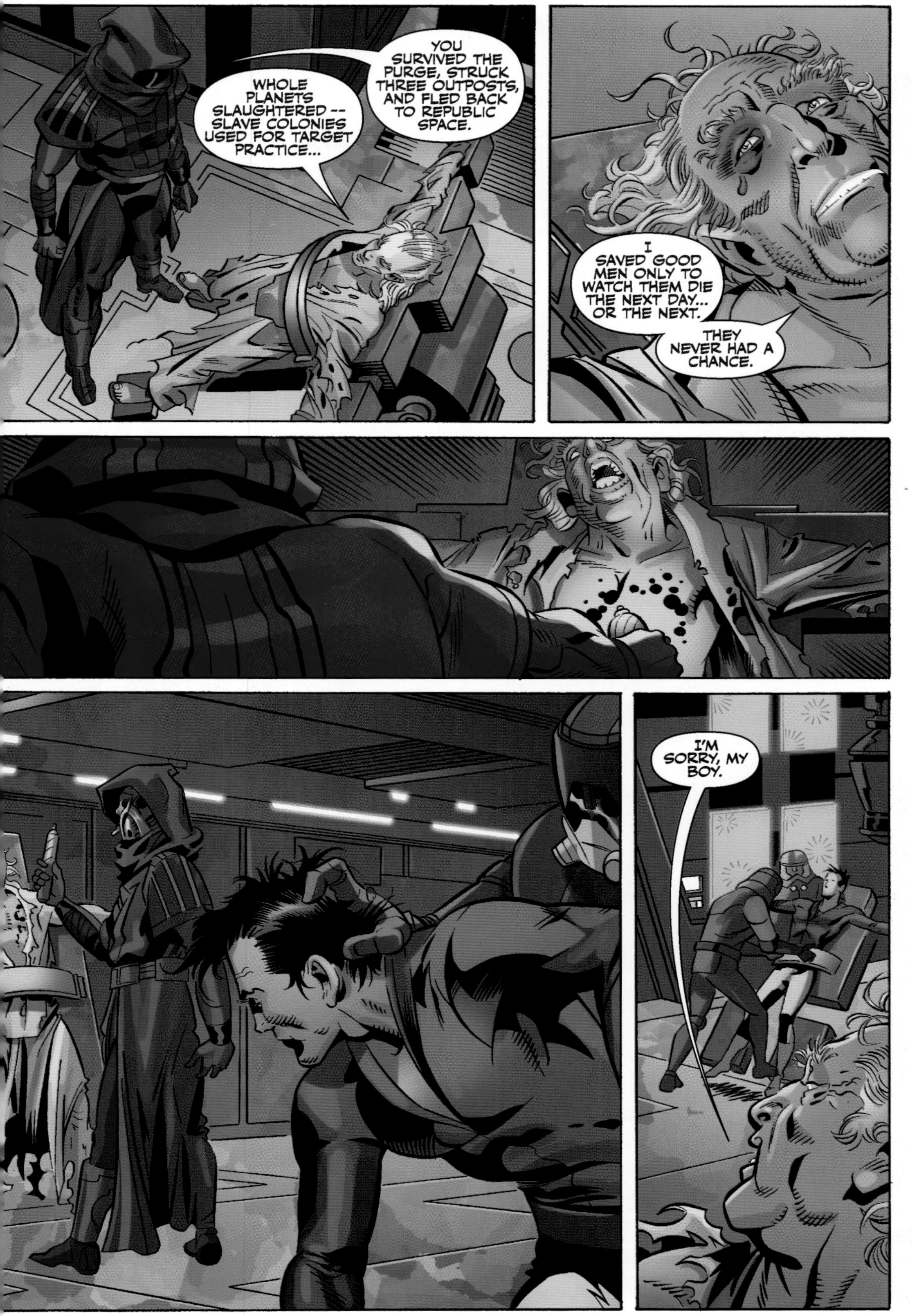
WHOLE PLANETS SLAUGHTERED -- SLAVE COLONIES USED FOR TARGET PRACTICE...
YOU SURVIVED THE PURGE, STRUCK THREE OUTPOSTS, AND FLED BACK TO REPUBLIC SPACE.
I SAVED GOOD MEN ONLY TO WATCH THEM DIE THE NEXT DAY... OR THE NEXT.
THEY NEVER HAD A CHANCE.
I'M SORRY, MY BOY.

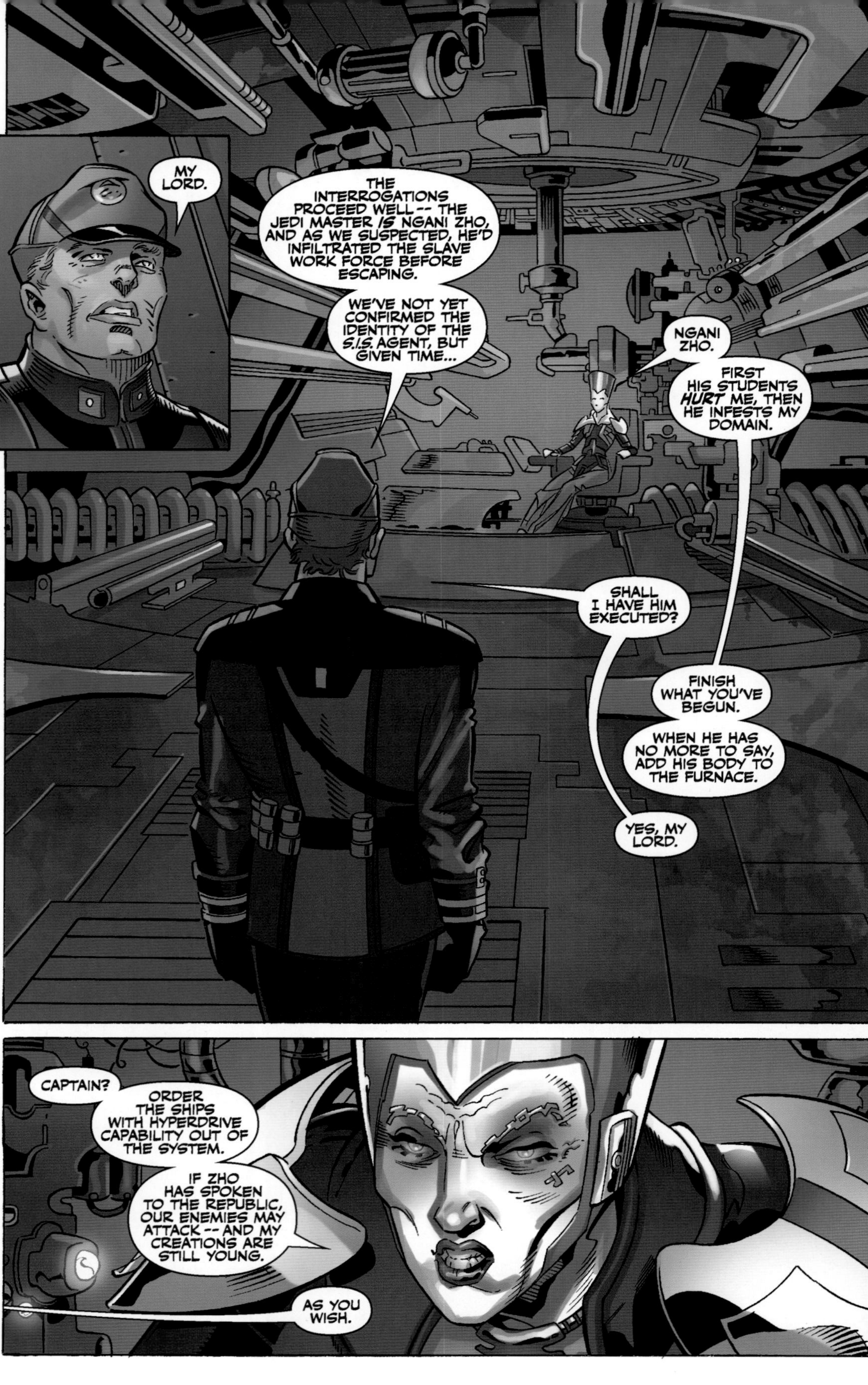
MY LORD.
THE INTERROGATIONS PROCEED WELL -- THE JEDI MASTER *IS* NGANI ZHO, AND AS WE SUSPECTED, HE'D INFILTRATED THE SLAVE WORK FORCE BEFORE ESCAPING.
WE'VE NOT YET CONFIRMED THE IDENTITY OF THE S.I.S. AGENT, BUT GIVEN TIME...
NGANI ZHO.
FIRST HIS STUDENTS *HURT* ME, THEN HE INFESTS MY DOMAIN.
SHALL I HAVE HIM EXECUTED?
FINISH WHAT YOU'VE BEGUN.
WHEN HE HAS NO MORE TO SAY, ADD HIS BODY TO THE FURNACE.
YES, MY LORD.
CAPTAIN?
ORDER THE SHIPS WITH HYPERDRIVE CAPABILITY OUT OF THE SYSTEM.
IF ZHO HAS SPOKEN TO THE REPUBLIC, OUR ENEMIES MAY ATTACK -- AND MY CREATIONS ARE STILL YOUNG.
AS YOU WISH.

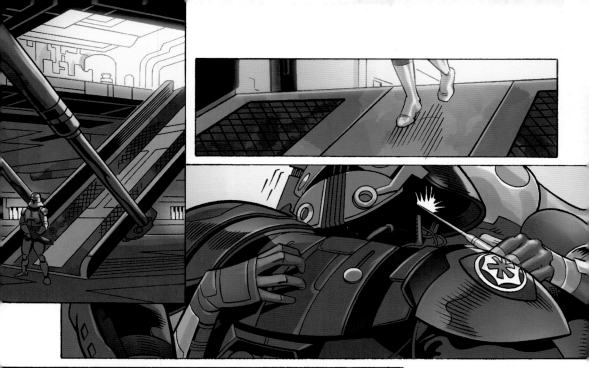

HUH.

STUPID HEAVY SOLDIER.

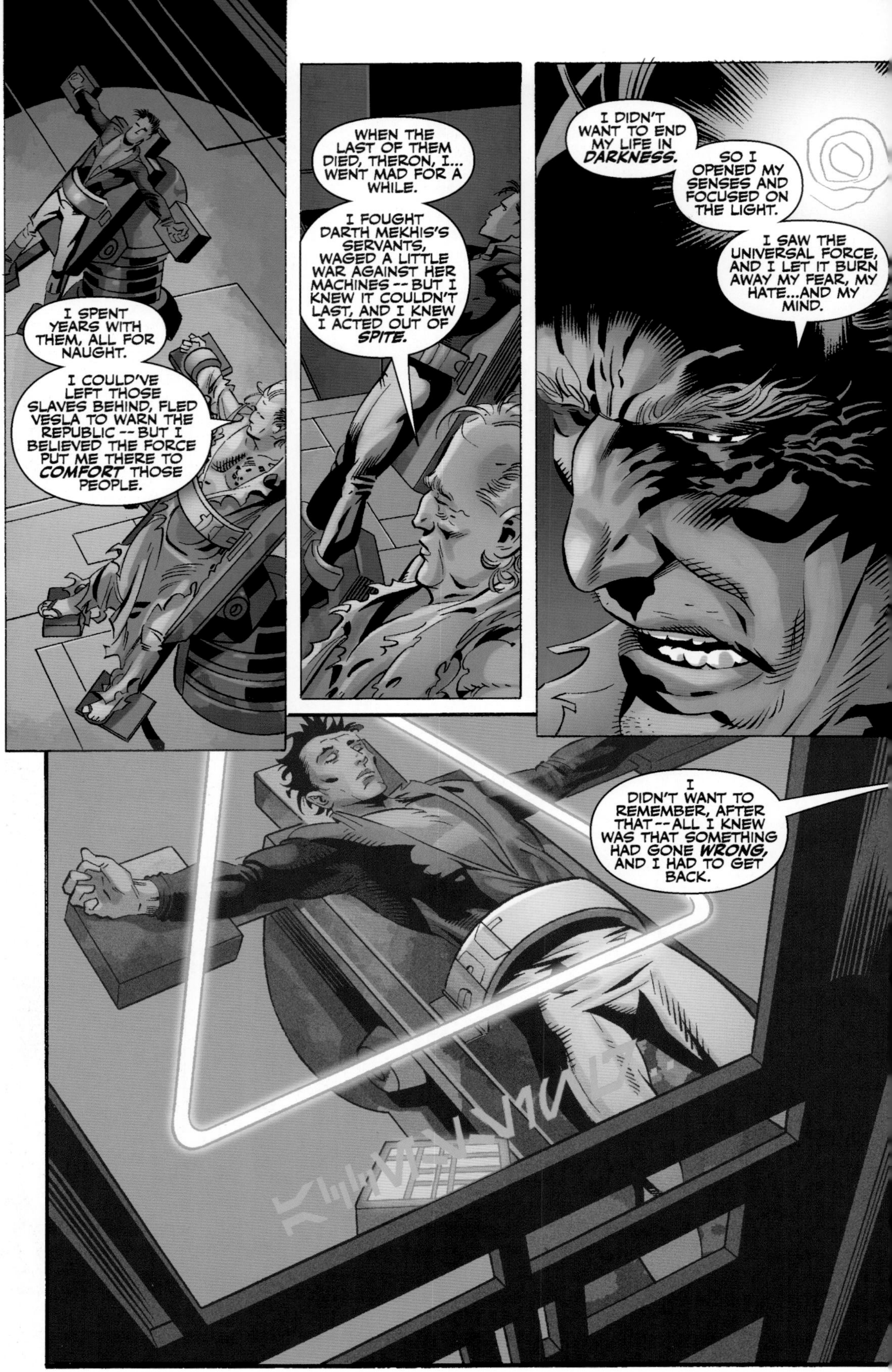
I SPENT YEARS WITH THEM, ALL FOR NAUGHT.
I COULD'VE LEFT THOSE SLAVES BEHIND, FLED VESLA TO WARN THE REPUBLIC -- BUT I BELIEVED THE FORCE PUT ME THERE TO COMFORT THOSE PEOPLE.
WHEN THE LAST OF THEM DIED, THERON, I... WENT MAD FOR A WHILE.
I FOUGHT DARTH MEKHIS'S SERVANTS, WAGED A LITTLE WAR AGAINST HER MACHINES -- BUT I KNEW IT COULDN'T LAST, AND I KNEW I ACTED OUT OF SPITE.
I DIDN'T WANT TO END MY LIFE IN DARKNESS.
SO I OPENED MY SENSES AND FOCUSED ON THE LIGHT.
I SAW THE UNIVERSAL FORCE, AND I LET IT BURN AWAY MY FEAR, MY HATE...AND MY MIND.
I DIDN'T WANT TO REMEMBER, AFTER THAT -- ALL I KNEW WAS THAT SOMETHING HAD GONE WRONG, AND I HAD TO GET BACK.

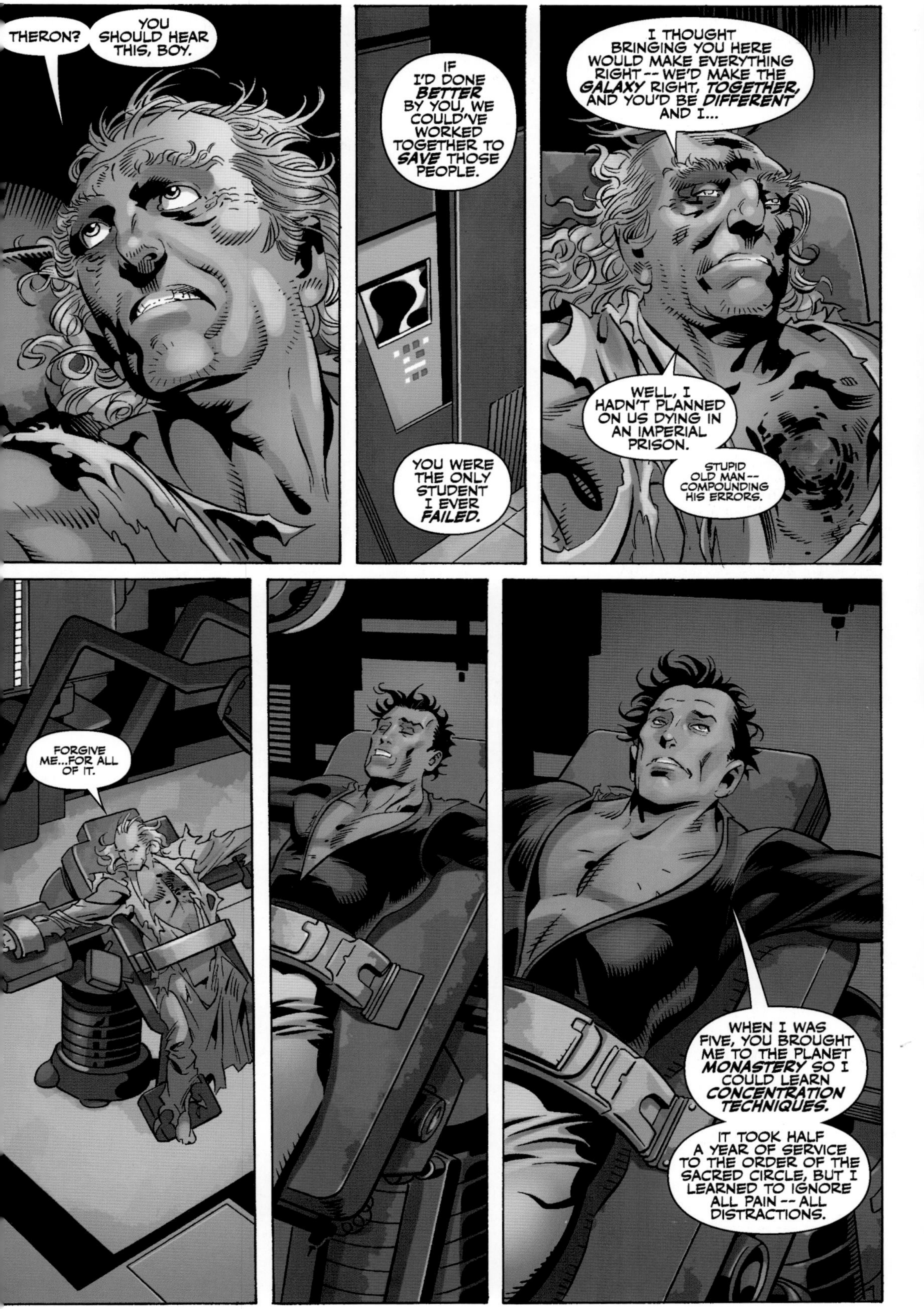
THERON?
YOU SHOULD HEAR THIS, BOY.
IF I'D DONE *BETTER* BY YOU, WE COULD'VE WORKED TOGETHER TO *SAVE* THOSE PEOPLE.
YOU WERE THE ONLY STUDENT I EVER *FAILED.*
I THOUGHT BRINGING YOU HERE WOULD MAKE EVERYTHING RIGHT -- WE'D MAKE THE *GALAXY* RIGHT, *TOGETHER,* AND YOU'D BE *DIFFERENT* AND I...
WELL, I HADN'T PLANNED ON US DYING IN AN IMPERIAL PRISON.
STUPID OLD MAN -- COMPOUNDING HIS ERRORS.
FORGIVE ME...FOR ALL OF IT.
WHEN I WAS FIVE, YOU BROUGHT ME TO THE PLANET *MONASTERY* SO I COULD LEARN *CONCENTRATION TECHNIQUES.*
IT TOOK HALF A YEAR OF SERVICE TO THE ORDER OF THE SACRED CIRCLE, BUT I LEARNED TO IGNORE ALL PAIN -- ALL DISTRACTIONS.

NEVER THOUGHT I'D NEED IT TO TUNE OUT YOUR SENTIMENTAL GIBBERISH.

I DON'T--

I'VE SPENT THE LAST TWELVE HOURS REBOOTING MY CYBERNETICS AND GAINING ACCESS TO PRISON SECURITY.

YOUR RESTRAINTS ARE NOW UNLOCKED.

HA!

ALWAYS WITH A PLAN, AREN'T YOU?

SOMEONE HAS TO BE.

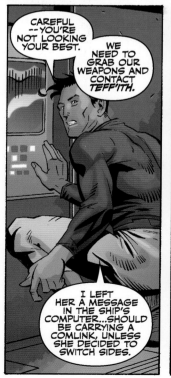

CAREFUL --YOU'RE NOT LOOKING YOUR BEST.

WE NEED TO GRAB OUR WEAPONS AND CONTACT *TEFF'ITH*.

I LEFT HER A MESSAGE IN THE SHIP'S COMPUTER...SHOULD BE CARRYING A COMLINK, UNLESS SHE DECIDED TO SWITCH SIDES.

SHE'S A CHILD, THERON.

EXPECT MORE FROM HER, AND SHE CAN SURPRISE YOU.

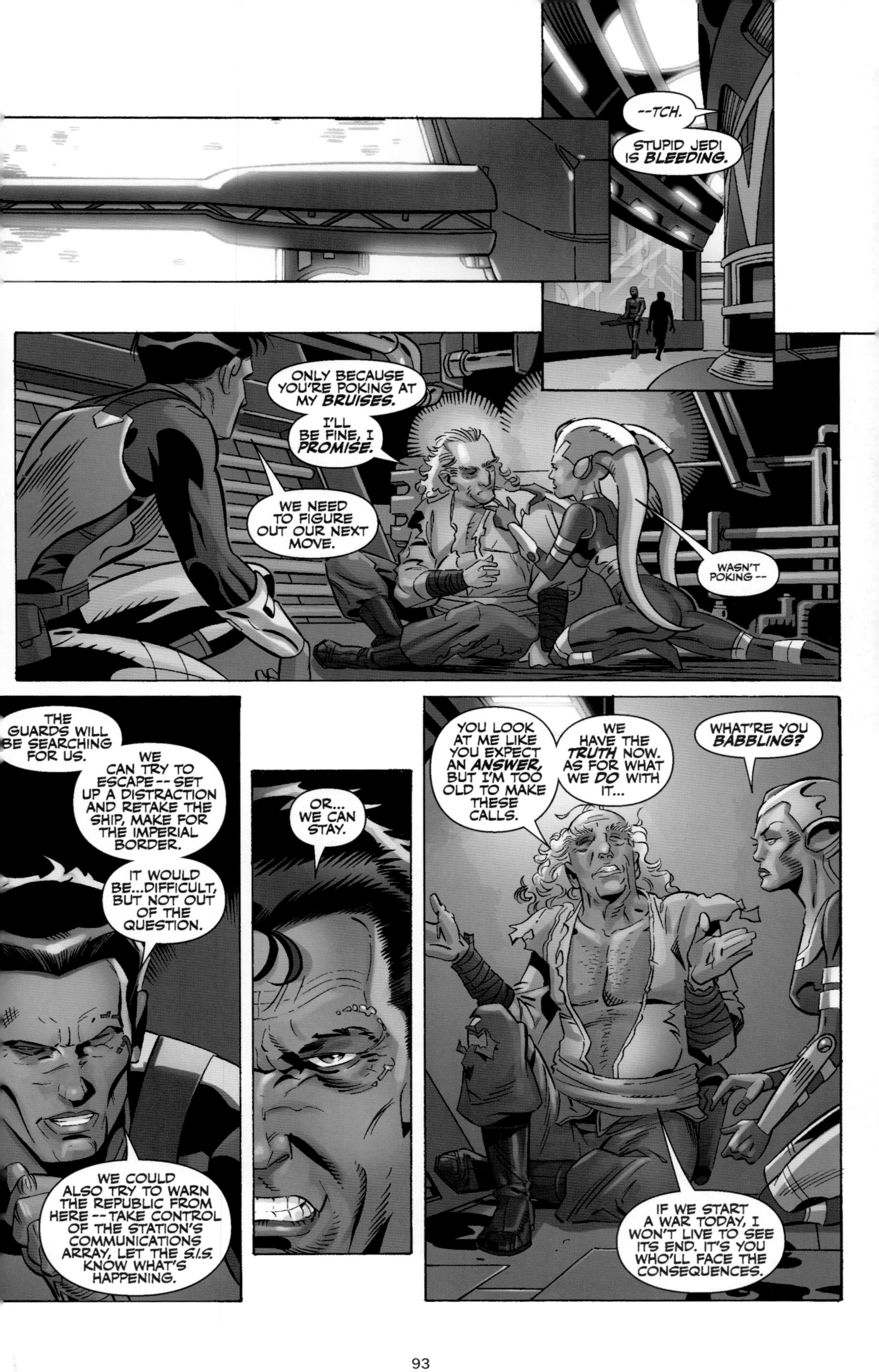
--TCH.
STUPID JEDI IS BLEEDING.
ONLY BECAUSE YOU'RE POKING AT MY BRUISES.
I'LL BE FINE, I PROMISE.
WASN'T POKING --
WE NEED TO FIGURE OUT OUR NEXT MOVE.
THE GUARDS WILL BE SEARCHING FOR US.
WE CAN TRY TO ESCAPE -- SET UP A DISTRACTION AND RETAKE THE SHIP, MAKE FOR THE IMPERIAL BORDER.
IT WOULD BE...DIFFICULT, BUT NOT OUT OF THE QUESTION.
WE COULD ALSO TRY TO WARN THE REPUBLIC FROM HERE -- TAKE CONTROL OF THE STATION'S COMMUNICATIONS ARRAY, LET THE S.I.S. KNOW WHAT'S HAPPENING.
OR... WE CAN STAY.
WHAT'RE YOU BABBLING?
WE HAVE THE TRUTH NOW. AS FOR WHAT WE DO WITH IT...
YOU LOOK AT ME LIKE YOU EXPECT AN ANSWER, BUT I'M TOO OLD TO MAKE THESE CALLS.
IF WE START A WAR TODAY, I WON'T LIVE TO SEE ITS END. IT'S YOU WHO'LL FACE THE CONSEQUENCES.

FAIR ENOUGH. TEFF'ITH?

JUST WANT *OUT.*

DON'T CARE WHAT *ELSE.*

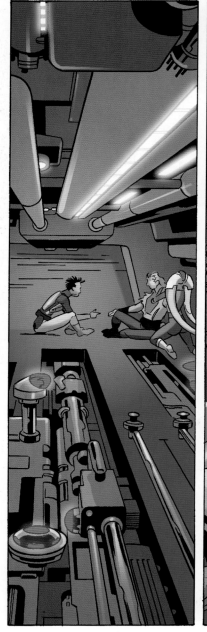

IF WE DON'T TAKE THIS CHANCE, THE EMPIRE WON'T GIVE US ANOTHER.

EVERY DAY THAT PASSES, THEY'LL BUILD MORE WEAPONS AND HARDEN VESLA'S DEFENSES.

SO HERE'S MY SOLUTION.

LET'S DESTROY THE SUN RAZER.

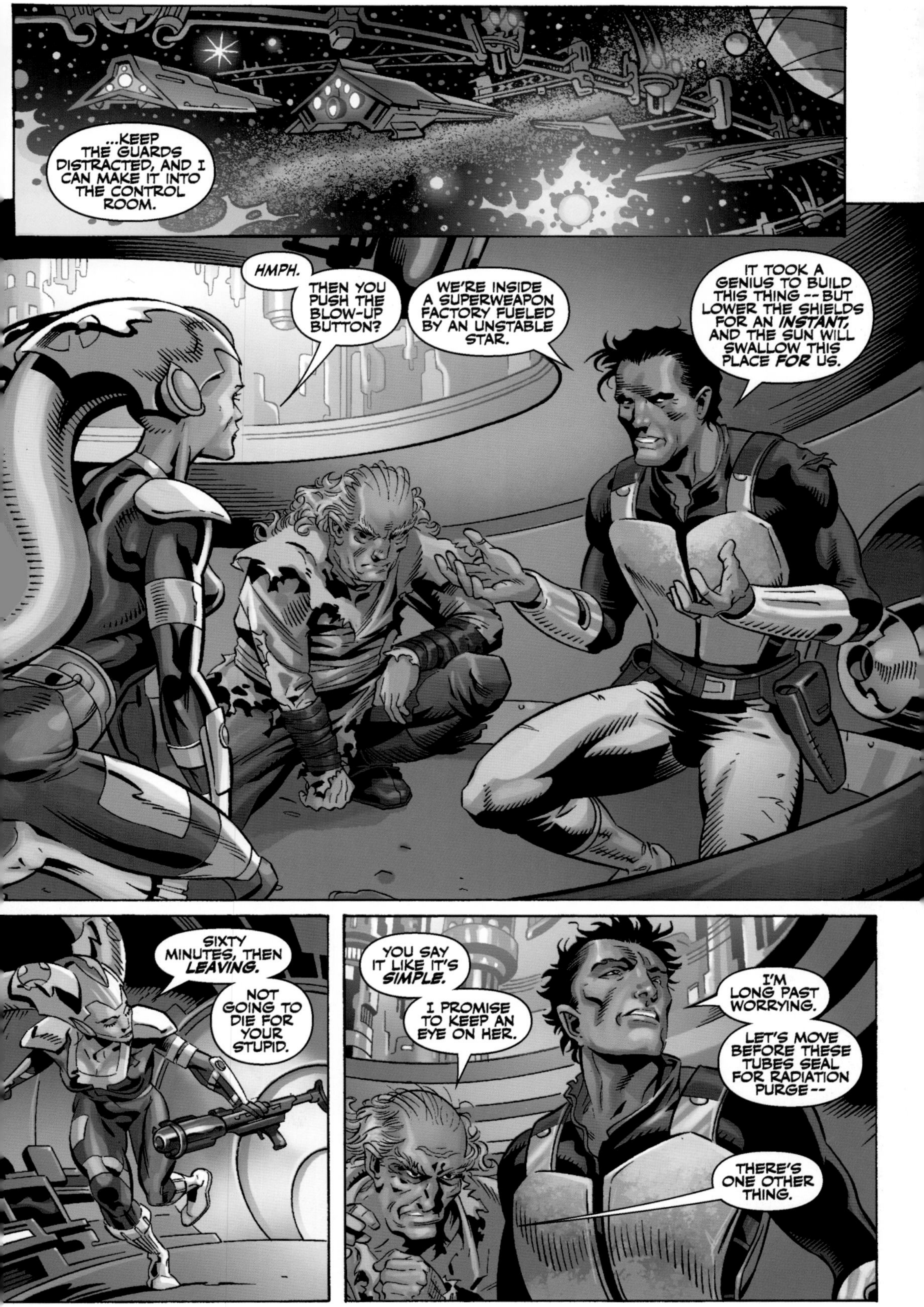
...KEEP THE GUARDS DISTRACTED, AND I CAN MAKE IT INTO THE CONTROL ROOM.
HMPH.
THEN YOU PUSH THE BLOW-UP BUTTON?
WE'RE INSIDE A SUPERWEAPON FACTORY FUELED BY AN UNSTABLE STAR.
IT TOOK A GENIUS TO BUILD THIS THING -- BUT LOWER THE SHIELDS FOR AN INSTANT, AND THE SUN WILL SWALLOW THIS PLACE FOR US.
SIXTY MINUTES, THEN LEAVING.
NOT GOING TO DIE FOR YOUR STUPID.
YOU SAY IT LIKE IT'S SIMPLE.
I PROMISE TO KEEP AN EYE ON HER.
I'M LONG PAST WORRYING.
LET'S MOVE BEFORE THESE TUBES SEAL FOR RADIATION PURGE --
THERE'S ONE OTHER THING.

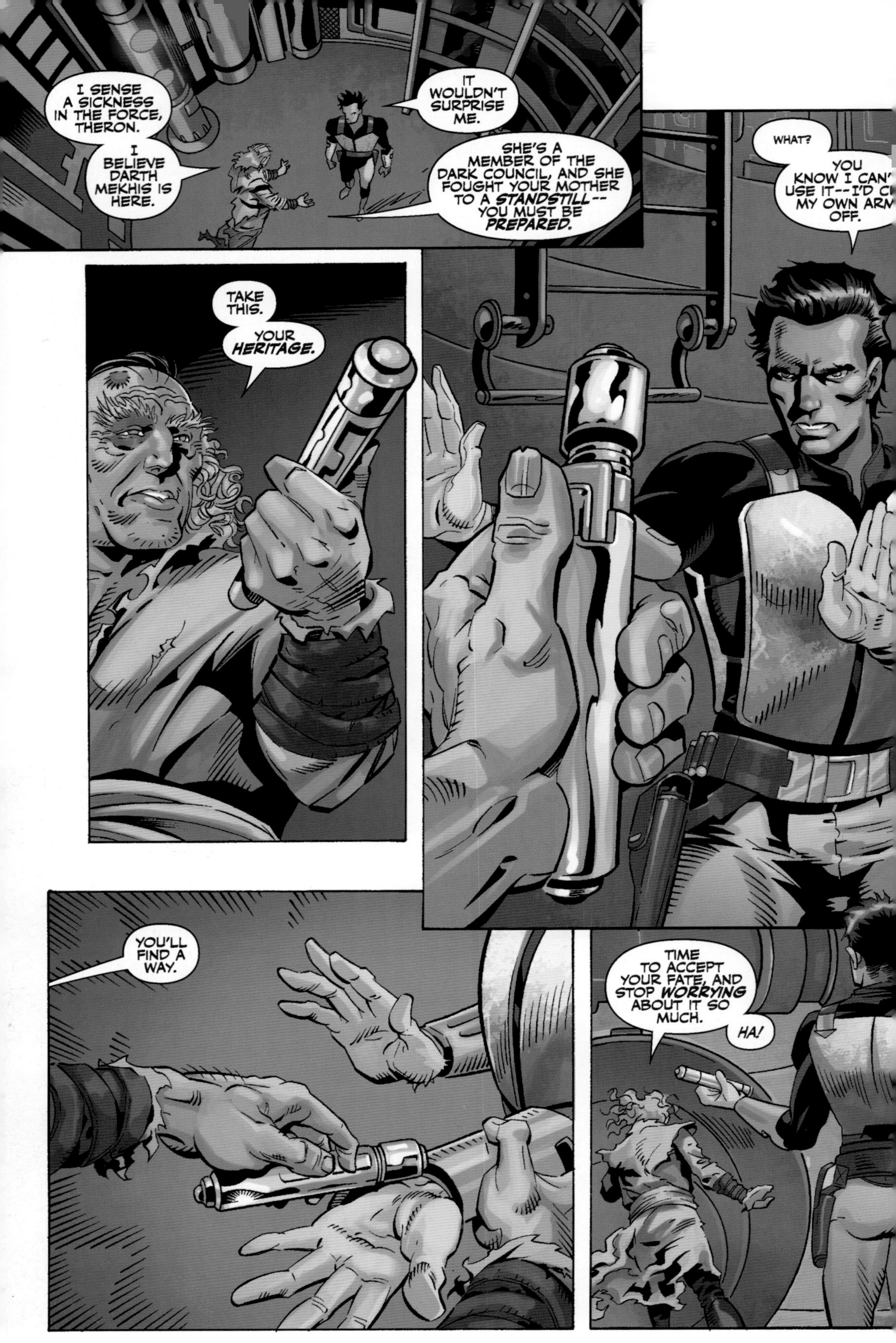
I SENSE A SICKNESS IN THE FORCE, THERON.
I BELIEVE DARTH MEKHIS IS HERE.
IT WOULDN'T SURPRISE ME.
SHE'S A MEMBER OF THE DARK COUNCIL, AND SHE FOUGHT YOUR MOTHER TO A STANDSTILL-- YOU MUST BE PREPARED.
TAKE THIS.
YOUR HERITAGE.
WHAT?
YOU KNOW I CAN' USE IT--I'D C MY OWN ARM OFF.
YOU'LL FIND A WAY.
TIME TO ACCEPT YOUR FATE, AND STOP WORRYING ABOUT IT SO MUCH.
HA!

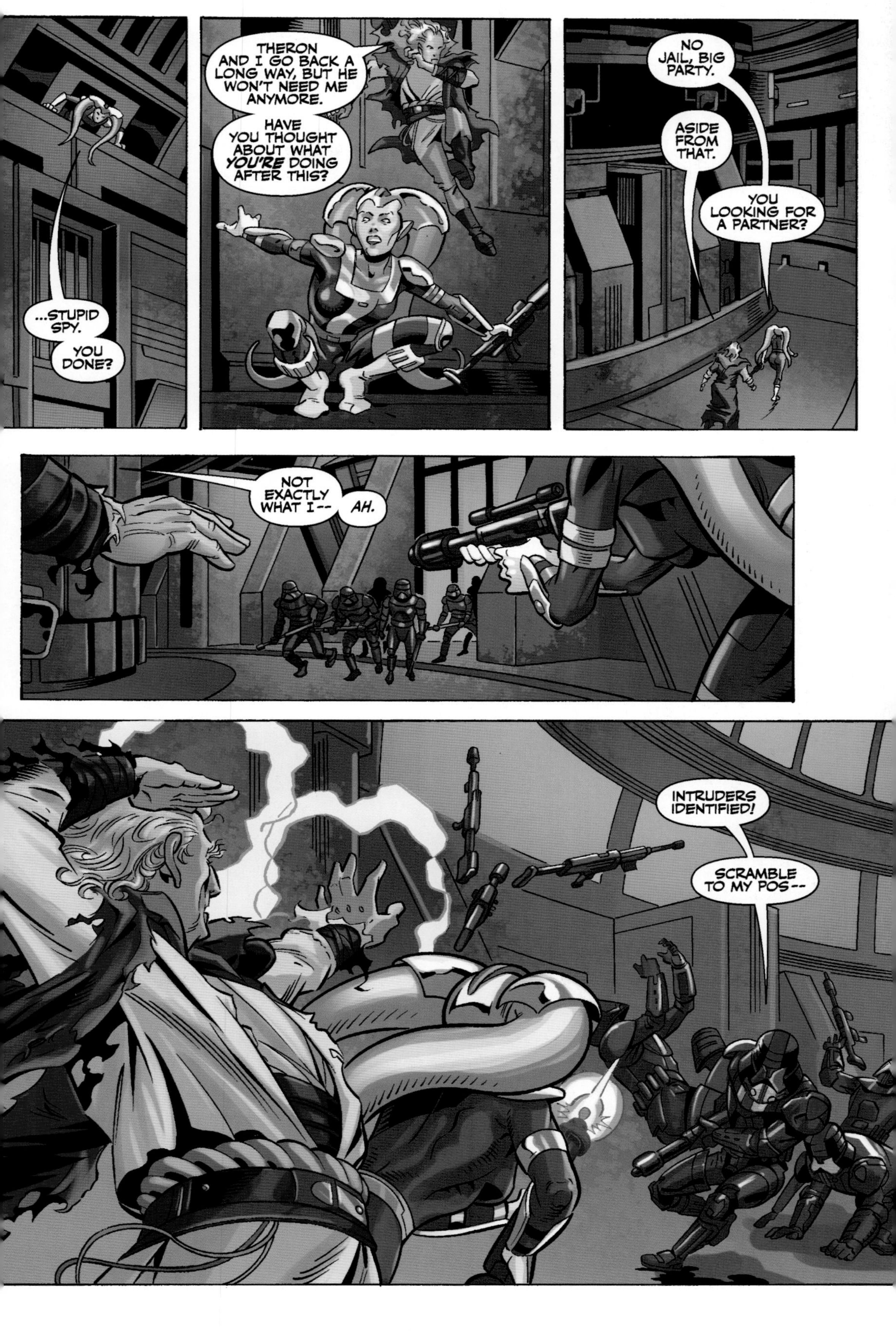
...STUPID SPY.
YOU DONE?
THERON AND I GO BACK A LONG WAY, BUT HE WON'T NEED ME ANYMORE.
HAVE YOU THOUGHT ABOUT WHAT *YOU'RE* DOING AFTER THIS?
NO JAIL, BIG PARTY.
ASIDE FROM THAT.
YOU LOOKING FOR A PARTNER?
NOT EXACTLY WHAT I--
AH.
INTRUDERS IDENTIFIED!
SCRAMBLE TO MY POS--

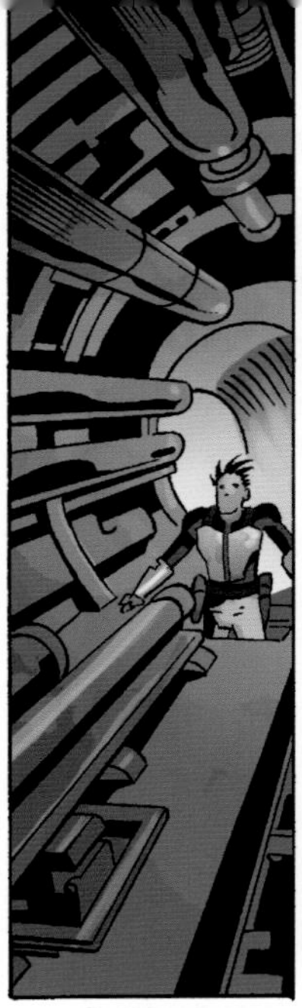
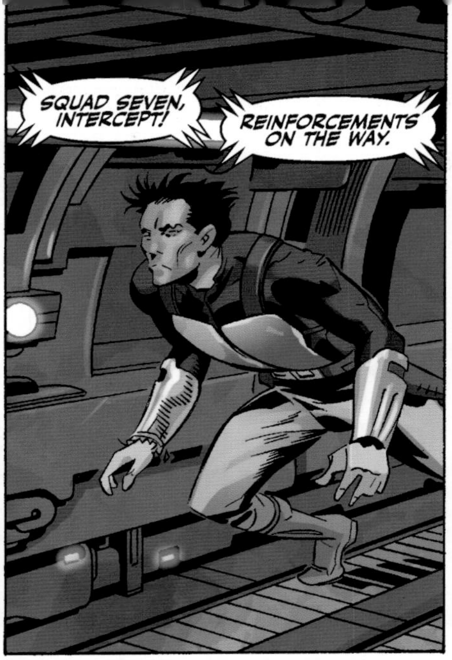
SQUAD SEVEN, INTERCEPT!
REINFORCEMENTS ON THE WAY.
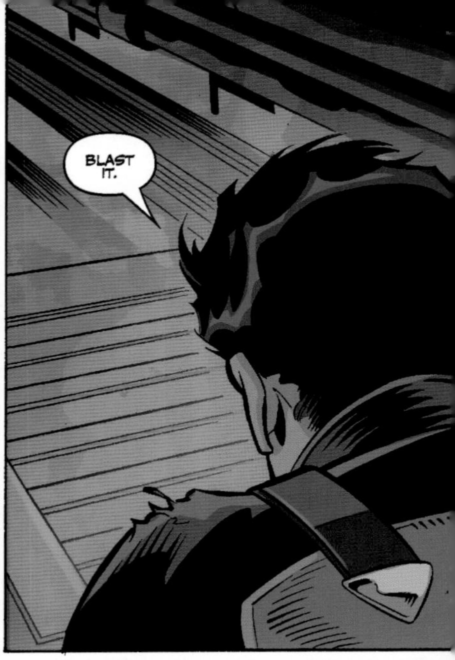
BLAST IT.
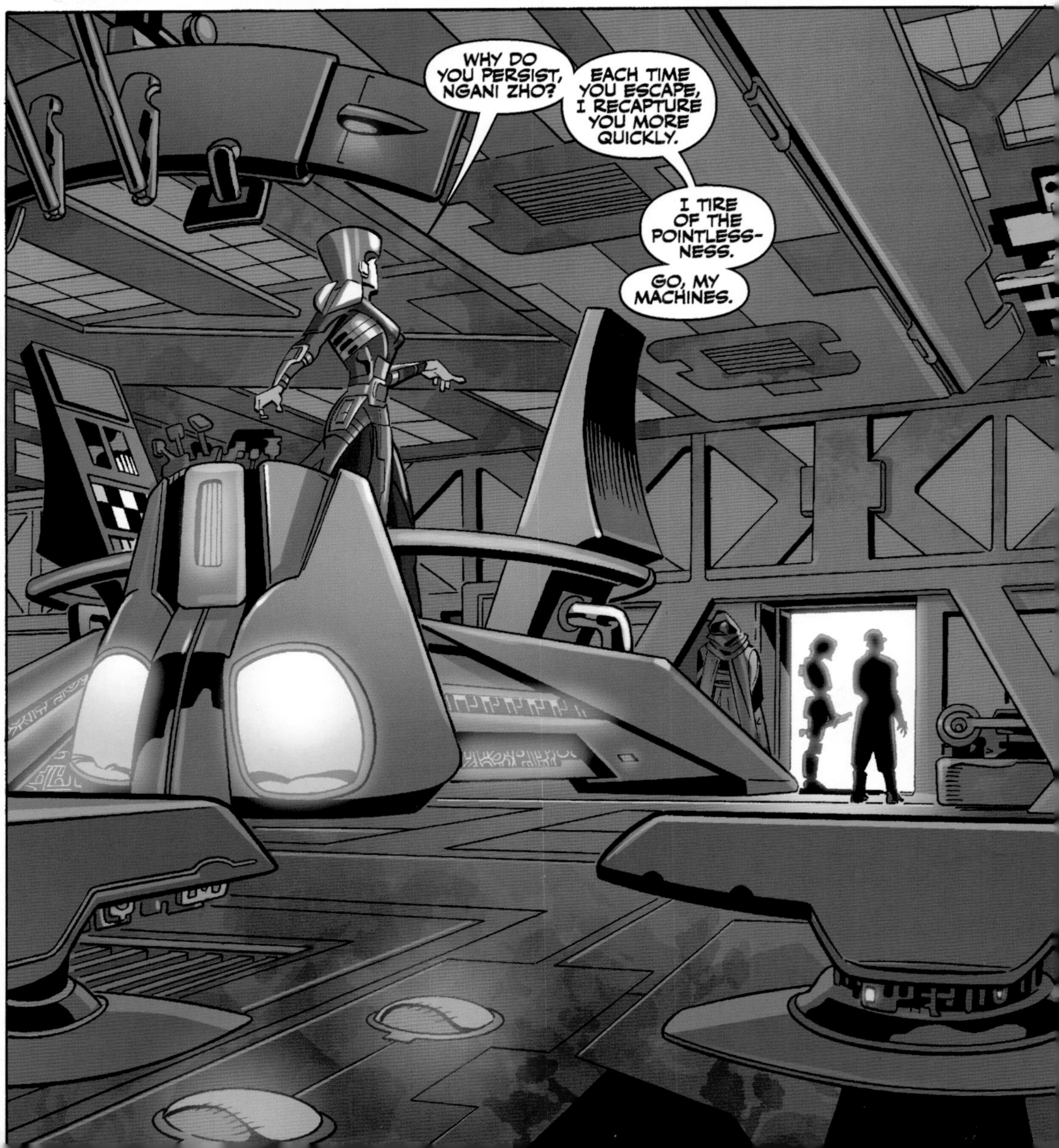
WHY DO YOU PERSIST, NGANI ZHO?
EACH TIME YOU ESCAPE, I RECAPTURE YOU MORE QUICKLY.
I TIRE OF THE POINTLESS-NESS.
GO, MY MACHINES.

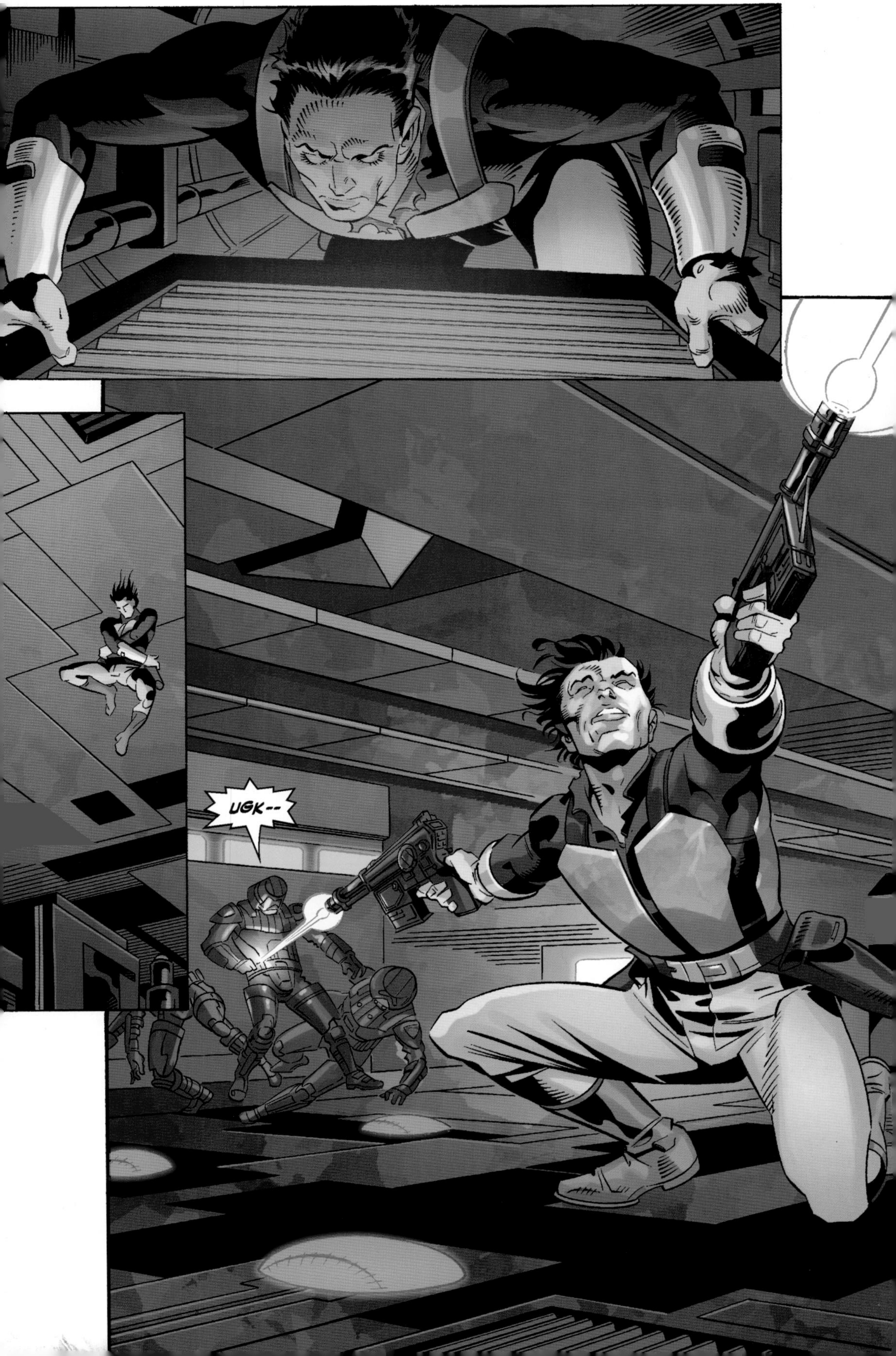
UGK--

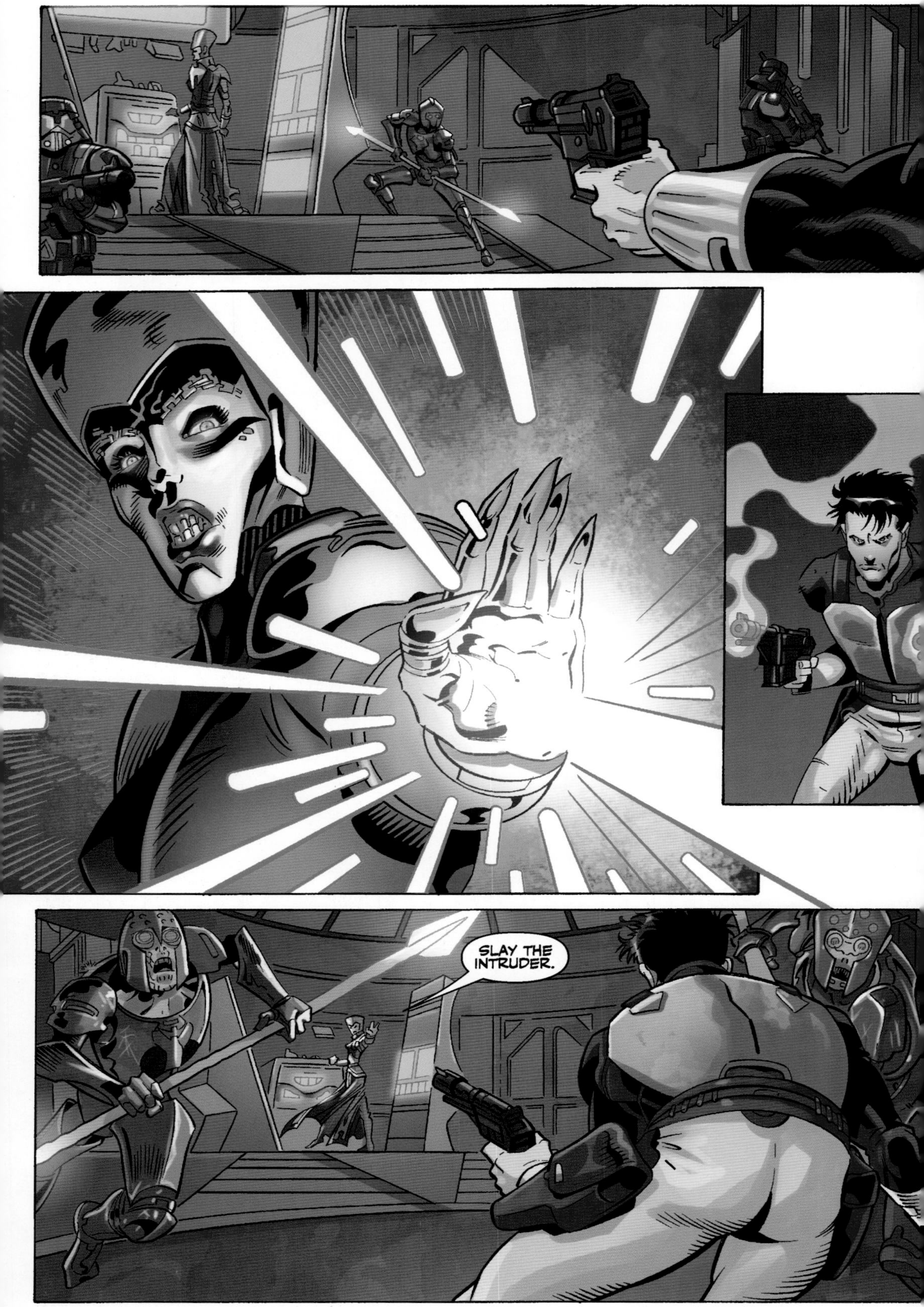
SLAY THE INTRUDER.

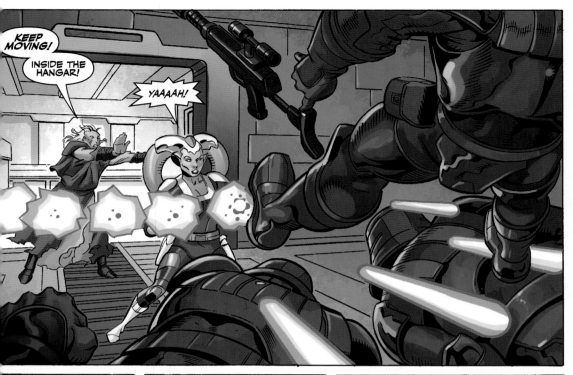

KEEP MOVING!

INSIDE THE HANGAR!

YAAAAH!

CLOSE, CURSE YOU!

CLOSE!

HA!

KRROMM

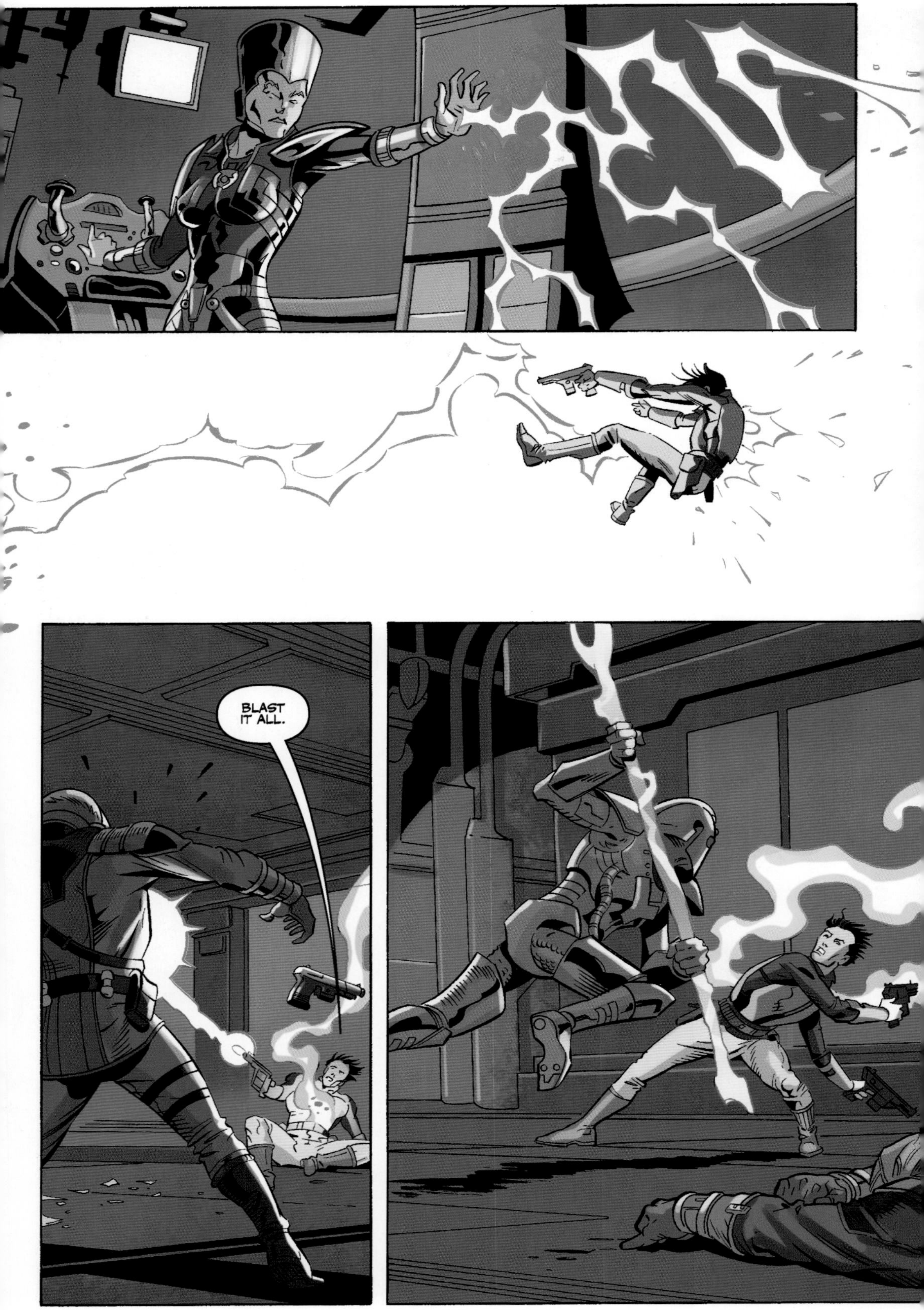
BLAST IT ALL.

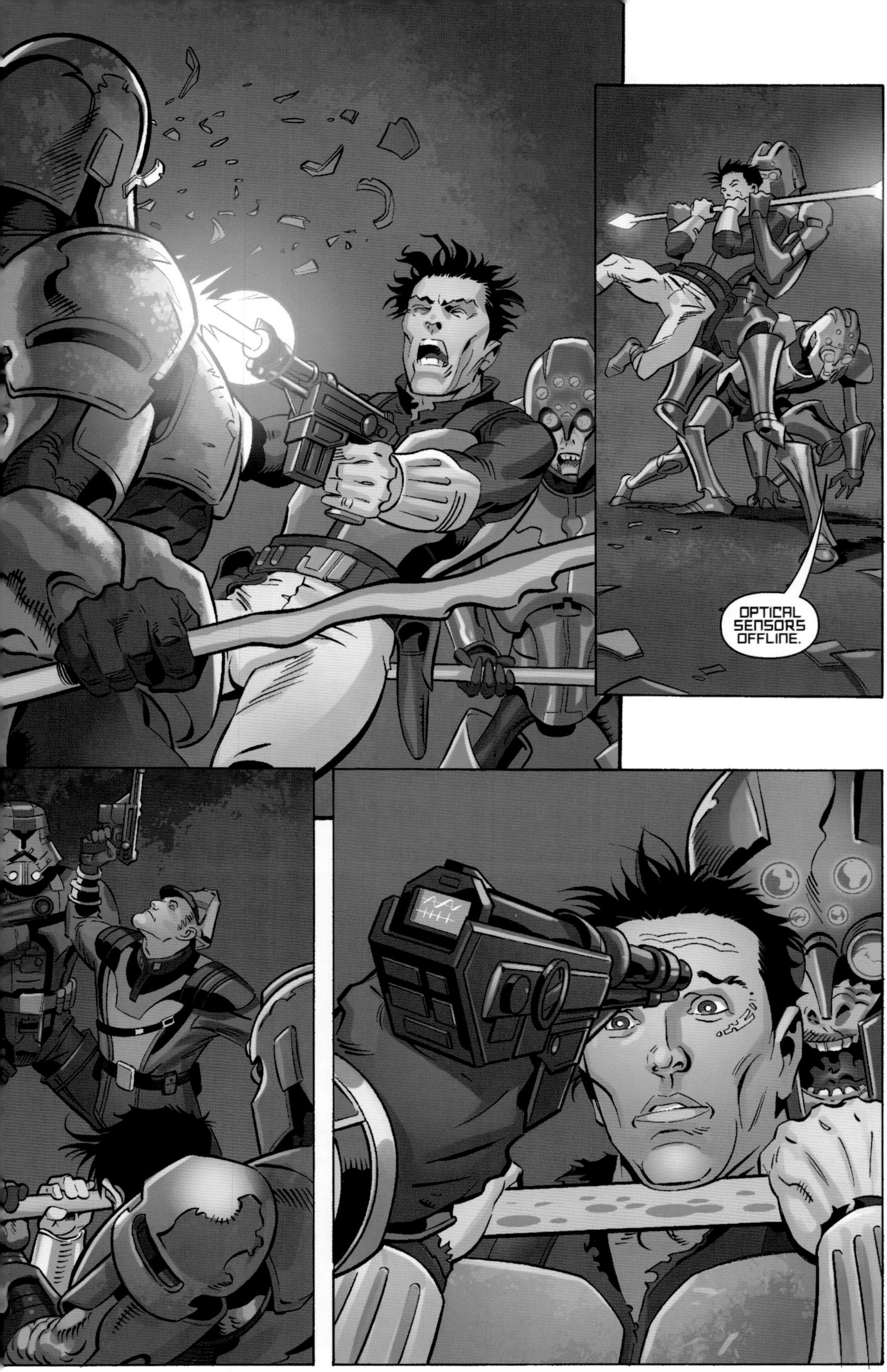
OPTICAL SENSORS OFFLINE.

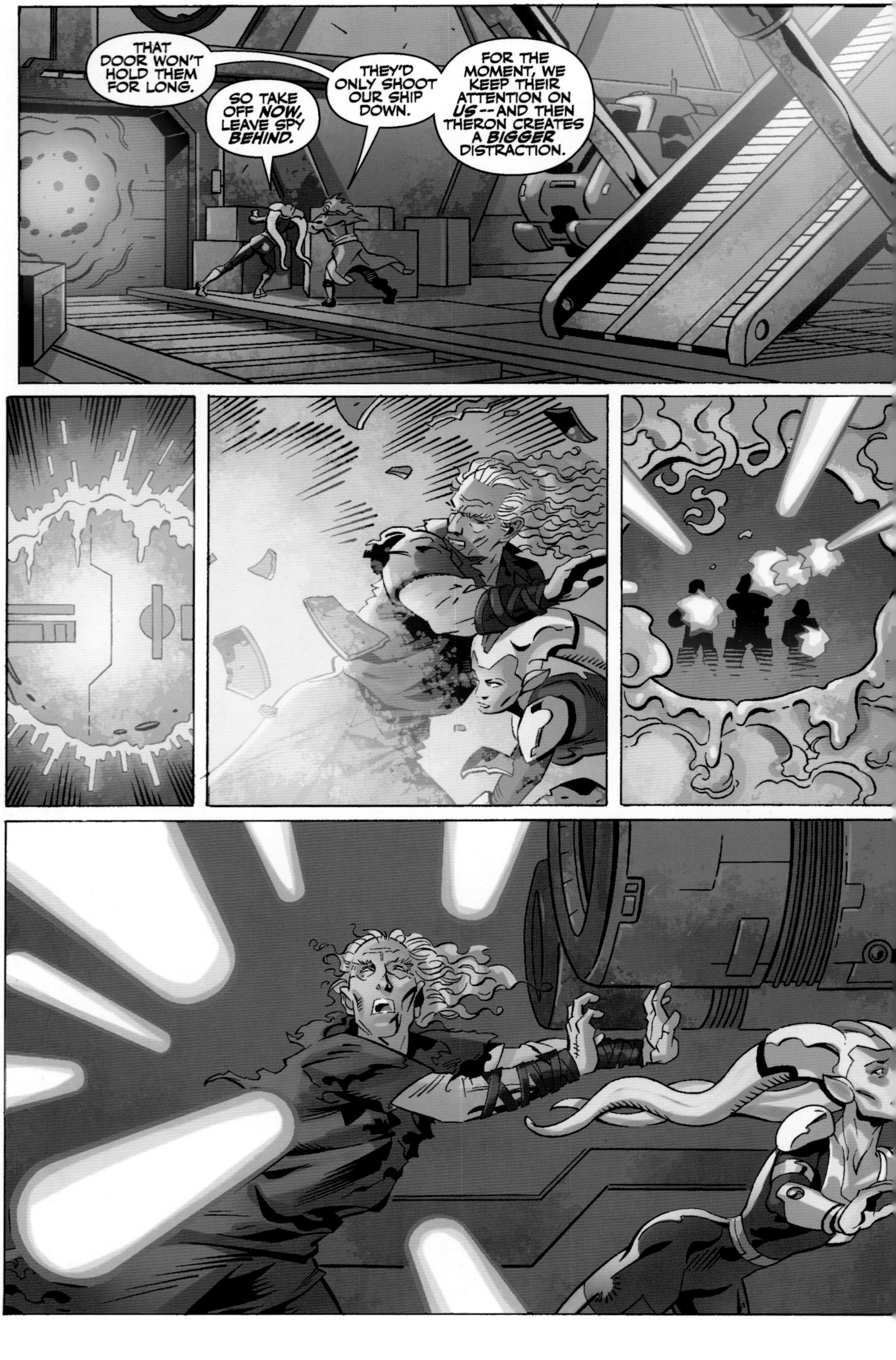

THAT DOOR WON'T HOLD THEM FOR LONG.
SO TAKE OFF NOW, LEAVE SPY BEHIND.
THEY'D ONLY SHOOT OUR SHIP DOWN.
FOR THE MOMENT, WE KEEP THEIR ATTENTION ON US--AND THEN THERON CREATES A BIGGER DISTRACTION.

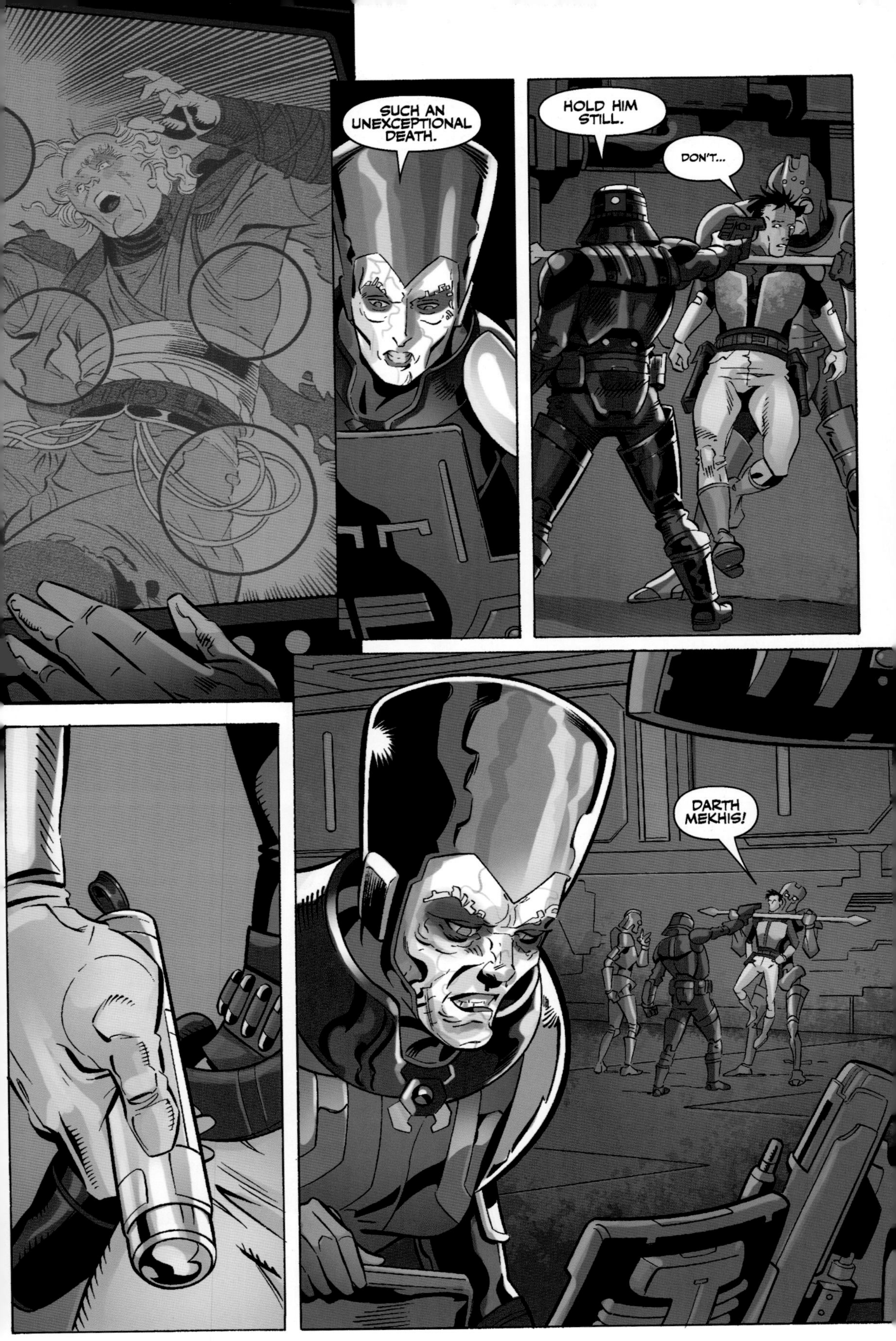
SUCH AN UNEXCEPTIONAL DEATH.
HOLD HIM STILL.
DON'T...
DARTH MEKHIS!

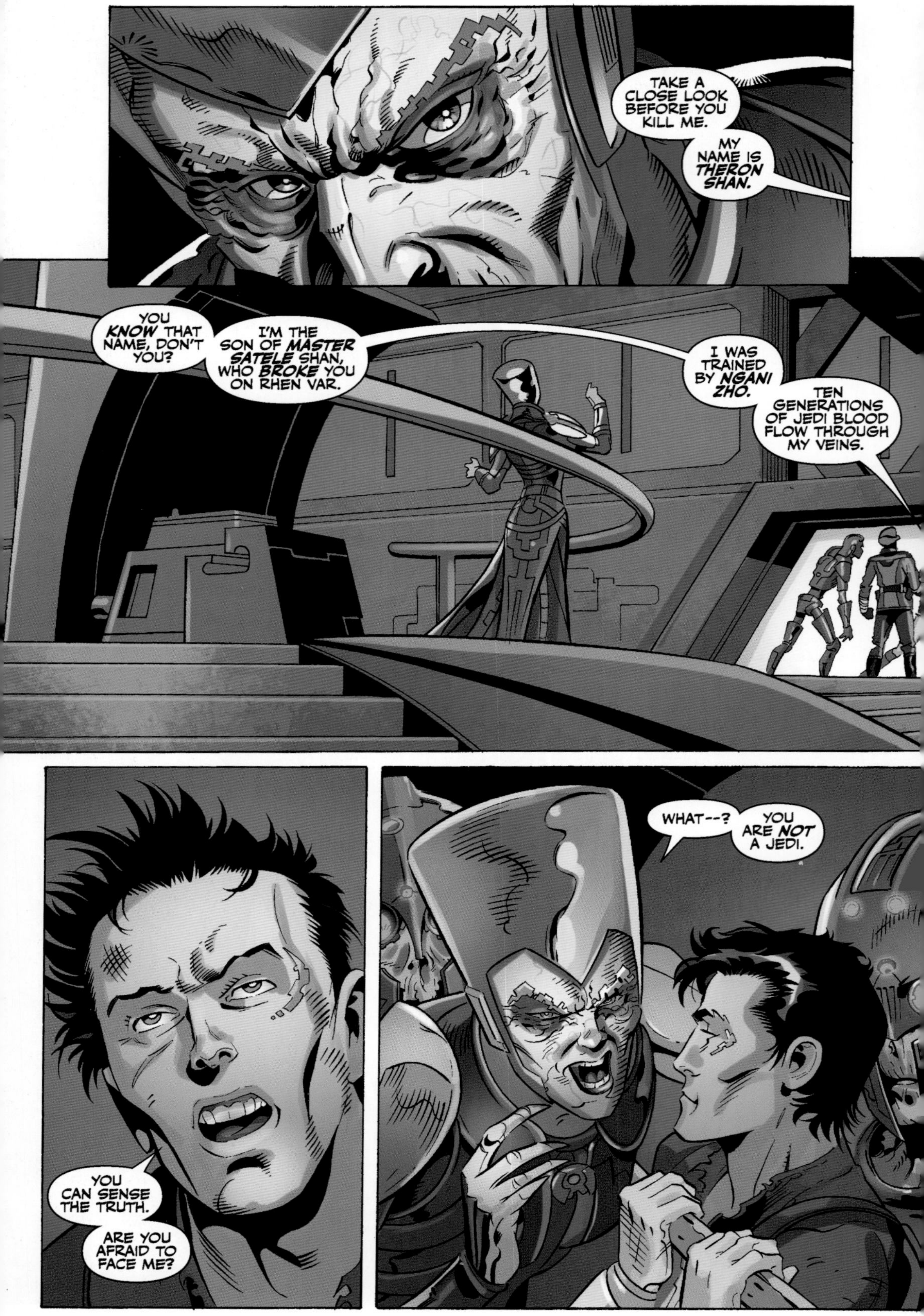

TAKE A CLOSE LOOK BEFORE YOU KILL ME.
MY NAME IS THERON SHAN.
YOU KNOW THAT NAME, DON'T YOU?
I'M THE SON OF MASTER SATELE SHAN, WHO BROKE YOU ON RHEN VAR.
I WAS TRAINED BY NGANI ZHO.
TEN GENERATIONS OF JEDI BLOOD FLOW THROUGH MY VEINS.
YOU CAN SENSE THE TRUTH.
ARE YOU AFRAID TO FACE ME?
WHAT--?
YOU ARE NOT A JEDI.

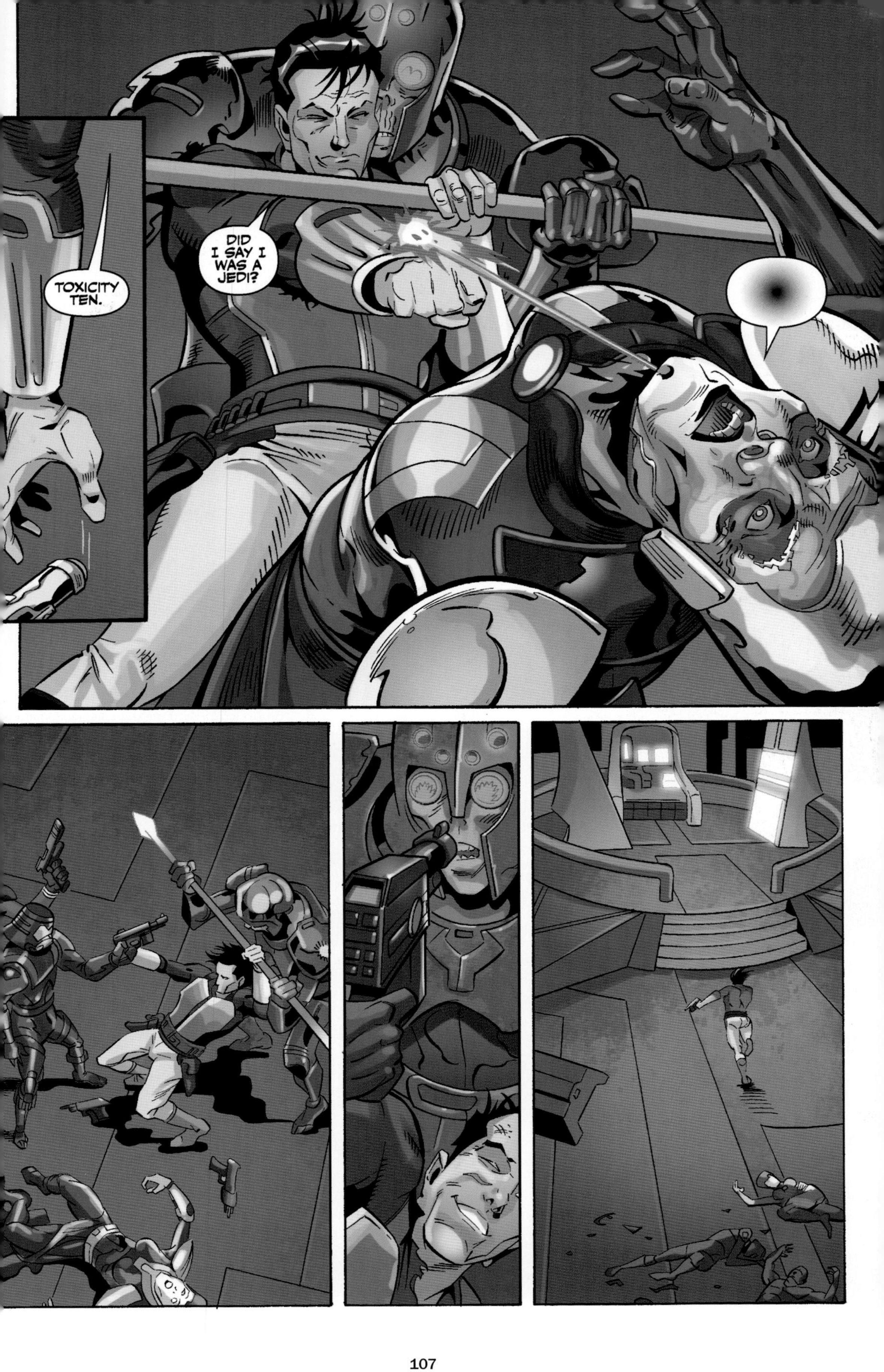
TOXICITY TEN.
DID I SAY I WAS A JEDI?

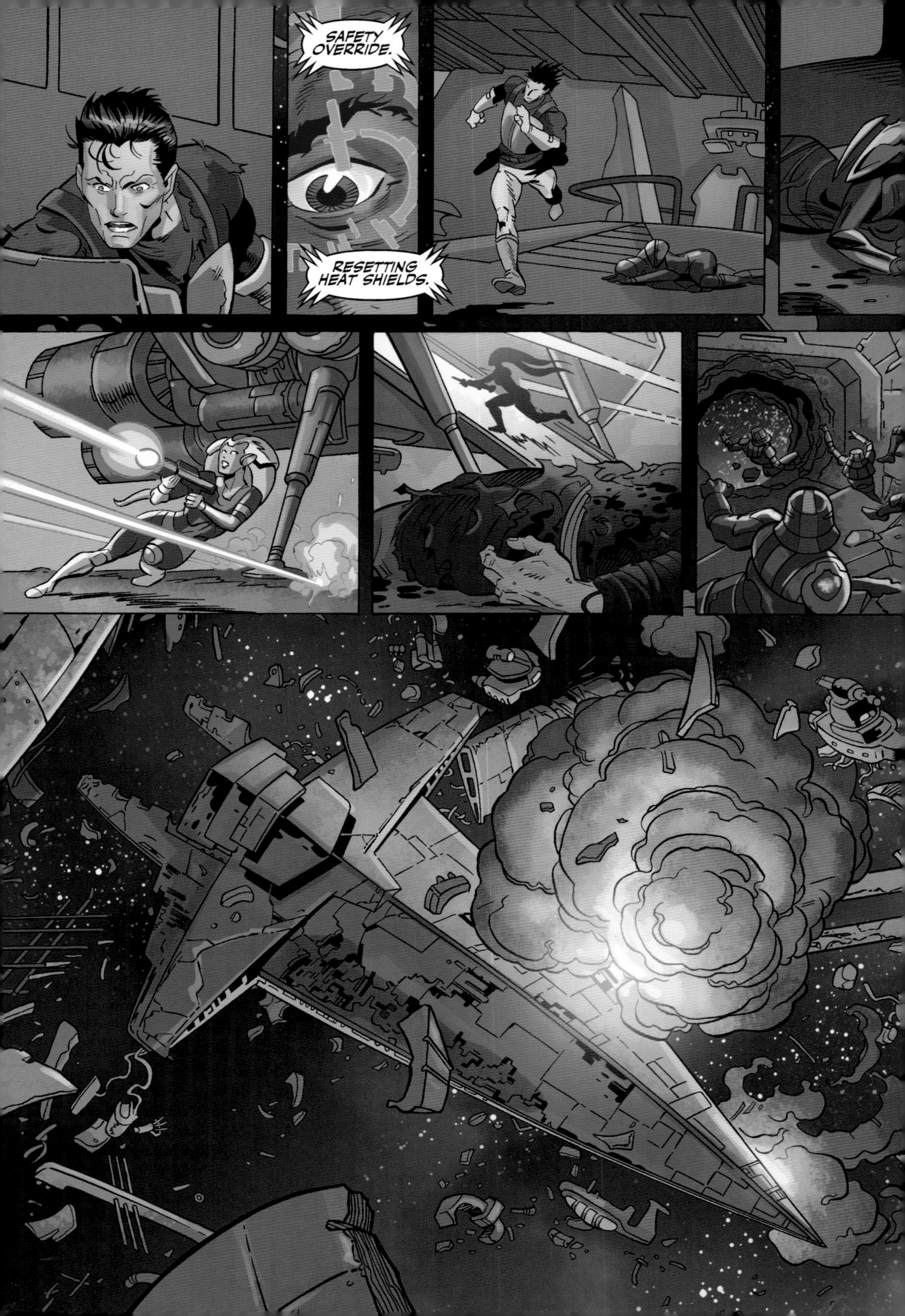
SAFETY OVERRIDE.
RESETTING HEAT SHIELDS.

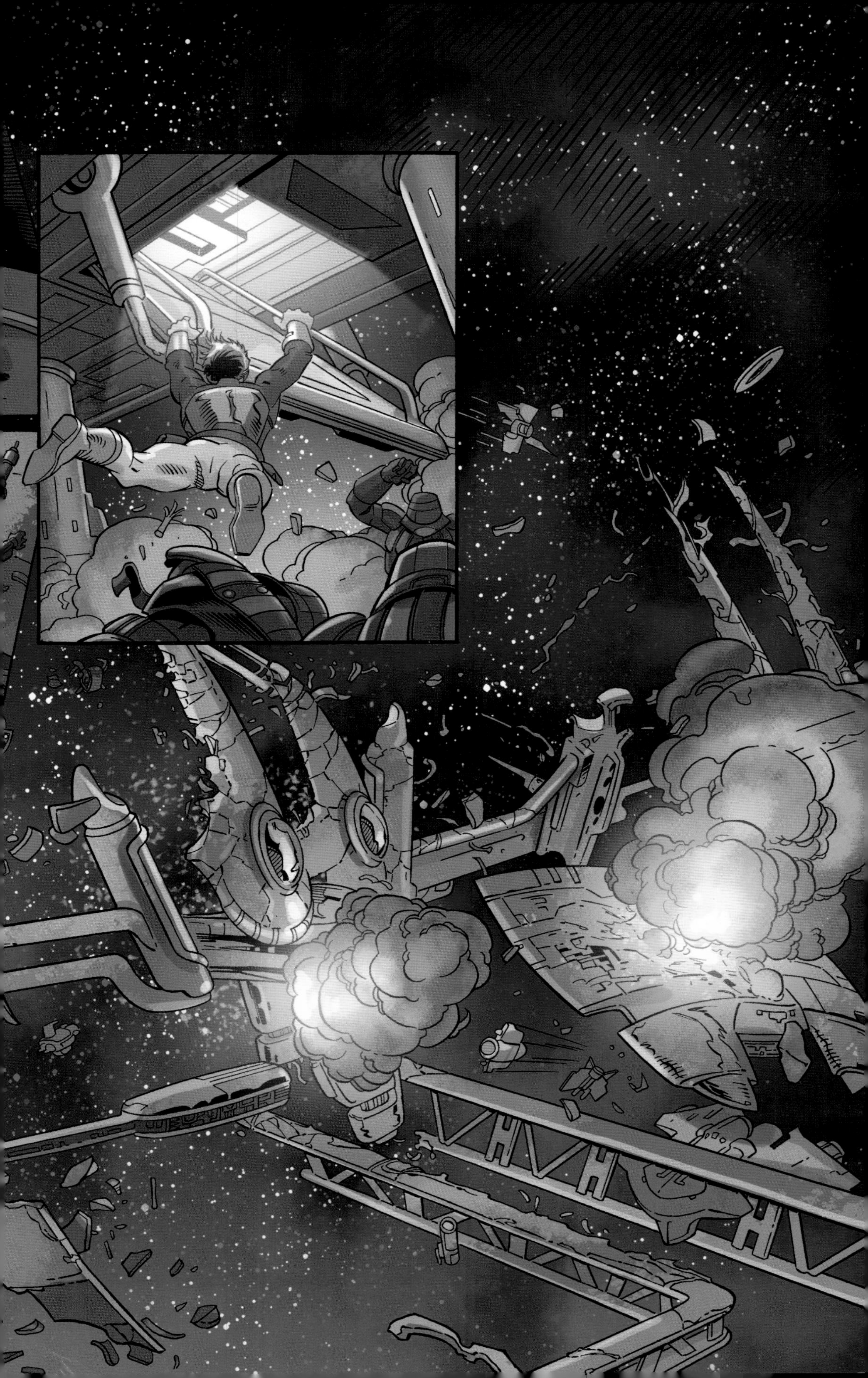

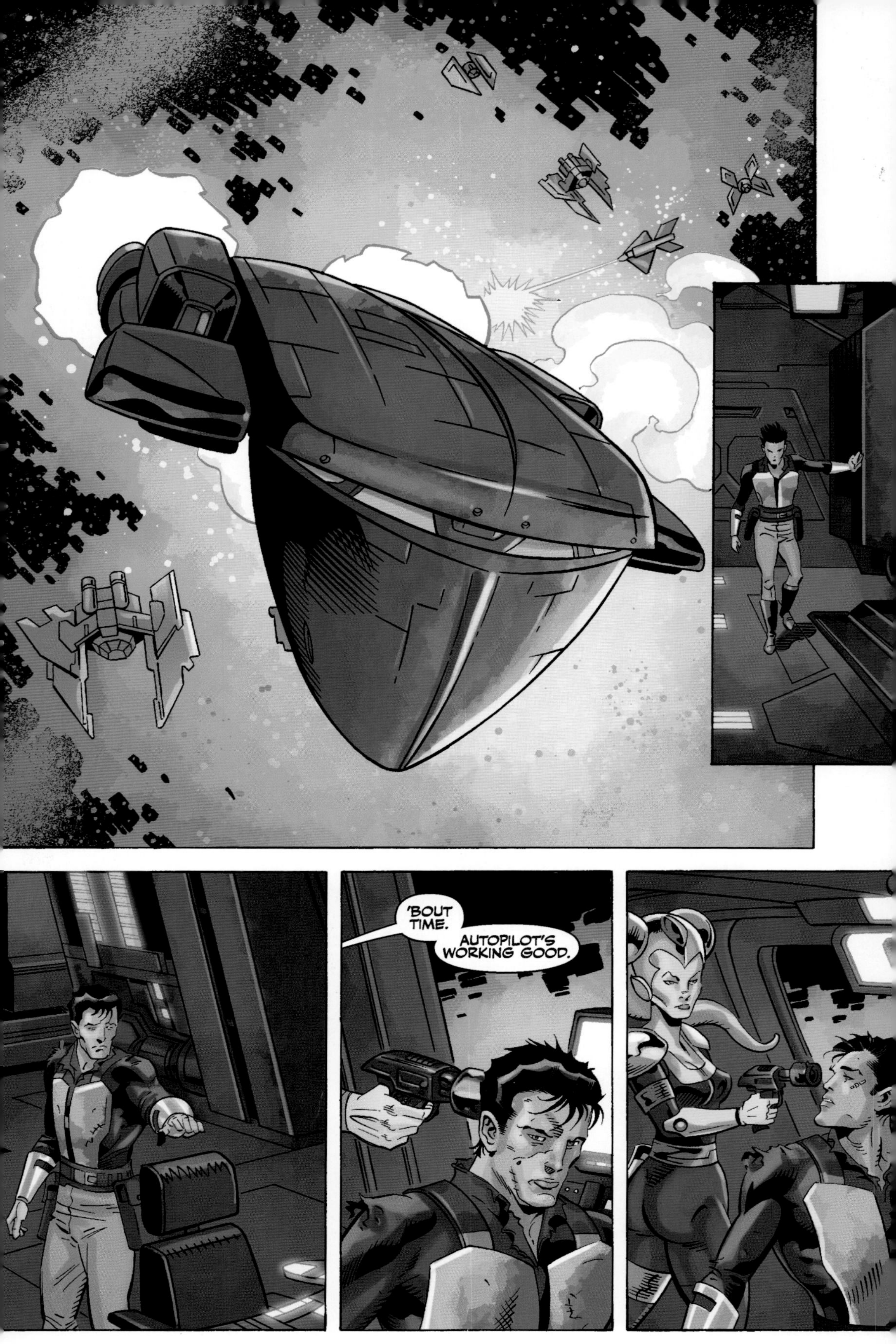
'BOUT TIME.
AUTOPILOT'S WORKING GOOD.

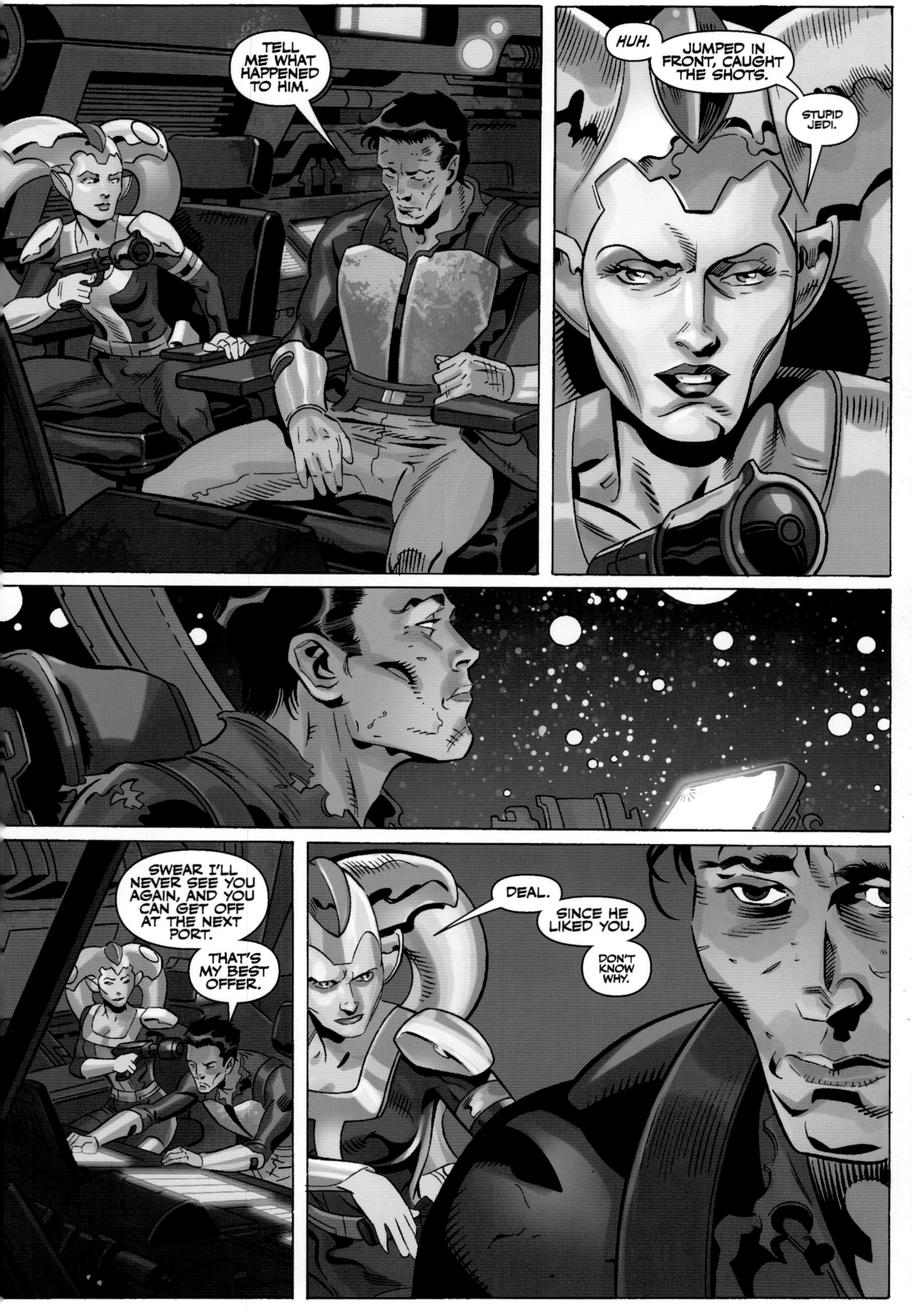
TELL ME WHAT HAPPENED TO HIM.
HUH.
JUMPED IN FRONT, CAUGHT THE SHOTS.
STUPID JEDI.
SWEAR I'LL NEVER SEE YOU AGAIN, AND YOU CAN GET OFF AT THE NEXT PORT.
THAT'S MY BEST OFFER.
DEAL.
SINCE HE LIKED YOU.
DON'T KNOW WHY.

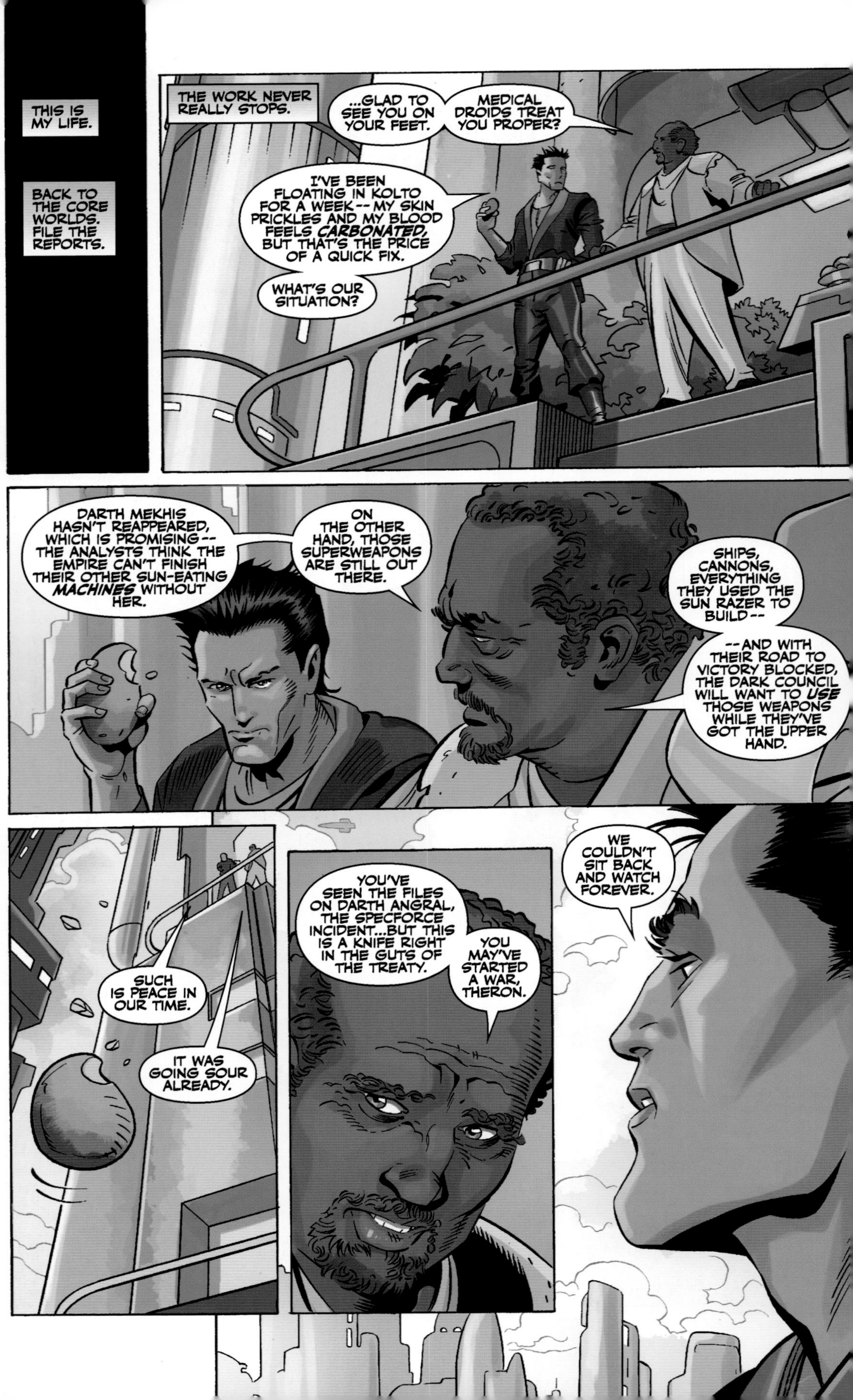
THIS IS MY LIFE.
BACK TO THE CORE WORLDS. FILE THE REPORTS.
THE WORK NEVER REALLY STOPS.
...GLAD TO SEE YOU ON YOUR FEET.
MEDICAL DROIDS TREAT YOU PROPER?
I'VE BEEN FLOATING IN KOLTO FOR A WEEK-- MY SKIN PRICKLES AND MY BLOOD FEELS CARBONATED, BUT THAT'S THE PRICE OF A QUICK FIX.
WHAT'S OUR SITUATION?
DARTH MEKHIS HASN'T REAPPEARED, WHICH IS PROMISING-- THE ANALYSTS THINK THE EMPIRE CAN'T FINISH THEIR OTHER SUN-EATING MACHINES WITHOUT HER.
ON THE OTHER HAND, THOSE SUPERWEAPONS ARE STILL OUT THERE.
SHIPS, CANNONS, EVERYTHING THEY USED THE SUN RAZER TO BUILD--
--AND WITH THEIR ROAD TO VICTORY BLOCKED, THE DARK COUNCIL WILL WANT TO USE THOSE WEAPONS WHILE THEY'VE GOT THE UPPER HAND.
SUCH IS PEACE IN OUR TIME.
IT WAS GOING SOUR ALREADY.
YOU'VE SEEN THE FILES ON DARTH ANGRAL, THE SPECFORCE INCIDENT...BUT THIS IS A KNIFE RIGHT IN THE GUTS OF THE TREATY.
YOU MAY'VE STARTED A WAR, THERON.
WE COULDN'T SIT BACK AND WATCH FOREVER.

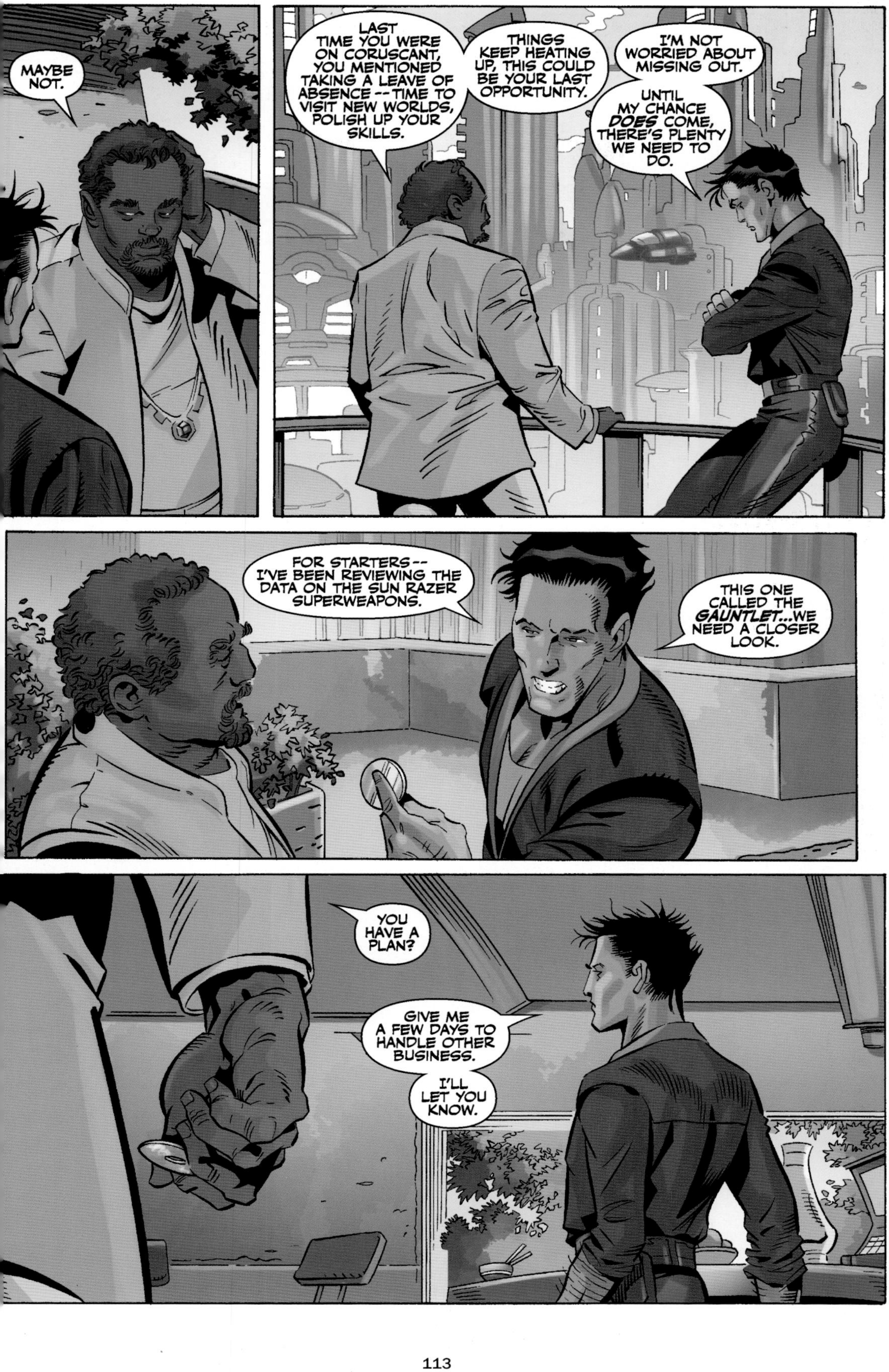
MAYBE NOT.
LAST TIME YOU WERE ON CORUSCANT, YOU MENTIONED TAKING A LEAVE OF ABSENCE--TIME TO VISIT NEW WORLDS, POLISH UP YOUR SKILLS.
THINGS KEEP HEATING UP, THIS COULD BE YOUR LAST OPPORTUNITY.
I'M NOT WORRIED ABOUT MISSING OUT.
UNTIL MY CHANCE *DOES* COME, THERE'S PLENTY WE NEED TO DO.
FOR STARTERS--I'VE BEEN REVIEWING THE DATA ON THE SUN RAZER SUPERWEAPONS.
THIS ONE CALLED THE *GAUNTLET*...WE NEED A CLOSER LOOK.
YOU HAVE A PLAN?
GIVE ME A FEW DAYS TO HANDLE OTHER BUSINESS.
I'LL LET YOU KNOW.

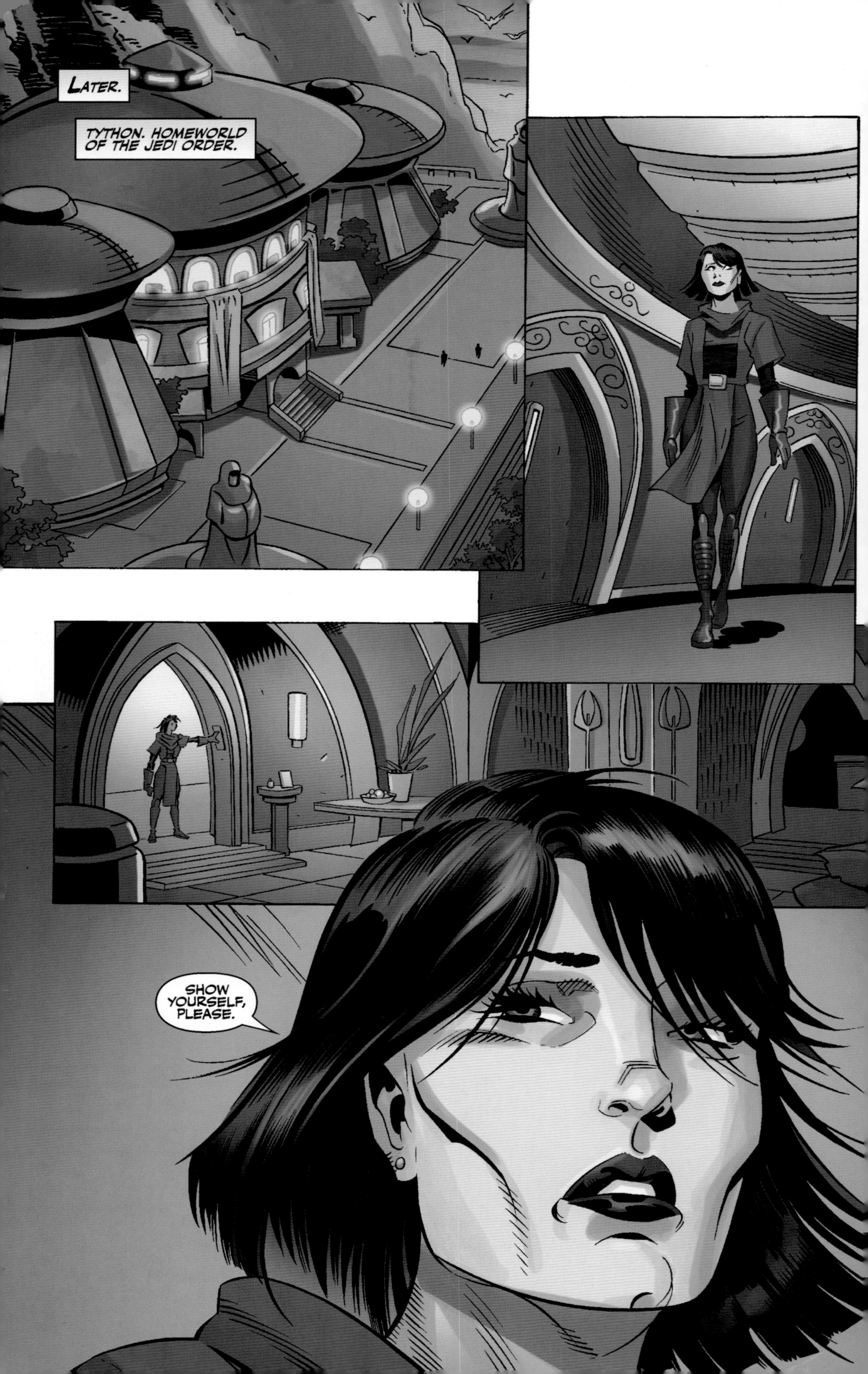
LATER.
TYTHON. HOMEWORLD OF THE JEDI ORDER.
SHOW YOURSELF, PLEASE.

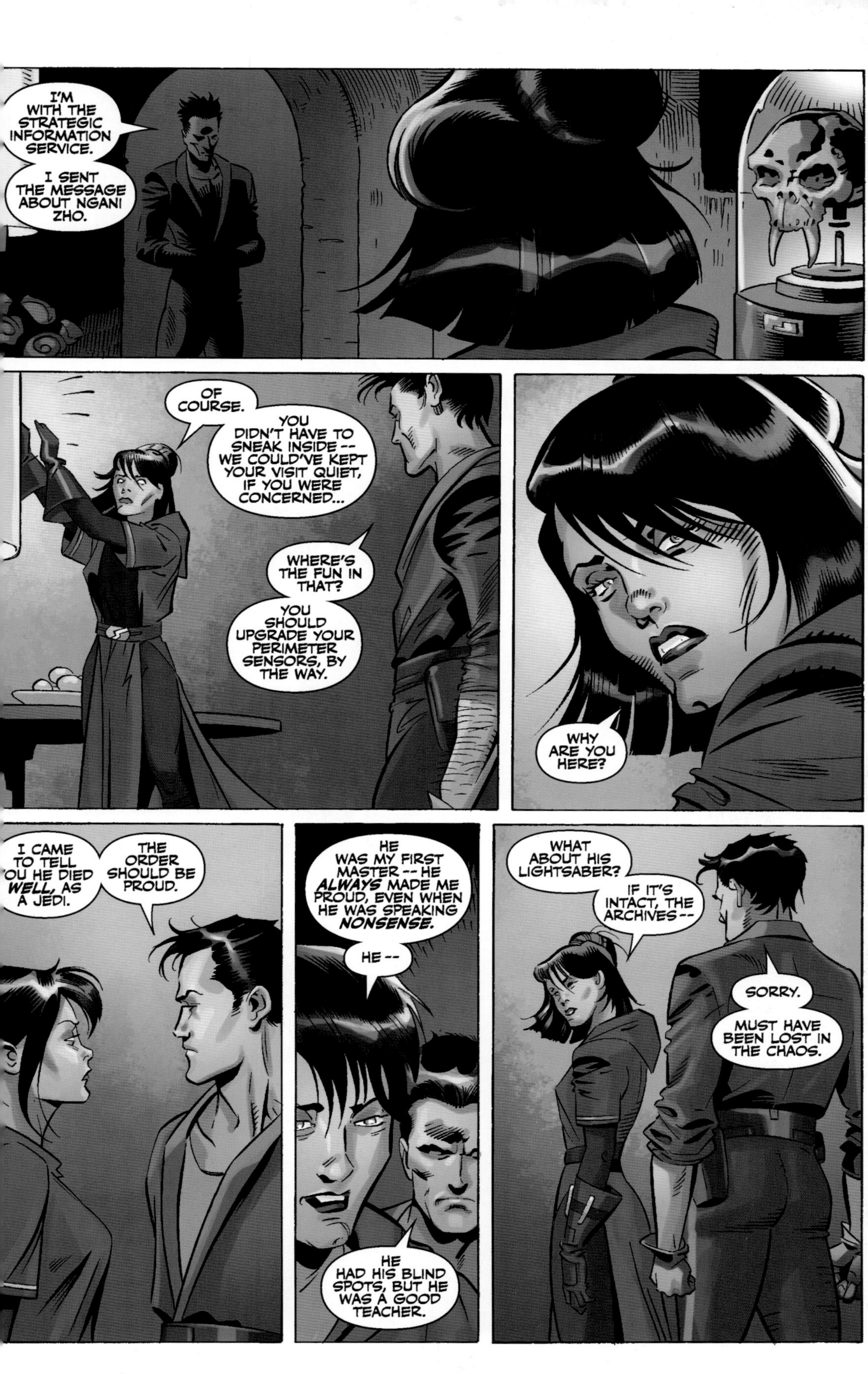
I'M WITH THE STRATEGIC INFORMATION SERVICE.
I SENT THE MESSAGE ABOUT NGANI ZHO.
OF COURSE.
YOU DIDN'T HAVE TO SNEAK INSIDE -- WE COULD'VE KEPT YOUR VISIT QUIET, IF YOU WERE CONCERNED...
WHERE'S THE FUN IN THAT?
YOU SHOULD UPGRADE YOUR PERIMETER SENSORS, BY THE WAY.
WHY ARE YOU HERE?
I CAME TO TELL OU HE DIED *WELL*, AS A JEDI.
THE ORDER SHOULD BE PROUD.
HE WAS MY FIRST MASTER -- HE *ALWAYS* MADE ME PROUD, EVEN WHEN HE WAS SPEAKING *NONSENSE.*
HE --
HE HAD HIS BLIND SPOTS, BUT HE WAS A GOOD TEACHER.
WHAT ABOUT HIS LIGHTSABER?
IF IT'S INTACT, THE ARCHIVES --
SORRY.
MUST HAVE BEEN LOST IN THE CHAOS.

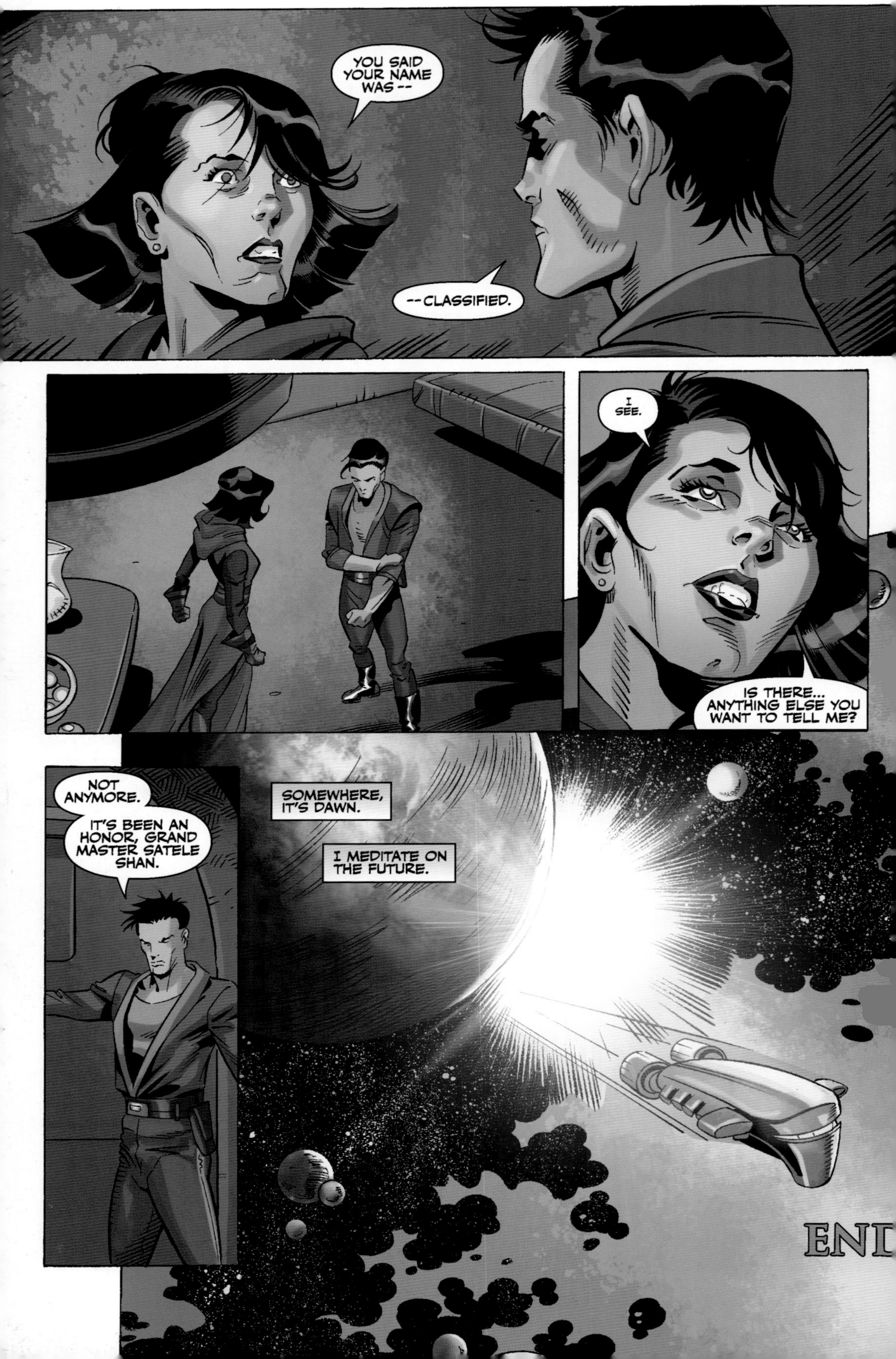
YOU SAID YOUR NAME WAS --
--CLASSIFIED.
I SEE.
IS THERE... ANYTHING ELSE YOU WANT TO TELL ME?
NOT ANYMORE.
IT'S BEEN AN HONOR, GRAND MASTER SATELE SHAN.
SOMEWHERE, IT'S DAWN.
I MEDITATE ON THE FUTURE.
END

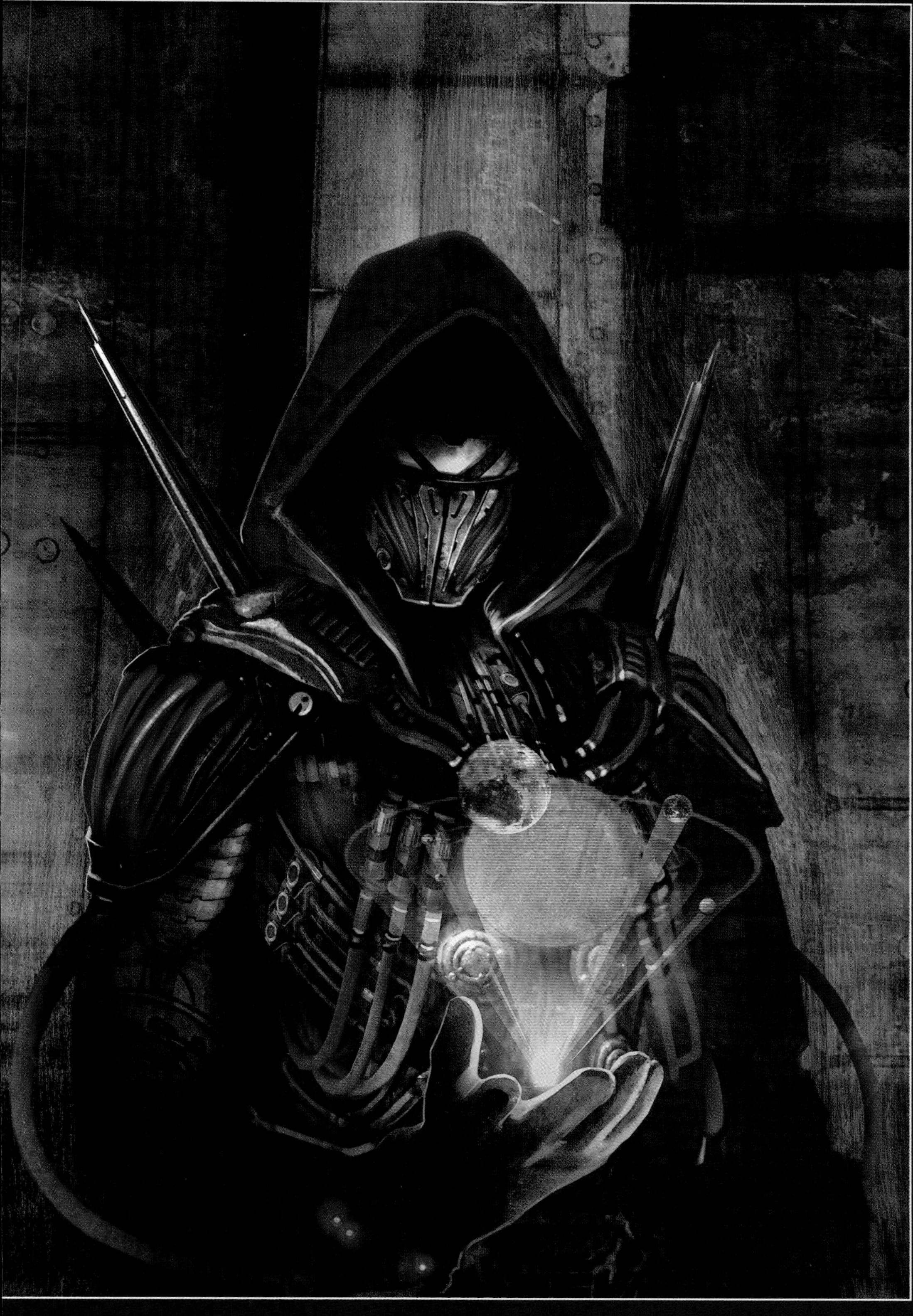

ILLUSTRATION BY
BENJAMIN CARRÉ

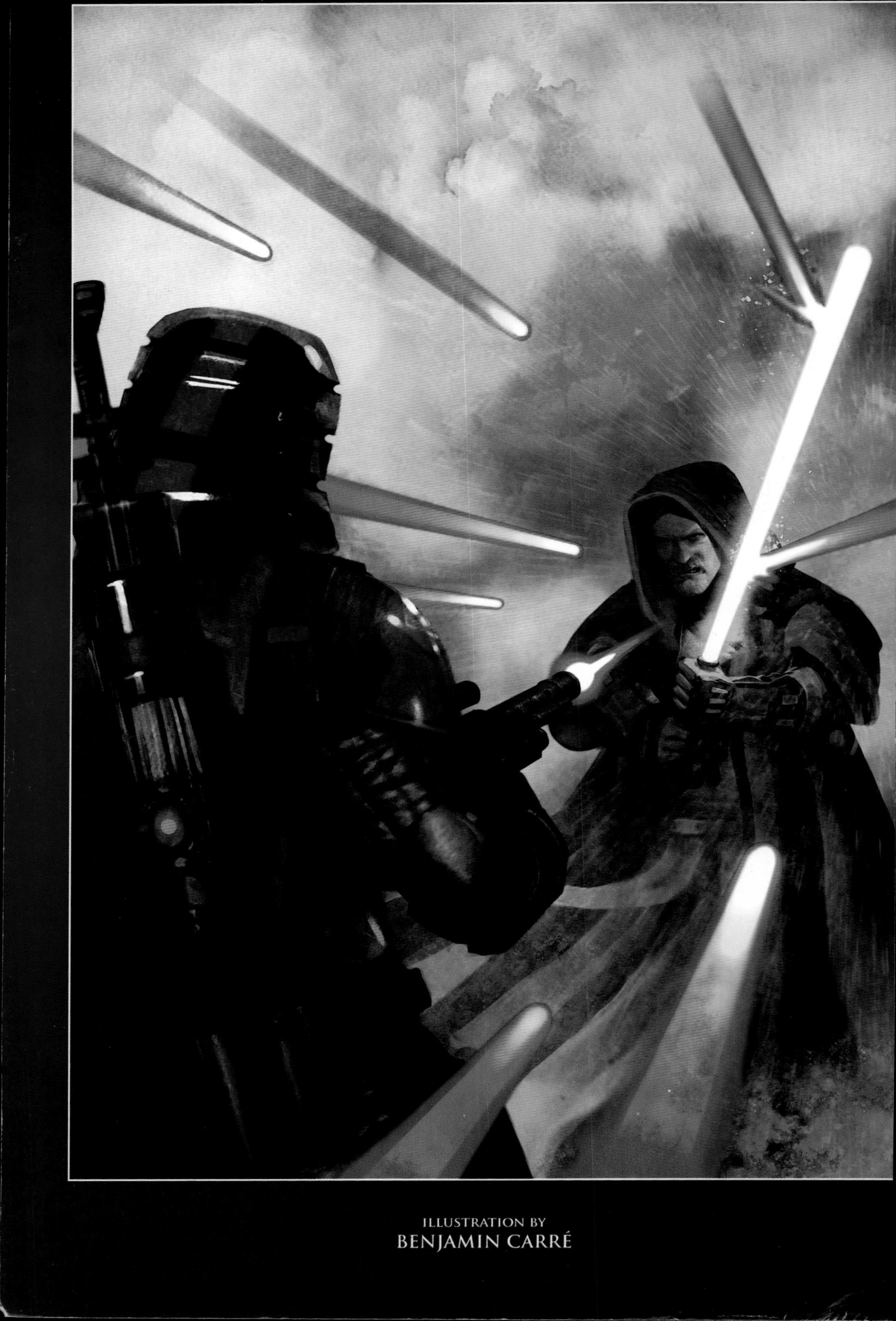

ILLUSTRATION BY
BENJAMIN CARRÉ

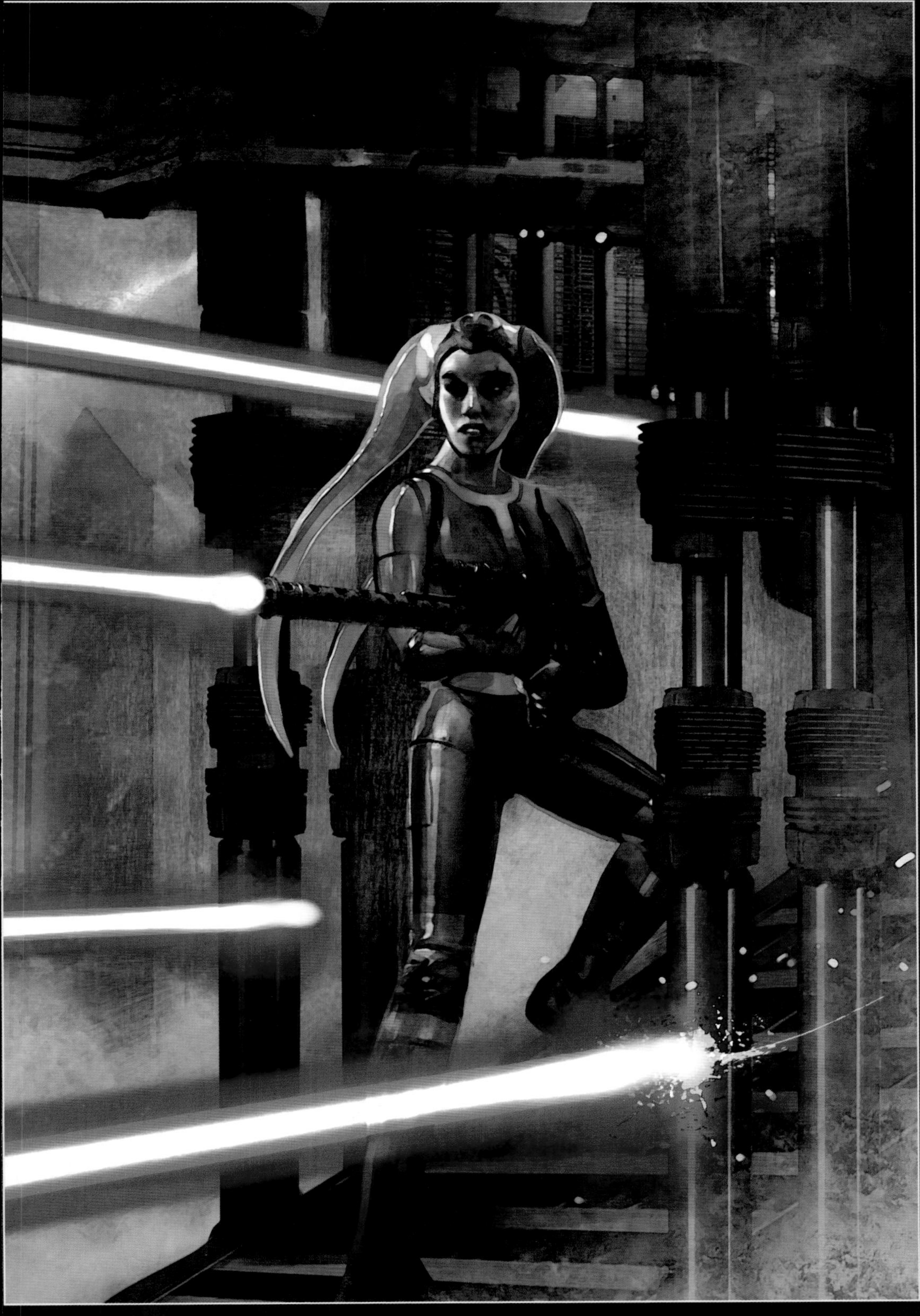

ILLUSTRATION BY
BENJAMIN CARRÉ

STAR WARS GRAPHIC NOVEL TIMELINE (IN YEARS

Omnibus: Tales of the Jedi—5,000–3,986 BSW4

Knights of the Old Republic—3,964–3,963 BSW4

The Old Republic—3653, 3678 BSW4

Knight Errant—1,032 BSW4

Jedi vs. Sith—1,000 BSW4

Omnibus: Rise of the Sith—33 BSW4

Episode I: The Phantom Menace—32 BSW4

Omnibus: Emissaries and Assassins—32 BSW4

Omnibus: Quinlan Vos—Jedi in Darkness—31–30 BSW4

Omnibus: Menace Revealed—31–22 BSW4

Honor and Duty—22 BSW4

Blood Ties—22 BSW4

Episode II: Attack of the Clones—22 BSW4

Clone Wars—22–19 BSW4

Clone Wars Adventures—22–19 BSW4

General Grievous—22–19 BSW4

Episode III: Revenge of the Sith—19 BSW4

Dark Times—19 BSW4

Omnibus: Droids—5.5 BSW4

Omnibus: Boba Fett—3 BSW4–10 ASW4

Underworld—1 BSW4

Episode IV: A New Hope—SW4

Classic Star Wars—0–3 ASW4

Omnibus: A Long Time Ago . . . —0–4 ASW4

Omnibus: At War with the Empire—0 ASW4

Omnibus: The Other Sons of Tattooine—0 ASW4

Omnibus: Early Victories—0–3 ASW4

Jabba the Hutt: The Art of the Deal—1 ASW4

Episode V: The Empire Strikes Back—3 ASW4

Omnibus: Shadows of the Empire—3.5–4.5 ASW4

Episode VI: Return of the Jedi—4 ASW4

Omnibus: X-Wing Rogue Squadron—4–5 ASW4

Heir to the Empire—9 ASW4

Dark Force Rising—9 ASW4

The Last Command—9 ASW4

Dark Empire—10 ASW4

Crimson Empire—11 ASW4

Jedi Academy: Leviathan—12 ASW4

Union—19 ASW4

Chewbacca—25 ASW4

Invasion—25 ASW4

Legacy—130–137 ASW4

Old Republic Era
25,000 – 1000 years before
Star Wars: A New Hope

Rise of the Empire Era
1000 – 0 years before
Star Wars: A New Hope

Rebellion Era
0 – 5 years after
Star Wars: A New Hope

New Republic Era
5 – 25 years after
Star Wars: A New Hope

New Jedi Order Era
25+ years after
Star Wars: A New Hope

Legacy Era
130+ years after
Star Wars: A New Hope

Vector
Crosses four eras in the timeline

Volume 1 contains:
Knights of the Old Republic Volume 5
Dark Times Volume 3
Volume 2 contains:
Rebellion Volume 4
Legacy Volume 6

BSW4 = before *Episode IV: A New Hope*. ASW4 = after *Episode IV: A New Hope*.